DISMANTLING THE DEMONIC KINGDOM ENCYCLOPEDIA

Identifying Demon Strongholds & Operations

Taquetta Baker

Book Synopsis

"*Dismantling The Demonic Kingdom Encyclopedia*" is designed to train and equip the reader on how to discern, overthrow, and be proactive against the wiles of demonic forces and systems that strive to steal, kill, and destroy the fruit and progress of people's lives, lineages, and destinies.

This kingdom encyclopedia provides descriptions on demonology, how they operate in different interactions and circumstances, and keys and strategies for how to dismantle and cast them out.

Learn the following:
- How to discern the hidden oppositions of the devil.
- How to discern and identify specific demonic spirits and spiritual attacks.
- How to identify and thwart attacks on people, bloodlines, ministries, businesses, regions, and spheres of influence.
- How to be delivered and healed, and how to walk with others as they process in deliverance, healing, and sustaining victory.
- Be enlightened in deliverance ministry, intercession, warfare, and regional reform that SHIFTS lives, destinies, and atmospheres.

Kingdomwellnesscenter@gmail.com
Kingdomshifters.com
KSWU.NET

Copyright 2022 – Kingdom Shifters Christian Empowerment Center. All rights reserved.

Images are either copyright-free, public domain images or used with permission of the graphic artist.

This book is protected by the copyright laws of the United States of America. This book may not be reprinted for commercial gain or profit. The use of occasional page copying for personal or group study is permitted and encouraged. Permission will be granted with a written request.

Taquetta's Bio

Taquetta was adopted by her aunt at two weeks old. She was raised with four brothers in East St. Louis and has been a fighter since she was a little girl. God has transformed that fighting personality into a spiritual warrior in his kingdom! She has a testimony of having her fists turned into hands of prayer, complete with a gift of healing and faith for miracles, signs, and wonders to manifest. God transformed Taquetta from one who frequented nightclubs and battled alcoholism to one with a strategy to empower others in destiny. Her name means "child of love," and she carries that mantle of unconditionally loving and restoring the unlovable.

Taquetta is gifted at empowering and assisting people with launching ministries, businesses, and books. She provides mentoring, counseling, coach, and destiny development through Kingdom Wellness Counseling and Mentoring Center. She has written her very own Kingdom Wellness Counseling Theory and will be launching a certified program to train mental health leaders, deliverers, and healings, in how to SHIFT people into sustainable wellness.

Taquetta flows through the wells of deliverance, revival reform, warfare, and worship. She carries the mantle, not only of her spiritual mother, Dr. Kathy Williams but also of her overseer and apostolic mother, Dr. Jackie Green. Her mantle includes an apostolic mandate of judging and establishing God's kingdom in people, ministries, communities, and regions. Taquetta has over 22 years of deliverance and warfare experience. She is skilled at dismantling principalities and strongholds in people, generations, and regions, and is keen on seeking God for strategic insight on how to overthrow the powers and systems of darkness.

Taquetta travels in foreign missions and throughout the United States. She has mentored and established dance, altar workers, deliverance, and prophetic ministries. Taquetta ministers in the areas of fine arts, all manners of prayer, fivefold ministry, deliverance, healing, miracles, atmospheric worship, apostolic reform, empowers and trains people in their destiny and life vision. She walks the walk and rejoices at the expansion of God's kingdom!

Taquetta's Credentials

- Founder of Kingdom Shifters Ministries (KSM), Indiana
- Founder of Kingdom Wellness Counseling and Mentoring Center
- Author of over 38 books and 2 prayer decree CD's
- Doctorate in Ministry from Rapha Deliverance University
- Master's Degree in Community Counseling with an emphasis on Marriage, Children and Family Counseling
- Bachelor's Degree in Psychology
- Associates Degree in Business Administration
- Certified Life Coach, Certified Professional Coach, Certified Executive Leadership Coach through Breakthrough Coaching and Leadership Academy
- Therapon Belief Therapist Certification from the Therapon Institute (faith-based counseling)
- Board of Directors for New Day Community Ministries, Inc.
- Graduate of Eagles Dance Institute under Dr. Pamela Hardy; licensed in the area of liturgical dance
- Apostolic Ordination by Bishop Jackie Green, Founder of JGM-National Prayer Life Institute (Phoenix, AZ)
- Previous ministry service as a prophet, visionary for Shekinah Expressions Dance Troupe, teacher, member of the presbytery, an overseer for altar workers' ministry

Table Of Contents

BOOK SYNOPSIS II
TAQUETTA'S BIO III
TAQUETTA'S CREDENTIALS IV
FOREWORD VI
FOREWORD VIII
HOW TO USE THIS ENCYCLOPEDIA 1
ALL AUTHORITY & POWER TO CAST OUT DEMONS 2
KEYS TO PRAYING THROUGH YOUR AUTHORITY 6
WARFARE LEVELS & TACTICS 24
DISCERNING OF SPIRITS 27
SPIRITUAL CLEANING! 33
MAINTAINING DELIVERANCE & HEALING 33
DEMONIC SPIRITS ABORT PROGRESS 52
DEMONIC SPIRITS THAT ATTACK IDENTITY 55
DEMONIC SPIRITS THAT ATTACK GOD'S WORD 75
DESTINY KILLING SPIRITS 81
SPIRITS THAT ATTACK CHILDREN 88
RELATIONSHIP DESTROYING DEMONS 103
SPIRITS THAT DEAL DEATH 113
DISMANTLING SEXUAL ACTS & DEMONS 118
SPIRITS THAT ATTACK MINISTERS 154
SPIRITS THAT ATTACKS VISIONS, TEAMS, & EVENT PLANNING 159
DEMONIC BINDINGS TO OLD PARADIGMS & SEASONS 193
THWARTING DEMONIC WITCHCRAFT ATTACKS 202
OVERTHROWING PRINCIPALITIES & STRONGHOLDS 218

FOREWORD

When he had disarmed the rulers and authorities [those supernatural forces of evil operating against us], He made a public example of them [exhibiting them as captives in His triumphal procession], having triumphed over them through the Cross. (Colossians 2:15) AMP

While reading Dr. Taquetta Baker's book "*Dismantling The Demonic Kingdom Encyclopedia*," I was reminded of the movie entitled, "*The Exorcist*" produced in 1973, about a twelve year old girl who was possessed by a mysterious entity, and her mother sought the help of two priests to "dismantle" the evil spirit and set her child free. The little girl was finally delivered after a gruesome process and it cost the life of both priests. The priest were not equipped to dismantle the strong demonic spirit(s) and it cost them their lives. The older priest died of a heart attack and the young priest was killed by the transference of the entity which entered him but left the girl free and delivered. This movie is somewhat of a prototype of the Church and it's spiritual impotence today. *The Church is busy having church, while dismantling nothing.*

I shared the movie, *The Exorcist*, to emphasize that the Church-at-large is not equipped to dismantle demonic kingdoms and that is why we need this book, or should I say "encyclopedia." I strongly recommend it for all Believers, and especially Church leaders and those called to the ministry of deliverance and total wellness.

This word "*dismantle*" literally means to take apart "*piece by piece*" or to strip down, pull down or bulldoze something, and in this case, it is demonic kingdoms. Jesus is our example for dismantling demonic kingdoms. He has already stripped them and triumphed over them, but the Church must maintain Jesus' authority over evil and dark kingdoms until He returns. Dr. Baker carefully prepares us in this book for the "*deliverers that must learn to dismantle darkness and evil,*" because she is called and mandated to train the Body of Christ in spiritual warfare. She states in her book that her heart is see the Church "*govern and not allow demons to cohabitate, or rule in our lives, families, generational lines, home, lands, regions and spheres.*"

Her series of books on raising up deliverers is right on time to stop the many casualties of war that will continue unless we take seriously the need to "*disciple the people of God how to dismantle demonic kingdoms and maintain our righteous position in Christ from generation to generation.*"

I sense that this book is not for the babe in Christ, but the Lord has given the revelation to Dr. Baker for a generation that is not "fearful and faithless" but hungry to see the Kingdom of God demonstrated in the earth. I believe Dr. Baker writes for generations that are not yet born, for they will arise, and as she stated: *"See Him and see heaven; hear Him and hear heaven; taste Him and taste heaven; discern Him and discern heaven."*

Dr. Baker is new breed and forerunner in the ranks of the "new voices" that will usher in "real church" that is arising out of the "a religious church," who are called to dismantle dark kingdoms and bring the glory and light of God's Kingdom on earth.

Following Hard After God,
Bishop Dr. Jackie L. Green, D. Min.
JGM Enternational Prayer Life Institute, Redlands, CA

FOREWORD

ATTENTION PLEASE - ATTENTION PLEASE - COME READ & BE FREE!

WOW, this encyclopedia clearly puts a WOE to the demonic structures that Satan has devised to destroy people, lands, communities, regions, and nations. Especially believers who are called to overthrow demons and demonic structures. This encyclopedia equips the reader with identifying demons by name, and provides scriptural revelation and principles to dismantle them, and their demonic systems.

Proverbs 4:7 says: *Wisdom is the principal thing; therefore, get the Wisdom and with all thy getting get Understanding.*

Dr. Baker provides wisdom and understanding. There is a treasure of revelation and impartation throughout this encyclopedia. I love the fact that Dr. Baker backs all her findings with the Word of God! This "Pocket Guide Encyclopedia" is an easy access for those who are involved in the ministry of counseling, deliverance, and spiritual warfare. This much needed warfare guide should be in every fivefold minister's and every mature believer's library. It is indeed a "carry with you manual" that tells on, exposes, and breaks the powers of the devil.

This encyclopedia is balanced and biblical, while exposing the truth regarding sexual demons. The chapter *Dismantling Sexual Demons* is raw. But let me tell you folks, it's REAL! Dr. Baker exposes the unadulterated truth about perverse acts and demonic bondages that most Christian folks want to keep hidden and out of the church. However, in order to truly be free, we need to admit what we are dealing with and use this encyclopedia to be set free.

Dr. Baker remind us that we do have power and authority over the works of the devil, that we have a rightful position and seat in God as born-again believers to be set free, and that it is time we take our position as sons and daughters of God to live well and FREE!

The *"Dismantling The Demonic Kingdom Encyclopedia" is* a slam-bam knock the devil in the head powerhouse manual. Get ready to be free and to aide others in obtaining victory with your pocket guide encyclopedia.

Well done Dr. Baker!
Prophet Cathy Fontenot
JGM-Enternational Prayer Commander

HOW TO USE THIS ENCYCLOPEDIA

If you have purchased any of my mantles, you are already aware that I provide revelation of how demonic spirits operate in most of them. This manual will include revelation from those books, along with new revelation and insight on demonic strongholds and their workings. It is intended to provide a comprehensive manual and training resource that can be utilized in ministry, deliverance, counseling, mentoring, discipleship, and in the everyday life of the believer, to dismantle the demonic attacks, systems, and kingdoms.

Some of the chapters will have the same demons listed as other chapters. However, the definition for how the demonic spirit operates will be tailored to that chapter and title. This is because a demon can have a specific assignment for a certain situation, event, or season of life, but still have the same name. My hope is that you will be able to go that specific chapter and gain entail based on how that demonic spirit is operating as it relates to what information you are seeking at that particular time.

I decree that as you partake of this manual, you will be empowered with confidence to walk in your divine authority as a believer who has power over all the power of the enemy. This book is to awaken your spiritual gates but not to take the place of God in discerning properly and effectively. Though demon names and workings will be listed in this manual.

It is important to seek God for revelation on how to utilize this information and insight on what demonic spirits and workings you are encountering. Do not just assume it is what is listed in this manual. Let this manual be a confirmation and further enlightenment of what God is speaking to you. God is the ultimate deliverer. He will keep you grounded with not being so focused on intellect, human strength, names, and relentlessly pursuing knowledge, that you do not rest and trust the truth that every demon is subject to you in this name. I decree this manual draws you closer to God while helping you to dismantle evil, set captives free while SHIFTING heaven to earth with sustaining success. **SHIFT!**

ALL AUTHORITY & POWER TO CAST OUT DEMONS

This information is from my book entitled, *"UNMASKING THE POWER OF THE SCOUTS, VOLUME I: GAINING INTEL FOR VICTORY OVER YOUR OPPOSITION."*

It is being provided with the intention to stir your authority so that as you SHIFT into the rest of this manual, you will advance inside the truth that you have all dominion over every demon, all unrighteousness, and the evil manner in the earth. As deliverers, we must embody this TRUTH and assert our kingly right to cast out, annihilate, and overthrow every demonic entity of witchcraft, demonology, lawlessness, and wickedness. For Jesus commissioned us to:

Matthew 10:8 Heal the sick, cleanse the lepers, raise the dead, cast out devils: freely ye have received, freely give.

Mark 16:17-18 And these signs shall follow them that believe; In my name shall they cast out devils; they shall speak with new tongues; They shall take up serpents; and if they drink any deadly thing, it shall not hurt them; they shall lay hands on the sick, and they shall recover.

<u>Cast Out is *ekballō* in Greek and means:</u>
- To eject (literally or figuratively)
- Bring forth, cast (forth, out), drive (out)
- Expel, leave, pluck (pull, take, thrust) out
- Put forth (out), send away (forth, out)
- Cast out, cast, bring forth, pull out, send forth, send out
- Drive out, to send out with the notion of violence
- To cast out of the world, i.e., be deprived of the power and influence he exercises in the world
- A thing: excrement from the belly into the sink
- To expel a person from the society, to banish from a family
- To compel one to depart; to bid one depart, in stern though not violent language
- To employed that the rapid motion of the one going is transferred to the one sending forth
- To command or cause one to depart in haste
- To draw out with force
- Tear out with implication of force overcoming opposite force
- To cause a thing to move straight on its intended goal
- To reject with contempt, to cast off or away
- To draw out, extract, one thing inserted in another
- To bring out of, to draw, or bring forth
- To except, to leave out, i.e. Not receive
- To lead one forth or away somewhere with a force which he cannot resist

Dictionary.com defines *cast* as:

Throw aside	Cast	Eject	Expel	Heave	Hurl	Launch
Expulsion	Fling	Pitch	Project	Shoot	Sling	Thrust
Toss	Drive	Discharge	Excrete	Eliminate	End	Terminate

As deliverers, we should not allow demons to cohabitate, negotiate, compromise, live, govern, or rule in our lives, families, generational lines, homes, lands, regions, spheres, ministries, business, organizations, destinies, visions, and callings. The kingdom should be our portion on earth as it is in heaven.

Matthew 28:18-19 And Jesus came and spake unto them, saying, All power is given unto me in heaven and on earth. Go ye therefore, and teach all nations, baptizing them in the name of the Father, and of the Son, and of the Holy Ghost.

The Message Bible Verse 18-20 Jesus, undeterred, went right ahead and gave his charge: "God authorized and commanded me to commission you: Go out and train everyone you meet, far and near, in this way of life, marking them by baptism in the threefold name: Father, Son, and Holy Spirit. Then instruct them in the practice of all I have commanded you. I'll be with you as you do this, day after day, right up to the end of the age."

Jesus was given two distinct dimensions of authority – heaven and earth. This authority was preeminent – supreme. It was non-negotiable! It was the highest honor bestowed upon him as the ruling savior who demonstrated with his very being that he embodied the eternal sovereign power of God. He then SHIFTED that authority onto us. It is now a part of our identity as his disciples and laborers on earth.

Ephesians 1:17-23 New International Bible I keep asking that the God of our Lord Jesus Christ, the glorious Father, may give you the Spirit of wisdom and revelation, so that you may know him better. I pray that the eyes of your heart may be enlightened in order that you may know the hope to which he has called you, the riches of his glorious inheritance in his holy people, and his incomparably great power for us who believe. That power is the same as the mighty strength he exerted when he raised Christ from the dead and seated him at his right hand in the heavenly realms, far above all rule and authority, power and dominion, and every name that is invoked, not only in the present age but also in the one to come. And God placed all things under his feet and appointed him to be head over everything for the church, which is his body, the fullness of him who fills everything in every way.

In this passage, Paul was praying that the believers would gain insight into this authority through the purposes and works of the cross. That such comprehension would SHIFT them into greater knowledge, revelation, understanding, intimacy, and covenant with Jesus. Paul reveals that this is a part of our God identity and kingly inheritance as sons of God and shared laborers in the faith. We must take our rightful place in sonship. We must assert our right to govern in both realms, live in heavenly realms, while utilizing our destinies and callings, and scouting authority to SHIFT heaven to earth. When we fail to do this, demons, and demonic systems takeover our spheres of influence and produce their sinful, destructive kingdom purposes in our midst.

I decree that as you study the scripture below, you receive an impartation of the truth that you have ALL POWER OVER ALL THE POWER OF THE ENEMY! I decree a fierce, bold, Jesus death-defying anointing embodies you where you fear nothing but Jesus.

Matthew 4:10 Then Jesus said to him, "Go, Satan! For it is written, 'YOU SHALL WORSHIP THE LORD YOUR GOD, AND SERVE HIM ONLY.'"

Luke 11:14 And He was casting out a demon, and it was mute; when the demon had gone out, the mute man spoke; and the crowds were amazed.

Matthew 8:16 When evening came, they brought to Him many who were demon-possessed; and He cast out the spirits with a word, and healed all who were ill.

Mark 1:34 And He healed many who were ill with various diseases, and cast out many demons; and He was not permitting the demons to speak, because they knew who He was.

Luke 4:41 Demons also were coming out of many, shouting, "You are the Son of God!" But rebuking them, He would not allow them to speak, because they knew Him to be the Christ.

Mark 1:39 And He went into their synagogues throughout all Galilee, preaching and casting out the demons.

Luke 13:32 And He said to them, "Go and tell that fox, 'Behold, I cast out demons and perform cures today and tomorrow, and the third day I reach My goal.'

Luke 4:35 But Jesus rebuked him, saying, "Be quiet and come out of him!" And when the demon had thrown him down in the midst of the people, he came out of him without doing him any harm.

Matthew 8:32 And He said to them, "Go!" And they came out and went into the swine, and the whole herd rushed down the steep bank into the sea and perished in the waters.
Mark 5:8 For He had been saying to him, "Come out of the man, you unclean spirit!"

Luke 8:29 For He had commanded the unclean spirit to come out of the man. For it had seized him many times; and he was bound with chains and shackles and kept under guard, and yet he would break his bonds and be driven by the demon into the desert.

Mark 9:25 *When Jesus saw that a crowd was rapidly gathering, He rebuked the unclean spirit, saying to it, "You deaf and mute spirit, I command you, come out of him and do not enter him again."*

Mark 7:26 *Now the woman was a Gentile, of the Syrophoenician race. And she kept asking Him to cast the demon out of her daughter.*

Matthew 8:31 *The demons began to entreat Him, saying, "If You are going to cast us out, send us into the herd of swine."*

Matthew 9:33 *After the demon was cast out, the mute man spoke; and the crowds were amazed, and were saying, "Nothing like this has ever been seen in Israel."*

Mark 16:9 *[Now after He had risen early on the first day of the week, He first appeared to Mary Magdalene, from whom He had cast out seven demons.*

Matthew 9:34 *But the Pharisees were saying, "He casts out the demons by the ruler of the demons."*

Matthew 12:24 *But when the Pharisees heard this, they said, "This man casts out demons only by Beelzebul the ruler of the demons."*

Matthew 12:27 *If I by Beelzebul cast out demons, by whom do your sons cast them out? For this reason, they will be your judges.*

Mark 3:22 *The scribes who came down from Jerusalem were saying, "He is possessed by Beelzebul," and "He casts out the demons by the ruler of the demons."*

Luke 11:15 *But some of them said, "He casts out demons by Beelzebul, the ruler of the demons."*

Luke 11:18-19 *If Satan also is divided against himself, how will his kingdom stand? For you say that I cast out demons by Beelzebul. "And if I by Beelzebul cast out demons, by whom do your sons cast them out? So they will be your judges.*

Matthew 12:26 *If Satan casts out Satan, he is divided against himself; how then will his kingdom stand?*

Luke 11:20 *But if I cast out demons by the finger of God, then the kingdom of God has come upon you.*

Matthew 12:28 *But if I cast out demons by the Spirit of God, then the kingdom of God has come upon you.*

KEYS TO PRAYING THROUGH YOUR AUTHORITY

Pray From Your Sonship Status
When we pray, we are praying from a place of sonship, redemption, what God has done for us through his works on the cross and who we are in him as sons and daughters and heirs to his kingdom.

Romans 8:15 *For you have not received a spirit of slavery leading again to fear [of God's judgment], but you have received the Spirit of adoption as sons [the Spirit producing sonship] by which we [joyfully] cry, "Abba! Father!*

Romans 8:19 *For [even the whole] creation [all nature] waits eagerly for the children of God to be revealed.*

Galatians 4:4-7 *But when the fulness of the time has come, God sent forth his Son, made of a woman, made under the law, To redeem them that were under the law, that we might receive the adoption of sons. And because ye are sons, God hath sent forth the Spirit of his Son into your hearts, crying, Abba, Father. Wherefore thou art no more a servant, but a son; and if a son, then an heir of God through Christ.*

Isaiah 53:5 *But He was wounded for our transgressions, He was bruised for our iniquities: the chastisement of our peace was upon him, and with his stripes, we are healed.*

Pray Through The Authority God Provide To You In Sonship
We are also praying through our authority via sonship. God has given us dominion in the earth, and power and authority over all the power of the enemy.

Genesis 1:26-28 *God said, Let Us [Father, Son, and Holy Spirit] make mankind in Our image, after Our likeness, and let them have complete authority over the fish of the sea, the birds of the air, the [tame] beasts, and over all of the earth, and over everything that creeps upon the earth. So God created man in His own image, in the image and likeness of God He created him; male and female He created them. And God blessed them and said to them, Be fruitful, multiply, and* *fill the earth, and subdue it [using all its vast resources in the service of God and man]; and have dominion over the fish of the sea, the birds of the air, and over every living creature that moves upon the earth.*

Psalm 82:6 *I have said, Ye are gods; and all of you are children of the Most High.*

John 10:34-35 *Jesus answered them, "Is it not written in your Law, 'I have said you are "gods"'? 35 If he called them 'gods,' to whom the word of God came – and Scripture cannot be set aside.*

Matthew 28:18-19 *Then Jesus came to them and said, 'All authority in heaven and on earth has been given to me. Therefore go and make disciples of all nations, baptizing them in the name of the Father and of the Son and of the Holy Spirit.*

Matthew 10:8 *Heal the sick, cleanse the lepers, raise the dead, cast out devils: freely ye have received, freely give.*

Matthew 18:18-20 *Verily I say unto you, Whatsoever ye shall bind on earth shall be bound in heaven: and whatsoever ye shall loose on earth shall be loosed in heaven. Again I say unto you, that if two of you shall agree on earth as touching anything that they shall ask, it shall be done for them of my Father which is in heaven. For where two or three are gathered together in my name, there am I in the midst of them.*

Luke 10:19 *Behold, I give unto you power to tread on serpents and scorpions, and over all the power of the enemy: and nothing shall by any means hurt you.*

Luke 11:20 *But if I with the finger of God cast out devils, no doubt the kingdom of God has come upon you.*

Romans 8:28-34 *And we know that all things work together for good to them that love God, to* **them who are the called according to his purpose.** *For whom he did foreknow, he also did predestinate to be conformed to the image of his Son, that he might be the firstborn among many brethren. Moreover whom he did predestinate, them he also called: and whom he called, them he also justified: and whom he justified, them he also glorified. What shall we then say to these things? If God is for us, who can be against us? He that spared not his own Son, but delivered Him up for us all, how shall he not with him also freely give us all things? Who shall lay anything to the charge of God's elect? It is God that justifieth. Who is he that condemneth? It is Christ that died, yea rather, that is risen again, who is even at the right hand of God, who also maketh intercession for us.*

Pray Through Your Personal Calling

God has called us to live his specific identity and likeness and has given us authority, governance, abilities, and capabilities in the earth according to who he has called us to be and do in the earth.

≈ **What has God called you to do on earth?** I am called as an apostle so that is my mantle and grace – apostolic grace.

≈ **What is the purpose of your calling?** I am called to deliver, heal, make well all people, and to raise up the younger generation in their destinies and calling where they sustain in personal generation inheritance. I am called to war and dismantle principalities and strongholds and to overthrow demonic kingdoms while SHIFTING in the kingdom of God in the earth through revival reformation.

≈ **What are your gifts?** I am gifted in counseling, teaching, training, equipping, releasing, delivering, healing, prophesying, interceding, working miracles, loving people like God loves people, fine arts ministry, administrating, scribing; I have the give of revelation, wisdom, counsel, understanding, knowledge, and might.

≈ **What is the well of anointing you are operating with?** Your well of anointing manifests in everything that you do. For example, if you teach, preach, paint, dance, intercede, that anointing will manifest. I operate through the well of deliverance, healing, SHIFTING, and transformation, so my well of anointing manifests in everything that I do. Everything I do and touch manifests a SHIFT!

Take some time to search God to these questions. Do not focus on if you can do it or not, how you are going to be equipped in it, that you have not arrived yet, etc. Just focus on journaling what he says, soaking and embodying it as truth, and reigning in the authority of what is the truth about you. This is important because it is your GOD-IDENTITY. So many people do not see prayers and prophecies manifest because they waver in their GOD-IDENTITY so the authority of the truth of who they are wains. David was anointed king in his youth and did not take the throne for years. But he never denied or rejected his calling to the throne. We must understand that who God called us to be. We must accept and embrace it so that all that we are to receive and achieve through it can be revealed and released to us.

Jeremiah 1:5 *Before I formed thee in the belly I knew thee; and before thou camest forth out of the womb I sanctified thee, and I ordained thee a prophet unto the nations.*

2Peter 1:10-11 *Wherefore the rather, brethren, give diligence to make your calling and election sure: for if ye do these things, ye shall never fall.*

Romans 12:1-21 *I beseech you therefore, brethren, by the mercies of God, that ye present your bodies a living sacrifice, holy, acceptable unto God, which is your reasonable service.*

John 6:44 *No man can come to me, except the Father which hath sent me draw him: and I will raise him up at the last day.*

Pray From The Third Heaven
Pray from the third heavens and from your rightful position – and seat - in God.

Ephesians 6:9 *And hath raised us up together, and made us sit together in heavenly places in Christ Jesus.*

By faith literally, start your prayer declaring and establishing yourself in the third heavens. Pray with a third heaven mindset and confidence as if you are looking down on the earth, your circumstances, demons, people, and life in general. Your life's intent should be to SHIFT heaven to earth. SHIFT what is in heaven into the earth realm.

Matthew 6:9-10 *After this manner, therefore, pray ye: Our Father which art in heaven, Hallowed be thy name. Thy kingdom come, Thy will be done in earth, as it is in heaven.*

Colossians 3:1-4 *If ye then be risen with Christ, seek those things which are above, where Christ sitteth on the right hand of God. Set your affection on things above, not on things on the earth. For ye are dead, and your life is hidden with Christ in God. When Christ, who is our life, shall appear, then shall ye also appear with him in glory.*

The phrase *"set your affection"* is one that requires obedience.

Set is a past tense word and is a stable place or position. *Set* also denotes an office and place of officiating and occupying. It is not a place you leave. Because it is past tense, it is a place you dwell, abide -establish residence in.

Affection in Greek is "*phroneo,*" and means:
1. Sentiment, opinion, interest, concern, care, savour
2. To be like-minded, to be of the same mind,
3. To have the understanding to be wise, to feel, to think divinely
4. Agree together, be harmonious, cherish the same views
5. To be of one party, to side with God
6. To judge oneself or ones opinion based on what God's opinion is

As we posture ourselves to have the same sentiments, opinions, interests, concerns, cares, as God, we SHIFT to living and reigning as judges and rulers from this seat of authority, grace, and dominion. As you practice this as a lifestyle, your spirit will automatically SHIFT you to a heavenly perspective where you easily see things like God sees them and hear God from his delights and perspective. You are able to automatically discern and operate through his holiness, righteousness, purity, love, plan, and purpose.

Philippians 4:8 *Finally, brethren, whatsoever things are true, whatsoever things are honest, whatsoever things are just, whatsoever things are pure, whatsoever things are lovely, whatsoever things are of good report; if there be any virtue, and if there be any praise, think on these things.*

Psalm 121:1-2 *I will lift up mine eyes unto the hills, from whence cometh my help. My help cometh from the Lord, which made heaven and earth.*

Isaiah 26:3 *Thou wilt keep him in perfect peace, whose mind is stayed on thee: because he trusteth in thee.*

Romans 12:2 *Do not conform any longer to the pattern of this world, but be transformed by the renewing of your mind.*

While seeking to sit in heavenly places as a lifestyle, it will be important to reject being dictated by your flesh, thoughts, and emotions. Many times we are yielding to how we feel, think, and the humanity of our fleshly and carnal desires. These perspectives are open doors to the enemy coming in and occupying us where we live below our heavenly authority and heritage, where we cannot reign in heavenly places with God. There will always be a war for our seats. As Paul says in *Romans 7:23*,

But I see another law in my members, warring against the law of my mind, and bringing me into captivity to the law of sin which is in my members.

James 4:7 *Submit yourselves therefore to God. Resist the devil, and he will flee from you.*

Prayer is from spirit to spirit – your spirit to God's spirit. It is not a consideration but a mandate.

John 4:24 *God is Spirit, and those who worship Him must worship in spirit and truth.*

A spirit-to-spirit connection with God is to be commonplace and is essential for the flourishing of every area of your life. Reject birthing or doing anything in your life outside of prayer. When you SHIFT to living in this mindset and mandate were communing with God is THE ESSENTIAL – your needful place = then nothing will separate you from him. You will sacrifice sleep, fellowships, and whatever else for him – to be with him. As you commune with him every day -all day – as a lifestyle, you will continuously evolve in prayer. He will constantly embody you, fill you, teach and train you, and use you for his glory.

Practice Making Heaven Your Established Home

To grow in your prayer life spend consistent time declaring by faith you are SHIFTING up in the heavens and you are surrounded, communing, and living in heaven - from a heavenly perspective, from heavenly fruit, fruit heavenly supply and provision; from who God is as ruler of all; your ruler who rules through you and supplies and guides your life and circumstances.

Ephesians 1:19-23 *And what is the exceeding greatness of His power toward us who believe, according to the working of His mighty power which He worked in Christ when He raised Him from the dead and seated Him at His right hand in the heavenly places, far above all principality and power and might and dominion, and every name that is named, not only in this age but also in that which is to come. And He put all things under His feet, and gave Him to be head over all things to the church, which is His body, the fullness of Him who fills all in all.*

Peering Into Heaven

Practice peering into heaven, peering into the rooms of heaven, peering into seeing God bless you, intervene for you, provide for you, protect you, guide you. Ask God to open the eyes of your understanding so you can peer into heaven through your spiritual senses.

Ephesians 1:18 *The eyes of your understanding being enlightened; that ye may know what is the hope of his calling, and what the riches of the glory of his inheritance in the saints.*

Seer Vision – (Excerpt from my book, *"Unmasking The Power Of The Scouts, Volume I: Gaining Intel For Victory Over Your Opposition."*) God will allow the eyes of your imagination and understanding to be open and empowered so you can peer into someone's life, ministry, business, situation, or region, so you can see what is or will occur. He may give you pictures, images, play-by-play, a spiritual tour, or full visions. God guides you in this. You do not open this portal yourself as then you have exposed yourself to what is called a "third eye" where you are receiving information illegally and through demonic assistance. The eyes of your understanding are a part of your spirit and thus what is being filtered into your imagination is from God's spirit to your spirit.

Some people see because they have the gift of a seer. Some can pray fiercely in the spirit for a significant length of time, then meditate on the Lord until he opens their understanding and imagination. If you do not flow in this area, then God may use you in other ways, such as:

- ≈ Day and night dreams and visions.

- ≈ Translations into regions of heaven, spiritual realms, demonic and witchcraft camps and kingdoms, people's homes, situations, communities, nations.

- Spiritual warfare as you intercede and stand in the gap for people, regions, and spheres (Study *Ephesians 6*).

- Your spiritual knower such that he downloads revelations and you just know information by his leading. God put it in us at creation to know Him *(Study Romans 1:19-21)*. This passage speaks about how we are without excuse when we reject knowing God because He created us to know Him, His character, and His nature. When we reject Him and choose another god, He turns us over to ourselves and to that which we choose to serve as to him, there is no excuse not to know Him. King David states the following:

    Psalm 51:6 Behold, thou desirest truth in the inward parts: and in the hidden part thou shalt make me to know wisdom.

    Psalm 139:14 I will praise thee; for I am fearfully and wonderfully made: marvellous are thy works; and that my soul knoweth right well

    Whether we acknowledge it or utilize it, have a knower in our soul that knows God, his voice, and his word.

- The mind of Christ – As we seek to possess the mind of Christ, he will give us his thoughts, insights, wisdom, revelations, knowledge, counsel, understandings, and instructions. We think like he thinks and possesses his ability to engage a matter through his intellect

    Philippians 2:5 Let this mind be in you, which was also in Christ Jesus.

- Sevenfold Spirit of The Lord – God will reveal mysteries through his spirit.

    Isaiah 11:2 And the spirit of the Lord shall rest upon him, the spirit of wisdom and understanding, the spirit of counsel and might, the spirit of knowledge and of the fear of the Lord.)

    John 16:13 Howbeit when he, the Spirit of truth, is come, he will guide you into all truth: for he shall not speak of himself; but whatsoever he shall hear, that shall he speak: and he will shew you things to come.

Ask God to open your spiritual eyes to,
- See Him and see heaven.
- Hear Him and hear heaven.
- Feel Him and feel heaven.
- Taste Him and taste heaven.
- Smell Him and smell heaven.

- Discern Him and discern heaven.
- Judge and distinguish what is and is not of him and of heaven.
- Engage him and engage heaven.

Hebrews 4:12 For the word of God is living and active, sharper than any two-edged sword, piercing to the division of soul and of spirit, of joints and of marrow, and discerning the thoughts and intentions of the heart.

John 14:2 In my Father's house are many mansions: if it were not so, I would have told you. I go to prepare a place for you.

Deuteronomy 28:12 The Lord will open for you His good storehouse, the heavens, to give rain to your land in its season and to bless all the work of your hand; and you shall lend to many nations, but you shall not borrow.

Jeremiah 50:25 The LORD hath opened his armoury, and hath brought forth the weapons of his indignation: for this is the work of the Lord GOD of hosts in the land of the Chaldeans.

1Corinthians 2:9 But as it is written, Eye hath not seen, nor ear heard, neither have entered into the heart of man, the things which God hath prepared for them that love him.

2Corinthians Paul the Apostle writes, "I know a person in Christ who fourteen years ago was caught up to the third heaven – whether in the body or out of the body I do not know; God knows.

Revelations 21:1-5 And I saw a new heaven and a new earth: for the first heaven and the first earth were passed away; and there was no more sea. And I John saw the holy city, new Jerusalem, coming down from God out of heaven, prepared as a bride adorned for her husband. And I heard a great voice out of heaven saying, Behold, the tabernacle of God is with men, and he will dwell with them, and they shall be his people, and God himself shall be with them, and be their God. And God shall wipe away all tears from their eyes; and there shall be no more death, neither sorrow, nor crying, neither shall there be any more pain: for the former things are passed away. And he that sat upon the throne said, Behold, I make all things new. And he said unto me, Write: for these words are true and faithful.

Ezekiel 8:3 He stretched out what looked like a hand and took me by the hair of my head. Then the Spirit lifted me up between earth and heaven and carried me in visions of God to Jerusalem, to the entrance of the north gate of the inner court, where the idol that provokes jealousy was seated.

Ezekiel 11:24 And the Spirit lifted me up and carried me back to Chaldea, to the exiles in the vision given by the Spirit of God. After the vision had gone up from me,

Ezekiel 43:5 Then the Spirit lifted me up and brought me into the inner court, and the glory of the LORD filled the temple.

Peering Into The Deep

Practice peering into the deep, the deep things of God, his mysteries, his sevenfold revelation, his insight, his understanding, his will, and purpose. Be obedient in prayer and in life to what he says so that deeper dimensions of his essence and mysteries can be revealed to you. Disobedience and not living as God requires hinders access. God reveals mysteries to his friends - his people. You are his if you keep covenant and obey his word.

Psalm 2:7 He stores up sound wisdom for the upright; He is a shield to those who walk in integrity.

I love this scripture. People always ask me how I scribe so many books. I pray in my prayer language all day long. I talk to God all through the day. I am always asking God questions, inquiring, seeking his will, purpose, and insight, and just, worshiping, reverencing, and honoring him. As a result, God constantly downloads his wisdom to me. I am adamant about releasing what God speaks to me whether praying, encouraging, preaching, teaching, equipping others, or scribing books. When I SHIFT into scribing a book, I usually have to break the book into a series because of the revelation God gives me. When I speak into people's lives, God usually gives me detailed strategies. I have wisdom stored up which generally allows me to have wisdom beyond my years and even into future generations.

Colossians 1:25-29 Whereof I am made a minister, according to the dispensation of God which is given to me for you, to fulfill the word of God; Even the mystery which hath been hidden from ages and from generations, but now is made manifest to his saints: To whom God would make known what is the riches of the glory of this mystery among the Gentiles; which is Christ in you, the hope of glory: To whom God would make known what is the riches of the glory of this mystery among the Gentiles; which is Christ in you, the hope of glory: Whereunto I also labour, striving according to his working, which worketh in me mightily.

Ephesians 6:19 And pray on my behalf, that utterance may be given to me in the opening of my mouth, to make known with boldness the mystery of the gospel.

Daniel 2:30 But as for me, this mystery has not been revealed to me for any wisdom residing in me more than in any other living man, but for the purpose of making the interpretation known to the king, and that you may understand the thoughts of your mind.

Daniel 2:23 "To You, O God of my fathers, I give thanks and praise, For You have given me wisdom and power; Even now You have made known to me what we requested of You, For You have made known to us the king's matter."

The mysteries of God are your right as sons of God.

Jeremiah 33:3 Call to Me and I will answer you, and I will tell you great and mighty things, which you do not know.

Ephesians 1:9 *He made known to us the mystery of His will, according to His kind intention which He purposed in Him.*

Luke 2:8 *And He said, "To you, it has been granted to know the mysteries of the kingdom of God, but to the rest, it is in parables so that seeing they may not see, and hearing they may not understand.*

1Corinthians 2:10 *For to us God revealed them through the Spirit; for the Spirit searches all things, even the depths of God.*

1Corinthians 2:9 *But just as it is written, "Things which eye has not seen and ear has not heard, And which have not entered the heart of man, All that God has prepared for those who love Him."*

Psalm 64:6 *They devise injustices, saying, "We are ready with a well-conceived plot;" For the inward thought and the heart of a man are deep.*

Job 38:16-17 *"Have you entered into the springs of the sea Or walked in the recesses of the deep? "Have the gates of death been revealed to you, Or have you seen the gates of deep darkness?*

Peer Into Your Situations

Practice peering into your situations and those you are praying for and seeking God for. Expect God to give you the answers, revelations, strategies, cures, and tangible manifestations you need to SHIFT heaven to earth – to produce his kingdom in your midst.

1Corinthians 6:2-4 *Do you not know that the saints will judge the world? And if you are to judge the world, are you not competent to judge trivial cases? Do you not know that we will judge angels? How much more the things of this life! Therefore, if you have disputes about such matters, appoint as judges even men of little account in the church!*

Use your spiritual discernment to see what operations are occurring. As you pray ask God,

- What's happening?
- Is God at work or the devil?
- Are good people or bad people at work and are they being used by God or the devil cause even good people can be intentional and unintentional open doors to demonic workings?
- What reasons is this occurring?
- What is God's position in this?
- What does God want my position and workings in this to be? This is important because sometimes we do more or less than God is requiring. We want to do

exactly what God desires and if he is not speaking, we want to be mindful of anything he has already spoken to us or to stand in faith and our right to have what he says according to his biblical word.

Daniel 2:19 *Then the mystery was revealed to Daniel in a night vision. Then Daniel blessed the God of heaven.*

Daniel 2:22 *"It is He who reveals the profound and hidden things; He knows what is in the darkness, And the light dwells with Him.*

Daniel 2:28 *However, there is a God in heaven who reveals mysteries, and He has made known to King Nebuchadnezzar what will take place in the latter days. This was your dream and the visions in your mind while on your bed.*

Daniel 2:47 *The king answered Daniel and said, "Surely your God is a God of gods and a Lord of kings and a revealer of mysteries since you have been able to reveal this mystery."*

Job 12:22 *He reveals mysteries from the darkness and brings the deep darkness into light.*

Job 33:15-18 *"In a dream, for instance, a vision at night, when men and women are deep in sleep, fast asleep in their beds – God opens their ears and impresses them with warnings to turn them back from something bad they're planning, from some reckless choice, and keep them from an early grave from the river of no return.*

2Kings 6:11-12 *Therefore the heart of the king of Syria was sore troubled for this thing; and he called his servants, and said unto them, Will ye not shew me which of us is for the king of Israel? And one of his servants said, None, my lord, O king: but Elisha, the prophet that is in Israel, telleth the king of Israel the words that thou speakest in thy bedchamber.*

Amos 3:7 *Surely the Lord GOD will do nothing, but he revealeth his secret unto his servants the prophets.*

Luke 5:22 *But when Jesus perceived their thoughts, he answering said unto them, What reason ye in your hearts?*

Psalm 139:2 *Thou knowest my downsitting and mine uprising, thou understandest my thought afar off.*

Peer Into Your Situations & Into The Devil's Camp
Practice peering into the devil's camp.

Numbers 14:38 *But Joshua the son of Nun, and Caleb the son of Jephunneh, which were of the men that went to search the land, lived still.*

New King James Bible But Joshua the son of Nun and Caleb the son of Jephunneh remained alive, of the men who went to spy out the land.

Matthew 12:25 And Jesus knew their thoughts, and said unto them, Every kingdom divided against itself is brought to desolation; and every city or house divided against itself shall not stand.

Luke 12:23 What you have spoken in the dark will be heard in the daylight, and what you have whispered in the inner rooms will be proclaimed from the housetops.

Please know that while you are not peering into the enemy's camp, he is indeed peering into your life. The devil and his imps are lurkers.

1Peter 5:8 Be sober, be vigilant; because your adversary the devil, as a roaring lion, walketh about, seeking whom he may devour.

Walketh about in Greek means, "to make use of opportunities, progress, regulate one's life, conduct one's life, pass one's life."

Seeking in Greek means, " to plot, inquire, endeavor, to seek in order to find, seek in order to find out, seek a thing, strive after, to crave, to demand something from someone."

Isn't that a trip….My Lord!

That should have made you ANGRY!!!

Ecclesiastes 10:20 Curse not the king, no not in thy thought; and curse not the rich in thy bedchamber: for a bird of the air shall carry the voice, and that which hath wings shall tell the matter.

Psalm 91 is all about being protected from lurking demons and their demonic attacks.

Psalm 91:5-6 Thou shalt not be afraid for the terror by night; nor for the arrow that flieth by day; Nor for the pestilence that walketh in darkness; nor for the destruction that wasteth at noonday.

Luke 20:20 So they watched him and sent spies, who pretended to be sincere, that they might catch him in something he said, so as to deliver him up to the authority and jurisdiction of the governor.

As you peer and God provides you with revelation, ask him the following:

- ≈ Who is the revelation for; you, someone in your family or friend, an acquaintance, your ministry or a specific ministry, the body of Christ, a community, region, or nation?

- ≈ Ask him for clarity on what demons and people are at work. If he does not reveal this information then be at peace with what he does reveal. Sometimes we know in part and someone else has the other piece of the revelation. It all will SHIFT together in His timing.

- ≈ Ask God what does he want you to do with the information; he may have you share it, he may not have you share it, he may just be sharing his heart and secrets, he may desire you to intercede, he may have you write a book about it, preach or teach on it. This is important because many people automatically assume that if God is revealing something to them, especially a warning, judgment, or information regarding demons and wickedness, they should sound the alarm. But this is not always the case. It is never good to be impulsive and irresponsible with the mysteries of God. So many have blasted forth without asking God his will and purpose, and without full revelation. This has resulted in people being hurt, them being rejected, and the body of Christ looking crazy and spooky spiritually. Ask God his intent so your heart can align with his purpose for HIS revelation.

- ≈ Ask him for more insight and if principalities and high places are involved, ask him how to disrupt, pull down, and overthrow their kingdoms. Do what as he leads. Nothing more and nothing less.

Pray The Word Of God

The biblical word of God is one of your greatest weapons of prayer. God responds to his word and operates through the truths, principles, stability, and standard of his word. God will not violate his word nor manipulate it to meet your will. Though God and his word are evolving, both are unchanging. God's word is set and will never change. We can interpret it 500 million ways, deny it, act as if it is insignificant or just another book, but his word is eternal. It will outlast every last one of us.

Proverbs 19:21 *There are many devices in a man's heart; nevertheless the counsel of the LORD, that shall stand.*

Psalm 119:89 *Your word, LORD, is eternal; it stands firm in the heavens.*

1Peter 21:5 *But the word of the Lord endures forever." And this is the word which was preached to you.*

Psalm 119:60 *The sum of Your word is truth, And every one of Your righteous ordinances is everlasting.*

Matthew 24:35 *Heaven and earth will pass away, but My words will not pass away.*

God's word also settles our victory and established the devil's fate. He has a time of roaming, but victory is already ours – WE WIN. He cannot handle the truth of our salvation and authority in God. When we are students of the word, we are able to war through the truth. It is the truth that sets us free. It is the truth that overthrows the enemy. As you pray and God reveals what you are praying for or you are led to pray different things, search out some scriptures to stand in and pray into as you entreat God via prayer. Study key words in the scripture and use the concordance and the dictionary to build your vocabulary and expand your prayer.

Pray Without Ceasing

Pray until you receive a breakthrough. I use my knowledge to determine if I have broken through or not. I have practiced tarrying with God until I experience a release in the spirit concerning whatever I am praying for until now my compacity for prayer is lengthy. I can pray consecutively and consistently for hours without becoming tired. I spend my free time even short times during the day praying and I make sacrifices to spend time in prayer and studying my word. I do not allow time or even the fact that I may have prayed for a specific area for hours to dictate my breakthrough. I allow the Holy Spirit – my knower – to guide me into the truth about what has happened in prayer and I am governed by the truth of whether I prayed through or not. I also do not allow religious cliché and ideologies to dictate my prayer time. Many believe that if they prayed once or for a long time that is enough and that it is a lack of faith to keep contending for a breakthrough. However, the Bible states the following:

1Thessalonians 5:16-18 *Rejoice always, pray without ceasing, give thanks in all circumstances; for this is the will of God in Christ Jesus for you.*

Philippians 4:6-7 *Be careful for nothing; but in every thing by prayer and supplication with thanksgiving let your requests be made known unto God. And the peace of God, which passeth all understanding, shall keep your hearts and minds through Christ Jesus.*

As the Lord leads, I may change my prayer such that I may decree and declare, spend time thanking God for what I am praying about, use soaking prayers, etc., but I do not cease on praying until I have SHIFTED heaven to earth. Until I have a strong knowing and tangible manifestation that breakthrough has SHIFTED into my midst – the situation I have prayed about.

Tread Down Your Enemies

When I am praying, I tread with God in the spirit. I seek to peer in like a literal trampling sword, seeking to tread down my enemies, do surgery by piercing the divide asunder of soul and spirit, while delivering, healing, and restoring whatever area my enemies sought to destroy or take as their own.

Hebrews 4:12 For the word of God is quick, and powerful, and sharper than any two-edged sword, piercing even to the dividing asunder of soul and spirit, and of the joints and marrow, and is a discerner of the thoughts and intents of the heart.

- ✓ A two-edged sword penetrates, divides, and cuts in **ANY** direction.
- ✓ The two-edged sword in you should be separating you from the people, lands, regions, spheres you prophesy to, and anything that is not of God.
- ✓ The two-edged sword should divide asunder what is soulish (e.g. fleshly, unhealthy feelings and emotions, vain thoughts, and imaginations) from what is of God's Holy Spirit.
- ✓ The two-edged sword should literally cut through hard matters and separate people, lands, regions, spheres, and the body of Christ from any joints and marrow – anything that has attached and presented itself as God and His kingdom.
- ✓ The two-edged sword should identify – produce discernment. It should be detecting whether what is being prayed for or prayed against, is producing God's will or the kingdom of heaven on earth.
- ✓ The two-edge sword is also a healer. God's word comes to deliver, heal, and produce his kingdom on earth.

Psalm 44:5 Through thee will we push down our enemies: through thy name will we tread them under that rise up against us.

Psalm 60:12 Through God we shall do valiantly: for he [it is that] shall tread down our enemies.

Psalm 91:13 Thou shalt tread upon the lion and adder: the young lion and the dragon shalt thou trample under feet.

Psalm 108:13 Through God we shall do valiantly: for he [it is that] shall tread down our enemies.

Isaiah 1:12 When ye come to appear before me, who hath required this at your hand, to tread my courts?

Isaiah 10:6 *I will send him against a hypocritical nation, and against the people of my wrath will I give him a charge, to take the spoil, and to take the prey, and to tread them down like the mire of the streets.*

Isaiah 14:25 *That I will break the Assyrian in my land, and upon my mountains tread him under foot: then shall his yoke depart from off them, and his burden depart from off their shoulders.*

Isaiah 63:3 *I have trodden the winepress alone; and of the people [there was] none with me: for I will tread them in mine anger, and trample them in my fury; and their blood shall be sprinkled upon my garments, and I will stain all my raiment.*

Isaiah 63:6 *And I will tread down the people in mine anger, and make them drunk in my fury, and I will bring down their strength to the earth.*

Jeremiah 25:30 *Therefore prophesy thou against them all these words, and say unto them, The LORD shall roar from on high, and utter his voice from his holy habitation; he shall mightily roar upon his habitation; he shall give a shout, as they that tread [the grapes], against all the inhabitants of the earth.*

Ezekiel 26:11 *With the hoofs of his horses shall he tread down all thy streets: he shall slay thy people by the sword, and thy strong garrisons shall go down to the ground.*

Zechariah 10:5 *And they shall be as mighty [men], which tread down [their enemies] in the mire of the streets in the battle: and they shall fight, because the LORD [is] with them, and the riders on horses shall be confounded.*

Malachi 4:3 *And ye shall tread down the wicked; for they shall be ashes under the soles of your feet in the day that I shall do [this], saith the LORD of hosts.*

Luke 10:19 *Behold, I give unto you power to tread on serpents and scorpions, and over all the power of the enemy: and nothing shall by any means hurt you.*

Joshua 1:3 *Every place that the sole of your foot shall tread upon, that have I given unto you, as I said unto Moses.*

<u>Tread is Pateo in Greek and means:</u>
1. To trample, crush with the feet, to advance by setting the foot upon, tread upon
2. To encounter successfully the greatest perils from the machinations and persecutions with which Satan would fain thwart the preaching of the gospel
3. To tread underfoot, trample on
4. To treat with insult and contempt
5. To desecrate the by devastation and outrage

Be intentional to kill the devil and his workings with your prayers in the same or greater manner that he is trying to kill you; and to receive miracles, signs, wonders, and breakthroughs, in the same or greater manner to which God is striving to bless you.

Pray In Your Prayer Language
If you have not received your prayer language, pursue God until your prayer language manifests in you. Your prayer language is the power of God's voice and spiritual utterance enduing, embodying, and empowering you.

Matthew 16:17 *And these signs will accompany those who believe: In my name, they will drive out demons; they will speak in new tongues.*

Acts 1:8 *But ye shall receive power, after that the Holy Ghost will come upon you: and ye shall be witnesses unto me both in Jerusalem, and in all Judaea, and in Samaria, and unto the uttermost part of the earth.*

Practice praying consistently so you can mature in the following:

- ≈ Knowing or having a sense of what you are praying against and what you are saying.

- ≈ Experiencing diverse kinds of tongues and spiritual tongues, where you sing, war, worship, praise through different wells of tongues and languages.

    1Corinthians 12:4 *Now there are diversities of gifts, but the same Spirit. You have to have the Spirit to have one of the 9 gifts of the Spirit.*

    1Corinthians 13:1 *Though I speak with the tongues of men and of angels, and have not charity, I have become as sounding brass or a tinkling cymbal.*

    1Corinthians 14:15 *What is it then? I will pray with the spirit, and I will pray with the understanding also: I will sing with the spirit, and I will sing with the understanding also.*

    2Corinthians 14:2 *For anyone who speaks in a tongue does not speak to people but to God. Indeed, no one understands them; they utter mysteries by the Spirit.*

- ≈ Living through your spirit, governing through your spirit, and manifesting the kingdom of heaven in the earth.

- ≈ Asserting power and confidence over all the power of the enemy.

I have an eBook that I would encourage you to purchase entitled, *"Holy Spirit As Friend"* that will teach you about the Holy Spirit, and how to grow in covenant friendship with him.

WARFARE LEVELS & TACTICS

This information will be *from my book entitled, "Unmasking The Power Of The Scouts, Volume I: Gaining Intel For Victory Over Your Opposition."* As you partake of the revelation in this book, it will be important to know a few keywords that may be utilized to explain demonic forces, and how they operate.

Ephesians 6:12-13 For we wrestle not against flesh and blood, but against principalities, against powers, against the rulers of the darkness of this world, against spiritual wickedness in high places. Wherefore take unto you the whole armour of God, that ye may be able to withstand in the evil day, and having done all, to stand.

It understands rankings and operates in levels of warfare.

Levels of Warfare

- **Ground Level Warfare** involves casting demons out of individuals, places, and things.

- **Occult Level Warfare** involves witchcraft, idolatry, or strategic organizations that are real powers of darkness, or spiritual wickedness in high places within a community or region. Examples, Freemasonry, Sororities, Fraternities, New Age Practices, Buddhism, Tibetan, Yoga, etc.

- **Strategic Level Warfare** is where principalities and territorial spirits are assigned by Satan to directly bind, influence, and govern the activities of communities, regions, states, and nations. They also coordinate demonic activities in political, governmental, economic, financial, educational, business, and entertainment arenas.

Spiritual Warfare – Whether we want to admit it or not, we are in a spiritual war. Jesus Christ came to break the powers of death and hell so that we can be restored in the blessings, favor, wellness, and eternity with God. We have to assert our right through the authority Jesus Christ has provided us through his blood, works on the cross, and resurrection, to have what he released unto us. The devil and his kingdom are constantly contending against what is rightfully ours. He wants us to live beneath or contrary to what God has ordained for us as his people. He will contend against us and God's kingdom until Jesus returns. We need to grasp this truth and SHIFT into our place as soldiers in the army of God.

Matthew 11:12 And from the days of John the Baptist until now the kingdom of heaven suffereth violence, and the violent take it by force.

Ephesians 6:12 *For we wrestle not against flesh and blood, but against principalities, against powers, against the rulers of the darkness of this world, against spiritual wickedness in high places.*

2Timothy 2:3-4 *Thou, therefore, endure hardness, as a good soldier of Jesus Christ. No man that warreth entangleth himself with the affairs of this life; that he may please him who hath chosen him to be a soldier.*

Apostle Jackie Green of JGM-Enternational Ministries defines spiritual warfare as the *"advanced and mature level of prayer and intercession that removes demonic strongholds that are blinding individuals, false religions, cities, and nations from receiving the gospel of Jesus Christ."*

Deliverance is about us asserting our right to what Jesus Christ freed us from and blessed us with when he shed his blood for us, died on the cross, and rose again with all power in his hands. He restored our right to live redeemed in the daily revival, renewal, blessings, and wellness of covenant destiny with God as a lifestyle.

2Corinthians 5:15 *And that he died for all, that they which live should not henceforth live unto themselves, but unto him which died for them, and rose again.*

John 3:16 *Now the Lord is the Spirit, and where the Spirit of the Lord is, there is freedom."*

Romans 4:25 *Who was delivered for our offenses, and was raised again for our justification.*

Galatians 4:4-7 *But when the right time came, God sent his Son, born of a woman, subject to the law. God sent him to buy freedom for us who were slaves to the law so that he could adopt us as his very own children. And because we are his children, God has sent the Spirit of his Son into our hearts, prompting us to call out, "Abba, Father." Now you are no longer a slave but God's own child. And since you are his child, God has made you his heir.*

Galatians 5:1 *So Christ has truly set us free. Now make sure that you stay free, and don't get tied up again in slavery to the law.*

Since salvation is our right as kingdom citizens, it is important to be offensive in knowing who and what we are combating so we can be effective in asserting our right to be delivered and set free. Such a posture requires us to be offensive in our salvation walk and in asserting power over the enemy.

Offensive Versus Defensive Warfare Tactics

Definition of Offensive:
1. Making an attack, aggressive, of relating to, or designed for attack
2. To be irritating or annoying, angering

3. Giving painful or unpleasant sensations: nauseous, obnoxious, causing displeasure or resentment, disrespectful, insulting; displeasing
4. The position or attitude of aggression or attack
5. An aggressive movement or attack
6. Attempting to score or one-up your opponent

Synonyms For The Word Offensive

Abhorrent	Abusive	Annoying	Biting	Cutting
Detestable	Disagreeable	Distasteful	Dreadful	Embarrassing
Evil	Foul	Ghastly	Grisly	Gross
Hideous	Horrible	Horrid	Impertinent	Insolent
Invidious	Irritating	Nauseating	Obnoxious	Offending
Repellent	Reprehensible	Repugnant	Repulsive	Revolting
Rotten	Rude	Shocking	Stinking	Terrible
Uncivil	Unmannerly			

On defense, you are trying to stop an opponent from their attack. On the offense, you are striving to attack your opponent while gaining leverage or victory before being attacked.

Matthew 11:12 And from the days of John the Baptist until now the kingdom of heaven suffereth violence, and the violent take it by force.

2Timothy 2:3 Thou therefore endure hardness, as a good soldier of Jesus Christ.

WE SHIFT TO BEING WARRIORS! Our praise and worship and ministry of dance in general, annihilate the enemies of God while ushering in his kingdom. SHIFT!

DISCERNING OF SPIRITS

Demons can operate in the following ways:

- ✓ In people whether believers or unbelievers.
- ✓ In the world and in ministries and churches
- ✓ Within an atmosphere and territory/region of a ministry.

These demonic spirits will oppress, depress, negatively influence, possess, or stronghold the communication, interaction, unity, personality, attitude, progress, the effectiveness of the ministry team or team members.

Demon Rankings

Demons are demonic forces, evil spirits, or devils that possess, depress, oppress, torment, influence, or stronghold a person, place, or thing. The way these demonic spirits attack is as follows:

- **Oppress** -to burden, restrain, weigh heavy upon, to put down; press down, subdue, or suppress an atmosphere or the soul, heart, or body of a person.
- **Depress** – to make sad or gloomy; lower in spirits; deject, dispirit, to lower in force, vigor, activity, etc.; weaken, make dull, a person or atmosphere.
- **Negatively influence** – cause confusion, discombobulation, double-mindedness, unexplainable weariness, tiredness or sluggardness, irritation, frustration, ungodly thoughts, thought racing within a person or atmosphere.
- **Possess** – to occupy, dominate, or control a person or atmosphere.

Strongholds are demonically possessed, demonically depressed, demonically gripping clutches, barriers, fortresses, walls, or entanglements that harass, influence, hinder and/or prevent a person from being free to walk in the full salvation of the Lord (*2 Corinthians 10:3-5, Ephesians 4:22-23, Matthew 16:19, Mark 3:27*).

Principalities are satanic princes and territorial spirits ruling over a nation, city, region, and community for the purposes of establishing Satan's demonic plan in people's lives and spheres.

Powers are high-ranking supernatural demons or demonic influences that cause evil and sin in the world.

Rulers of Darkness are demonic forces that govern deception and manipulative hardships and catastrophes that are generally produced by witchcraft, manipulation of the weather, and worldly systems; they operate in cultures and countries such that idolatry and sin reign in the earth.

Spiritual Wickedness in High Places are evil plots and deceptions, and demonic attacks directed in and against the church and God's people for the purposes of hindering, contaminating, and demolishing God's will on earth.

Territorial Spirits entail any demonic spirits that rule over a specific area of people, land, region, district, or body of water. These demonic spirits assert jurisdiction of these areas and will fight not to relinquish them. A territorial spirit can be a principality, power, ruler spirit, or can be spirits operating under and with these systems of demons.

Generally, territorial spirits are already in the area you are striving to occupy as they tend to squat over that particular sphere and assert their influence. Or they enter the area when you are striving to expand your authority, reach, and governance in that area, and war with you in an effort to hinder your expansion, authority, reach, governance, and your right to have what is rightfully yours. As you contend with them, they work with the demons and systems of principalities, powers ruling spirits, spiritual wickedness in high places to overthrow you and push you out of the territory you are seeking to occupy.

Territorial spirits are haughty, prideful, and stubborn. They do not back down nor will they relent easily. If the territorial spirits can overthrow you, it will try to occupy and reign with you – amongst you. The system that operates with territorial spirits will track you and follow you and then seek to hinder or take up residents in your new place, even as it contends for the old area it has attacked you in. Do not compromise and yoke with territorial spirits. When you do, they will have you submitting to their unrighteousness and evil system that disregards your worth, while draining you of your success, time, attention, abilities, and calling.

2Corinthians 6:14 Be ye not unequally yoked together with unbelievers, for what fellowship hath righteousness with unrighteousness? And what communion hath light with darkness?

This spirit will also use manipulation and trickery to frustrate you and get you to give up territory. It will use people and systems to change what has been promised or stated to you concerning the area you are seeking to occupy, especially if it is tied to expansion and promotion. It will seek to have you compromising or remaining stagnant as you are reluctant or fear fighting for your right to have what you are worth, what is promised, and what God has said is yours. It will be important to stand your ground, know your divine truth, and not yield to the manipulation, intimidation, confusion, and trickery plans of the enemy.

Many people will say, God, sent me to a particular region to live, release a ministry or business, but when they move there and warfare manifests, they dread the move instead of recognizing that territorial spirits are not going to allow them to just move in without a fight. Or they will SHIFT to their next position on their job, in relationships, within the family lineage, or their sphere of influence and is challenged when they are faced with conflict.

Territorial spirits will make you feel like you do not belong or supposed to have the space that you have already been given access to. BUT THESE DEVILS AND THEIR SYSTEMS ARE LIARS!

1Chronicles 4:10 And Jabez called on the God of Israel, saying, Oh that thou wouldest bless me indeed, and enlarge my coast, and that thine hand might be with me, and that thou wouldest keep me from evil, that it may not grieve me! And God granted him that which he requested.

The Amplified Bible *Jabez cried to the God of Israel, saying, Oh, that You would bless me and enlarge my border, and that Your hand might be with me, and You would keep me from evil so it might not hurt me! And God granted his request.*

The Message Bible *Jabez prayed to the God of Israel: "Bless me, O bless me! Give me land, large tracts of land. And provide your personal protection – don't let evil hurt me." God gave him what he asked.*

This scripture is a weapon against territorial spirits as it can be used to seek God for his blessings, provision, and protection against the territorial spirit.

Monitoring & Tracking Spirits may also be called watcher spirits, squatter spirits, scanner spirits, and demonic agents. They are demonic spirits or behaviors of demonic spirits where they track people's lives, monitor their habits, relationships, successes, actions, and behaviors, and seek ways to possess, oppression, depress, stronghold, alter, influence, torment, attack their lives and create situations to sabotage their destiny. These spirits work as destiny-killing spirits. They work to collaborate with as a demonic confederacy with systems of principalities, powers, territorial spirits, ruler spirits, spiritual wickedness in high places to gain entail on people so they seek ways to infiltrate people's lives.

Witchcraft Practices
Witchcraft is the practice of magic, especially black magic; it is the utilization of spells and the invocation of demons to bind people, families, ministries, businesses, organizations, land, atmospheres, climates, regions, and nations. Some people engage in witchcraft for entertainment, curiosity, or ignorance. Those that dedicate their lives to it use it to acquire personal success and advancement, power, fame, rank in spiritual realms, spheres, and to obtain high ranking positions and platforms in the natural.

As deliverers, it is important to study witchcraft and gain intel on their operations. One of your mandates as a scout is to deal with spiritual wickedness in high places and to pull down high places. Witchcraft has become more prevalent and blatant and confrontation of witches, warlocks, and witchcraft is essential for cleansing the land and airways of regions and dispelling spells sent about the ministers, ministries, organizations, and businesses of God.

Witches are known to come to services posing as saints while releasing spells against the people and purposes of God. They are known to cast spells on ministers and against events. As a scout, you may even encounter witches in your dream realm, during Holy Spirit translations, or during intercessory and spiritual warfare. Deliverers are not afraid of witches and witchcraft. Know your authority and gain intel on how witchcraft operates so you can quickly discern and dispel its workings.

Some witchcraft practices include:

Sorcery	Magic	Witching	Wizardry
Black Magic	White Magic	Candle Magic	Spells
Hexes	Vexes	Hoodoo	Voodoo
Wicca	Mojo	Chants	Demonic Crossroads
Santeria	Yoruba Religion	Hinduism	New Age Practices
Horoscopes	Tarot Readings	Psychic Readings	Chain Letters
Familiar Spirits	Spirit Guides	High Priest/Priestess	Demonic Omens
Necromancy	Yoga	Shamanism	Fortune Telling
Hypnotism	Acupuncture	Psychic Powers	Superstition
Reincarnation	Ouija Boards	Fengshui	Good Luck Charms
Buddhism	Tibetan	Freemasonry	Eastern Stars
Sororities/Fraternities	Psychic Readings	Witchery	Pagan Holidays
Chakras	Kundalini	Astrology	Tarot Cards
Numerology	Dream Catchers	Palm Readings	Fortune Cookies
Ley Lines	Incantations	Psychological Warfare	Demonic Crossroads/Spirits of the Crossroads

Because we are all working out our salvation, demons can be intertwined in a person's soul, heart, mind, and body. They can also be intertwined within the personality of a person, which can sometimes cause them to go unnoticed. This being the case, it is not always obvious that a demon is at work in a person's life.

1John 4:1-2 *Beloved, believe not every spirit, but try the spirits whether they are of God: because many false prophets are gone out into the world. Hereby know ye the Spirit of God: Every spirit that confesseth that Jesus Christ is come in the flesh is of God.*

Try in the Greek is *dokimazō* and means:
1. To test (literally or figuratively); by implication, to approve, allow, discern, examine
2. To test, examine, prove, scrutinize (to see whether a thing is genuine or not)
3. To recognize as genuine after examination, to approve, deem worthy

Whether a person is good or bad, our friend or our enemy, our family member or a stranger, we have the right to try their spirit at any given time to examine if they are operating in the Holy Spirit, a Demonic Spirit or a Human Spirit:

- ❏ **The Holy Spirit** - is God's Spirit living inside of us (*John 14:26, Acts 1:8 Romans 8:26, Galatians 5:22-23, Isaiah 11:12*).

- ❏ **Demonic Spirits** - are demonic forces, evil spirits or devils that possess, oppress, torment, or influence a person, place, or thing (*1Peter 5:8, Revelation 16:14, Ephesians 6:10-18, 1Corinthians 11:14, Mathew 12:43-45, Matthew 13:22*).

- ❏ **Human Spirit** is in operation when a person is ruled or driven by his or her will, soul, and/or heart desires or by the flesh (*Hebrews 4:12, 1Corinthians 2:14, Jude 19, Romans 8:16*).

We try every spirit using the gift of discerning of spirits found in *1Corinthians 12:10*:

To another the working of miracles; to another prophecy; to another discerning of spirits; to another divers kind of tongues; to another the interpretation of tongues.

Discernment in the Greek language is *diakrisis* and means "*judicial estimation, discern, disputation.*" It comes from a word meaning to separate thoroughly, withdraw, oppose, discriminate, decide, hesitate, contend, makes to differ, doubt, judge, be partial, stagger, waver. So if you wrestle with a wavering in what you discern, now you know why. These words describe the process the receiver of discernment goes through! When the discerner is confronted with something that appears good on the outside but is not, it becomes a stumbling block to his spirit. His flesh sees good signs, but his spirit is disputing, opposing, hesitating, contending, differing, doubting, staggering, and wavering against the outward appearance. Discernment is an internal war as one grapples to line up what they perceive, with who God is, and what is being offered.

Matthew 15:26 lets us know that deliverance is the children's bread. That means believers can have demonic spirits and that deliverance is for the believer. We are exposing these demonic forces not to embarrass people or for leaders and members to be rebuking one another. The purpose is so we can more adequately discern how demonic forces are infiltrating our lives, practices, and ministries to undermine and lessen our effectiveness, unity, progress, and maturity in the call and gifting of dance ministry. The more discerning we are, the more we can:

- Free ourselves and atmospheres of these demonic forces
- Mature in operating and manifesting the pure power of God
- Unify as an effective praise and worship army of God

This book will provide balanced wisdom on how and when to confront and/or be delivered from these demonic forces.

SPIRITUAL CLEANING!
MAINTAINING DELIVERANCE & HEALING

From my book entitled, *"Healing The Wounded Leader."*

This chapter will provide you with strategies for equipping yourself and those you minister to with tools to sustain deliverance and sustaining wellness. *Matthew* records a conversation between Jesus and the disciples where Jesus not only instructs them to heal, cleanse, raise, and cast but reminds them that they have to also receive from that level of ministry. Remember Jesus healing Peter's mother-in-law? Lazarus? Those who followed Jesus had first-hand experience of how his ministry changed their lives. I decree that you shall be fully armored to break the power and stronghold of the devil as your revelation and arsenal become empowered with truth and weaponry to dismantle, seize, and invalidate the enemy. **SHIFT!**

Matthew 10:8 *Heal the sick, cleanse the lepers, raise the dead, cast out devils: freely ye have received, freely give.*

<u>*Spiritual Cleansing*</u> – The discipline of purging and purifying the mind, body, and soul of impurities that cause a plethora of negative influences. While there are multiple styles of including this practice, every faith-based counselor is equipped to support the client in spiritual cleansing. The New Testament language of origin is Greek. The word leprosy is *leora* which refers to scaliness (or the skin); an offensive and dangerous cutaneous (akin) disease that will eventually pervade the entire body. Cleanse is *katharizo* which means to make clean or in a moral sense, to free from defilement and faults, to purify from wickedness, or to consecrate.

Leprosy is an infectious disease that causes disfiguring sores, nerve damage, and progressive debilitation. In the Bible, lepers were outcasts because of their highly contagious nature. It is intriguing that leprosy begins on the surface (skin) and then works its way to the internal organs, eventually resulting in death.

Lepers are isolated, in part, because of how others react to them. The way the disease physically alters a person, the fear others had about the disfigurement, and the fear of contracting leprosy were factors in the isolation. Judaism includes laws to mandate separation.

Leviticus 13:45-46 *And the leper in whom the plague is, his clothes shall be rent, and his head bare, and he shall put a covering upon his upper lip, and shall cry, Unclean, unclean. All the days wherein the plague shall be in him he shall be defiled; he is unclean: he shall dwell alone; without the camp shall his habitation be.*

Numbers 5:1-3 *And the LORD spake unto Moses, saying, Command the children of Israel, that they put out of the camp every leper, and every one that hath an issue, and whosoever is defiled by the dead: Both male and female shall ye put out, without the camp shall ye put them; that they defile not their camps, in the midst whereof I dwell.*

God gave Moses clear instructions about lepers and the necessity of separating them from the community.

Let's take a moment to explore the comparison between leprosy and sin:

- o Sin causes us to be unclean, impure, unhealthy.
- o Our sin contaminates and influences others; it pollutes society and the world at large.
- o We think people cannot see our sins, but sins can be seen in our presentation, disposition, personality, clothing, conversation, perceptions, communication, interactions, relationships, how we handle situations, and how we live our lives (***Proverbs 4:23***).
- o Sin causes a separation from God's presence and his plan for our lives.
- o Sin defames God and tarnishes his reputation, especially when we are living a life of sin while contending that we serve God.

When considering the concept of cleansing the lepers or shall we say cleansing sins, it is important to cleanse the infection and cleanse what is causing the infection.

Matthew 8:1-4 *When he was come down from the mountain, great multitudes followed him. And, behold, there came a leper and worshipped him, saying, Lord, if thou wilt, thou canst make me clean. And Jesus put forth his hand, and touched him, saying, I will; be thou clean. And immediately his leprosy was cleansed. And Jesus saith unto him, See thou tell no man; but go thy way, shew thyself to the priest, and offer the gift that Moses commanded, for a testimony unto them.*

For many individuals, willpower is their primary strength used to stop sinning. When using willpower the person is operating through self-control. The person is striving to control their impulses and choices. But if one cannot keep themselves from engaging in the sin, how can he or she stop themselves from never doing it again? A person needs more willpower. God has provided us with Holy Ghost power!

A positive attribute of leprosy is its appreciation for pain.

"References to leprosy have a different emphasis in the New Testament. They stress God's desire to heal. Jesus freely touched people with leprosy. While people with leprosy traditionally suffered banishment from family and neighbors, Jesus broke from the tradition. He treated lepers with compassion, touching and healing them.

Although we cannot know all the reasons that God allows disease into our lives, Biblical leprosy is a powerful symbol reminding us of sin's spread and its horrible consequences. Like leprosy, sin starts out small but can then spread, leading to other sins and causing great damage to our relationship with God and others."[1]

Ephesians 3:16 *He would grant you, according to the riches of His glory, to be strengthened with power through His Spirit in the inner man.*

God's Holy Ghost power empowers a person to grow strong, so he or she can withstand sin and worldliness. The Holy Spirit instills sensitivity to negativity.

The Amplified Bible *May He grant you out of the rich treasury of His glory to be strengthened and reinforced with mighty power in the inner man by the [Holy] Spirit [Himself indwelling your innermost being and personality].*

Even if the person uses their own will to stop sinning, they are still unclean if they do not allow God's Holy Ghost's power to cleanse them from sin.

In ***Matthew 8:1-4***, Jesus laid hands on the lepers and they were made clean. This is miraculously awesome and is a form of deliverance and healing that many have experienced when encountering Jesus. Even with this miraculous cleansing, the leper still had to make a lifestyle change to remain clean.

- o He could not return to the leper camp as he would risk being contaminated again.
- o If his leprosy was a sin issue, then he had to reframe from that sin to maintain his deliverance and healing.
- o Even as the leper's community had changed, his relationships and interactions had to be changed.

The leper's identity and lifestyle had to change to maintain his healing. Such a change requires processing to wholeness. This requires a relationship with God beyond just the initial encounter of deliverance and healing. A person must journey with him in a lifestyle change, learn his plan for maintaining healing, and walk that plan out as a daily lifestyle.

---

[1]Allen L. Gillen. (2007, June 10). Biblical leprosy: Casting light on the disease that shuns. Retrieved from *Answers in Genesis* website at https://answersingenesis.org/biology/disease/biblical-leprosy-shedding-light-on-the-disease-that-shuns/

This brings us to this scripture:

Isaiah 64:6 *But we are all as an unclean thing, and all our righteousnesses are as filthy rags; and we all do fade as a leaf; and our iniquities, like the wind, have taken us away.*

<u>Unclean</u> is *tame* in Hebrew and means:
1. To be unclean, become unclean, become impure, regard as unclean
2. To be or become unclean, to defile oneself, be defiled
    a. Sexually
    b. Religiously
    c. Ceremonially
    d. By idolatry
3. To profane (God's name)

<u>Filth</u> is *ed* in Hebrew and means:
1. To set a period, the menstrual flux, soiling, filthy
2. Menstruation
    a. A filthy rag, stained garment
    b. Figuratively of best deeds of guilty people

The Amplified Bible *For we have all become like one who is unclean [ceremonially, like a leper], and all our righteousness (our best deeds of rightness and justice) is like filthy rags or a polluted garment; we all fade like a leaf, and our iniquities, like the wind, take us away [far from God's favor, hurrying us toward destruction].*

Even the righteousness of a person needs cleaning in God's eyes. Just like we cleanse our physical body, it is necessary to cleanse the inner person. When we cleanse our physical bodies, we are detailed in making sure we clean every part of our bodies. We even purchase the correct hygienic products to ensure that we remain clean. When we find a product that does not work, we move on to different products until we find out what works best. We need this same standard for our spiritual lives. And because our righteousness is filthy, we should be cleaning our souls, hearts, minds daily just like we do our physical bodies. For even when we think we are clean, to God, there are still areas that need cleansing.

Let's explore the Holy Spirit equipping you with delivery and healing techniques sufficient for cleansing the life of those you will counsel.

<u>**Soaking Prayer & Cleansing**</u> – Sometimes in order for an item to get cleaned, it has to be soaked for a period of time. Depending on the composite of the stain and the item that is stained, an item may require lengthy soaking and continuous soaking and purifying before the stain is removed. This is the same for our bodies, souls, minds, will, identity, personality, emotions, etc. Soaking prayer and cleansing denote a time of intimate

prayer, meditating, resting, and communing with the Lord. It is a focused time of being with the Lord and allowing him to build a relationship or to cleanse stubborn and difficult areas of a person's life. While the terminology may be new for many, the concept is likely something that is already a spiritual practice. As you learn the tools and strategies below, you will learn to use some of these tools such as the blood of Jesus, the Glory of God, the fire of the Holy Spirit, word of God, etc., during their intimate time of soaking, to deliver, heal, purge, and cleanse themselves of ungodly or unhealthy attributes, infestations, manifestations, and strongholds.

- *Psalm 4: 4* *Meditate within your heart on your bed, and be still.*
- *Psalm 16:11* *Thou wilt shew me the path of life: in thy presence [is] fulness of joy; at thy right hand [there are] pleasures forevermore.*
- *Psalm 27:8* *My heart has heard you say, "Come and talk with me." And my heart responds, "LORD, I am coming.*
- *Psalm 51:7* *Purge me with hyssop, and I shall be clean: wash me, and I shall be whiter than snow.*
- *Psalm 51:7* *Soak me in your laundry and I'll come out clean, scrub me and I'll have a snow-white life. (MSG)*
- *Psalm 145:18* *The LORD [is] nigh unto all them that call upon him, to all that call upon him in truth.*
- *Jeremiah 29:13* *And ye shall seek me, and find [me], when ye shall search for me with all your heart.*
- *Luke 11:9* *And so I tell you, keep on asking, and you will receive what you ask for. Keep on seeking, and you will find. Keep on knocking, and the door will be opened to you.*
- *Matthew 11:28-30* *Come to Me, all you who labor and are heavy laden, and I will give you rest. Take My yoke upon you and learn from Me, for I am gentle and lowly in heart, and you will find rest for your souls. For My yoke is easy and My burden is light.*

<u>**Infilling of the Holy Spirit**</u> - (**Acts 1-2, Acts 13:22** *And the disciples were continually filled with joy and with the Holy Spirit*). All of us receive the Holy Spirit upon us when we accept Jesus as our personal savior. When I speak of infilling, I am referencing speaking in tongues where God's voice and power speak through us and empower us as believers. When God's power flows through us, his voice equips us with greater

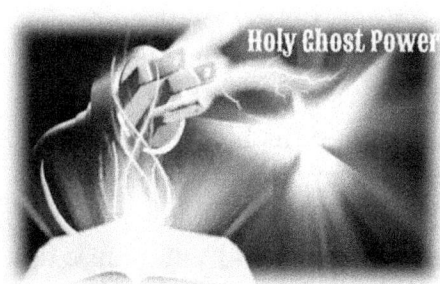

heavenly sound and power to annihilate the enemy. There are some things the enemy will not respond to in our voice, but he will if we speak in our heavenly prayer language of tongues. If you are not filled with the Holy Spirit, spend time asking God to fill you and posture yourself in soaking prayer so he can release your prayer language to you. You can also ask someone to pray for you and you can pray for others to receive the infilling of the Holy Spirit. You and others who desire to be filled need to study the purpose of doing so, while asking the Holy Spirit to manifest his voice through you all. Spend time praying in your prayer language daily and encourage others to spend time empowering themselves in their prayer language consistently. I encourage people to speak in tongues while in the shower or driving to work. These are perfect times, because the person is generally alone, and can focus. Let the person know that they do not have to know what they are saying or even have a prayer focus. The more they speak in tongues and just focus on being empowered in God, the more they will know what they are saying and praying, and the more the Holy Spirit will guide them in knowing what to pray for, against, and how to use their prayer language to cleanse themselves of the filth of the enemy. (*John 16:13 Howbeit when he, the Spirit of truth, is come, he will guide you into all truth: for he shall not speak of himself; but whatsoever he shall hear, that shall he speak: and he will shew you things to come*).

<u>Spirit of Lord</u> – Empowers the believer with the wisdom, revelation, knowledge, counsel, understanding, and guidance needed to handle one's daily affairs and journey in a destiny lifestyle with the Lord. (***Isaiah 11:2*** *And the spirit of the LORD shall rest upon him, the spirit of wisdom and understanding, the spirit of counsel and might, the spirit of knowledge and of the fear of the LORD*). Study the attributes of the spirit of the Lord, seek God for the importance of these attributes as it relates to their deliverance and healing, and declare continually that they are consumed in the spirit of wisdom, revelation, understanding, etc. until it becomes part of your identity. Refuse to accept and cleanse all confusion, ignorance, foolery, witchcraft, bewitchment, mind control, mind blinding/binding, lack of knowledge, lack of guidance, etc. Assert your right to have the spirit of the Lord teaching you all things and practice living by his leading. (***John 14:26*** *But the Comforter, which is the Holy Ghost, whom the Father will send in my name, he shall teach you all things, and bring all things to your remembrance, whatsoever I have said unto you*).

<u>Fruit of God</u> – Fills, restores, produces, reproduces (***Galatians 5:22-23*** *But the fruit of the Spirit is love, joy, peace, long suffering, gentleness, goodness, faith, Meekness, temperance: against such there is no law*). Cleanse all defiled, demonic, and unhealthy fruit that does not represent the character and nature of God, while filling yourself up with spiritual fruit that represents his character and nature.

<u>Blood of Jesus</u> – Purges, purifies, redeems, reconciles, sanctifies, sanitizes, forgives, heals, and frees a person from death (***Ephesians 1:7*** *whom we have redemption through his blood, the forgiveness of sins, according to the riches of his grace*). We hear a lot about pleading the blood, but the blood is an application. Jesus applied his blood to our sins and sicknesses, and through his perfected blood, we were redeemed and made whole. Believers can apply the blood of Jesus to their soul, heart, mind, thoughts, personality, character, identity, righteousness, body, command redemption, life, and wholeness to come. Believers can soak themselves in the blood of Jesus until they see breakthroughs in these areas or as a daily application of being cleansed and free in the redeeming blood power of Jesus.

Binding, Loosing & Casting Out Devils – Delivers the person from demons, and strongholds (**Matthew 16:19** *And I will give unto thee the keys of the kingdom of heaven: and whatsoever thou shalt bind on earth shall be bound in heaven: and whatsoever thou shalt loose on earth shall be loosed in heaven*). Bind means *"to knit, chain, tie, and to fasten, put under subjection, to forbid, prohibit, declare to be illicit."* Loose means to *"loosen, cast off, break (up), destroy, dissolve, (un-)loose, melt, put off, to declare unlawful, to overthrow."* Believers possess the power to bind demons and demonic kingdoms and forbid them to remain inside of them and others. Believers can bind themselves, others, their ministry, their atmosphere, the land, and region to God and his kingdom. Believers can also lose themselves from demonic powers, and forbid and overthrow their working in their lives, lives of others, their ministry, the atmosphere, the land, and region.

Casting Out Devils – Deliverance ministry is a part of our rights and health as believers of Jesus Christ. It is the believer's daily manna and authority to be free of demons and their demonic stronghold. Jesus has given us power over all the power of the enemy. *Cast out* means to *"eject with violence, drive (out), expel, leave, pluck (pull, take, thrust) out, put forth (out), send away."* Cast the devil out of your life and the life of others so you all can be free of demonic fruit, filth, oppression, depression, and possession.

- *Matthew 10:8* Heal the sick, cleanse the lepers, raise the dead, cast out devils: freely ye have received, freely give.
- *Luke 10:19* Behold, I give unto you power to tread on serpents and scorpions, and over all the power of the enemy: and nothing shall by any means hurt you.
- *Luke 11:20* But if I with the finger of God cast out devils, no doubt the kingdom of God is come upon you.

It is important to assert power and authority over the enemy because he is always trying to claim rights to the believer and what belongs to us. The devil is not passive and is always seeking to possess, devour, and destroy what is ours. Be offensive and aggressive in letting the devil know that he cannot have your life, family, ministry, atmosphere, land, region, nation.

Breaking Curses – A curse is a solemn utterance intended to invoke a supernatural power to hinder blessings, inflict harm, judgment, or punishment, on a person, group of people, generational line, place, situation, or thing. Curses can enter a person's life:

> *Word Curses* – Words carry power. We can curse ourselves by what we speak and others can speak words that inflict curses in our lives.

- ***Proverbs 12:18*** *The words of the reckless pierce like swords, but the tongue of the wise brings healing. (NIV)*
- ***Proverbs 13:3*** *Be careful what you say and protect your life. A careless talker destroys himself. (GNT)*
- ***Proverbs 18:21 NIV*** *The tongue has the power of life and death, and those who love it will eat its fruit. (NIV)*
- ***James 3:10*** *Out of the same mouth proceedeth blessing and cursing. My brethren, these things ought not so to be.*

<u>Generational Curses</u> – Curses are passed down through the family line from one generation to the next, due to sin, transgressions, ungodly or unhealthy behavioral cycles, patterns, and customs. When parents and older family members do not reject or conquer these issues, the children and other family members become susceptible to them or have a propensity for them. These curses must be verbally broken and triumphed over, for the fullness of salvation to operate in a person's life and in their family line.

- ***Exodus 34:7*** *Keeping mercy for thousands, forgiving iniquity and transgression and sin, and that will by no means clear [the guilty]; visiting the iniquity of the fathers upon the children, and upon the children's children, unto the third and to the fourth [generation].*
- ***Numbers 14:18*** *The LORD [is] longsuffering, and of great mercy, forgiving iniquity and transgression, and by no means clearing [the guilty], visiting the iniquity of the fathers upon the children unto the third and fourth [generation].*
- ***Deuteronomy 5:9*** *Thou shalt not bow down thyself unto them, nor serve them: for I the LORD thy God [am] a jealous God, visiting the iniquity of the fathers upon the children unto the third and fourth [generation] of them that hate me.*

<u>Witchcraft/Occult Curses</u> – Curses are released by witches, warlocks, and those involved in witchcraft and/or occult practices. Such people engage in witchcraft, satanism, new age religions, magic, psychic powers, occult activities while releasing curses via rituals, spells, hexes, incantations, jinxes, sorcery, bewitchment, telepathy, demonic prayers, love potions, and other demonic activities. They may also use demonic spirits to aid them in carrying out their curses or demonic assignments.

- ***Deuteronomy 18:10-11*** *Let no one be found among you who sacrifices their son or daughter in the fire, who practices divination or sorcery, interprets omens, engages in witchcraft, or casts spells, or who is a medium or spiritist or who consults the dead.*
- ***Numbers 22-24*** *Balaam refused to speak what God did not speak and would not curse the Israelites, even though King Balak of Moab offered him money. People will actually higher those who operate in witchcraft and occult practices to curse others.*

- ***Ephesians 5:16*** *Above all, taking the shield of faith, wherewith ye shall be able to quench all the fiery darts of the wicked.*

It is important to receive personal, generational, regional, cultural freedom from negative words spoken over your life sent to you, or curses implemented due to personal and generational sins, and occult practice (***Galatians 3:13*** *Christ hath redeemed us from the curse of the law, being made a curse for us: for it is written, Cursed is every one that hangeth on a tree*). Teach clients how to:

o Identify curses and where they are originating from.
o Repent for personal, generational, regional, and cultural strongholds.
o Break curses and lose the blood of Jesus to cleanse the curse and all filth associated with it.
o Bind and cast out any spirits operating behind the curse.
o Declare their freedom through Jesus Christ (***2Corinthians 3:17*** *Now the Lord is that Spirit: and where the Spirit of the Lord is, there is liberty*).
o Fill themselves back up with the fruit, promises, prophecies, and blessings of God.

The most powerful book I ever read and worked through regarding breaking curses was, "Repentance Cleansing your Generational Bloodline," by Natasha Grbich. I highly recommend it to you and to those you minister to.

<u>*Word of God*</u> – Discerns, divides what is of God and what is not of God, cuts out, does surgery, instills God's truth, will, and plan (***Hebrews 4:12*** *For the word of God is quick, and powerful, and sharper than any two-edged sword, piercing even to the dividing asunder of soul and spirit, and of the joints and marrow, and is a discerner of the thoughts and intents of the heart*). Teach clients to:

o Use the word of God to divide what is of God in their lives your life from what is not of him.
o Use the word of God to extract what is not of God from your soul, heart, mind, body, and spirit.
o Use the word of God to overthrow every lie that the enemy uses to keep you bound to demons.
o Use the word of God to cut out any word, character trait, hurt, pain, and flaw that keeps you bound to demons.
o Spend time studying, meditating on, and soaking in the word of God. Allow God's word to go inside of your (heart, mind, soul, identity), and cleanse everything that is contrary to the word of God for your life.

- Study and meditate on God's word and be refilled in his truth concerning their identity, purpose, destiny, and who he is as daddy God, Lord and Savior, ruler and king of their lives.

Fire of God – Burns out, fuses, refines, purges, purifies, consumes, and tests (***Malachi 3:2-3*** *But who may abide the day of his coming? and who shall stand when he appeareth? for he is like a refiner's fire, and like fullers' soap: And he shall sit as a refiner and purifier of silver: and he shall purify the sons of Levi, and purge them as gold and silver, that they may offer unto the Lord an offering in righteousness*). Sometimes when demons are cast out, their deposits, residue, and attributes are still lodged in the person. The fire of God can be used to purge and burn out these demonic deposits. A person can also be purified and refined with the fire of God. Demons hate the fire of God and the blood of Jesus. Fire is a judgment to demons. The fire of God can be used to torment demons and send them fleeing from a person's life, bloodline, ministry, land, atmosphere, and region. (***Revelations 20:10*** *And the devil that deceived them was cast into the lake of fire and brimstone, where the beast and the false prophet are, and shall be tormented day and night forever and ever*).

Fullers' Soap – Entails a washing by trampling, treading, stamping, scrubbing. It is likened to trampling or scrubbing something hard until it is clean. (***Malachi 3:2-3*** *But who may abide the day of his coming? and who shall stand when he appeareth? for he is like a refiner's fire, and like fullers' soap: And he shall sit as a refiner and purifier of silver: and he shall purify the sons of Levi, and purge them as gold and silver, that they may offer unto the Lord an offering in righteousness*). When there are things in you or others that require deep cleansing, the fuller soap of God can be used to scrub and trample them out.

Power of God – Delivers, overthrows demonic powers and governments, releases the virtue and government of God, releases miracles, signs, and wonders (***Acts 1:8*** *But ye shall receive power, after that the Holy Ghost is come upon you: and ye shall be witnesses unto me both in Jerusalem, and in all Judaea, and in Samaria, and unto the uttermost part of the earth*). Use the power of God to annihilate the powers of the enemy (***Luke 10:19*** *Behold, I give unto you power to tread on serpents and scorpions, and over all the power of the enemy: and nothing shall by any means hurt you*). Study the power of God so you will know their authority and ability to recreate and create body parts, birth forth things that you need, bring excellency to your heart, mind, and soul, release virtue into your life, and annihilate the power of the enemy, such that it brings transforming deliverance and healing.

The glory of God – Much of what the believer needs and desires from God is inside his glory. The Glory refreshes fills, refills, fulfills, creates, recreates, revives, renews, makes whole, establishes the presence of God, draws us into intimacy and relationship with God, while instilling God's character, nature, truth, knowledge, revelation, and pleasures forevermore (***Psalm 16:11*** *Thou wilt shew me the path of life: in thy presence is* *fulness of joy; at thy right hand there are pleasures for evermore*). Every believer should be living inside the presence of God. This is where the believer's direction of life is revealed. As the believer walks in alignment with God, continual fulness of joy and pleasures of God should be evident in their lives. If the believer is living in the glory of God, they should be living a fulfilled life no matter what trials and tribulations may occur. Seek God for revelation on how to build a relationship with him where you abide in his presence. Engage his presence to be refreshed, fulfilled, and filled and encourage you to continually cultivate your life and atmosphere in his presence so you can be true glory carriers of the Lord (***John 15:4*** *Abide in me, and I in you. As the branch cannot bear fruit of itself, except it abide in the vine; no more can ye, except ye abide in me*).

Rivers of Living Water – Stirs, replenishes, breeds life, vitality, beauty, youthfulness, creativity, strength, efficiency, and releases what is inside of them to whatever you are sending it to (***John. 7:38*** *He that believeth on me, as the scripture hath said, out of his belly shall flow rivers of living water*). Spend time cleansing and stirring the rivers that are inside of you, such that their inner wells incite pure waters as whatever is in you will be released into the things God has granted to your hands.

Pluck Out – Roots out, pulls down, destroys, and throws down (***Jeremiah 1:10*** *See, I have this day set thee over the nations and over the kingdoms, to root out, and to pull down, and to destroy, and to throw down, to build, and to plant*). Some demonic spirits and ungodly attributes are embedded in a person's foundation and need to be uprooted. They can be a root that has been there for years or can be rooted generationally, so keep that in mind. Learn how to:

- o Pluck out demons.
- o Command demons and strongholds that are lodged deep within to come up out of them by the root.
- o Cut the root in pieces then pull them out.

A person may have to pull down ideation or attribute, such as pulling down strongholds, imaginations, and prideful spirits that have exalted themselves above God and have exalted themselves as idols in their lives.

Please know that you cannot be nice to demons and or compromise with wickedness. Our mission as believers has to be to destroy the forces of darkness just like they want to destroy us. The devil understands he is in a fight and will do whatever is necessary to gain entry and control to a believer's life. Believers must be warriors and be willing to pluck up, root out, toes, trample, etc., to assert authority over demons and their powers. The process of plucking up may require a constant contending to uproot demons and their contaminations out of their life and the lives of others.

Hammer Down – Walls, barricades, barriers, hindrances, and blockages, have to be hammered down (*Jeremiah 23:29 Is not my word like as a fire? saith the LORD; and like a hammer that breaketh the rock in pieces?*) Sometimes these fortifications are made by the believer, sometimes the words and ideologies of others cause these walls and barriers, and sometimes they are made by the devil. Either way, they need to come down. Use the hammer of God to break down walls and barriers that have been erected to hinder breakthroughs.

Run Through Troops – Blast through troops that keep you bound or that may be blocking your breakthrough (*Psalm 18:30 For by thee I have run through a troop; and by my God have I leaped over a wall*). If you read **Psalm 18:30-51**, you will determine that it is the power of God that enables you to do this. When you find yourself in tough life situations, ganged up on by demons or you come up against a stronghold that does not want to budge in your life, ask God to empower you to run through troops. Then as you pray and deal with these situations in your natural life, use your faith, power, and authority to blast through these bondages.

Resist the Devil – Stand against, oppose, withstand, set against the devil and all that concerns him (*James 4:7 Submit yourselves therefore to God. Resist the devil, and he will flee from you*). Before demons and filth will leave the believer, they must fall out of agreement with it. The devil and his filth cannot stay if there is nothing in the believer wanting or aiding him to remain. Break every covenant with it, divorce it, hate it, dread it being in you, and resist it from being a part of your life. Spend time breaking covenants with the devil, sin, pleasures of sin, mindsets, errors, and anything that keeps you in a relationship with the enemy and his filthiness.

Breaking Soul ties – Soul ties can be godly or ungodly in nature. In the same way, generational curses are passed down, soul ties are transferred from one person to the other person and vice versa. Soul ties can be formed through close friendships and interactions, covenants, vows, commitments, promises, physical intimacy, etc. A person can also have a soul tie by having an unhealthy attachment to something or someone that has taken the place of God in their lives or that has become an addiction in their lives. A person's soul, heart, mind, and body can be intertwined, bound, knitted, or in covenant with that person, place, or thing. In addition, a person can exchange parts of themselves with the person they are in a soul tie with. Parts of their personality, soul, heart, thoughts, mindsets, character, nature, and other deposits, infuse them and begin to influence and live in the person and vice versa. Also, whomever they have had a relationship with and have not cleansed themselves of is being passed on to those two people.

Visualization of a Knot

A soul tie is knotting together. Consider the visualization. A piece of rope has a beginning and an ending that are each easy to identify. A person is free to choose which end is which because it won't matter UNTIL the person decides to put the piece of rope to work.

Now, look at it again.

Once the rope has been knotted, it is not a simple task to identify the beginning and the ending. Did you know that rope is made by taking multiple fibers called slivers and twisting those into strands until there is a continuous and unified piece? The rope has something called tensile strength which is the maximum capacity to carry weight and stretch. Adding a knot will increase the strength of the bond by at least fifty percent. Have you ever had a knot in a shoestring? Have you ever used the point of something to get into the knot to loosen it? In a soul tie, it often takes something sharp to get in between the knot and loosen.

- ***Hebrews 4:12** For the word of God is quick, and powerful, and sharper than any twoedged sword, piercing even to the dividing asunder of soul and spirit, and of the joints and marrow, and is a discerner of the thoughts and intents of the heart.*

A person is free of knots until they are tied to someone. Suddenly what was simple and clear is complex and difficult and its presence strengthens a bond that can be empowering and challenging. That is why many people who know they are in a soul tie and admittedly want out of the soul tie still have such a struggle to be free. With soul ties, the more entangled the soul tie becomes, the more difficult it becomes to tell where one person starts and the other ends and vice versa.

Soul ties are often provoked by external circumstances that feel uncontrollable by those affected, so the distorted attempt to address the issue is the cause of the knotting and entangling. The more knotting occurs, the less room there is for anyone else to be involved. The cycle continues to deepen and is dependent on isolating those in the soul tie to believe that the solution can only happen if the other person is involved. That is why women who are victimized by domestic violence continue to return to, "Nobody will love you as I love you." It is what keeps believers in unhealthy church settings with the voice of leadership saying, "But God assigned you to this ministry." It becomes a covenant of soulish perversion. If you leave a rope knotted for a lengthy period of time, the friction of the rope in the knot will discolor the rope and cause fraying of the material. The longer a person stays in a soul tie, the more alteration takes place within the original nature of the person(s) which is why there is a great need for deliverance, counseling, and submission to the healing process

Godly Soul ties – Soul ties can be godly and healthy. They possess the fruit and nature of God and empower a person's life, ministry, purpose, and destiny. A healthy soul tie has God's character, nature, fruit, will, and plan for their lives, a person can be tied to good things, but they may not necessarily be God's design.

- ***1Samuel 18:1*** *And it came to pass, when he had made an end of speaking unto Saul, that the soul of Jonathan was knit with the soul of David, and Jonathan loved him as his own soul.*

Knit is *qâŝar* in Hebrew and means:
1. To tie, physically (gird, confine, compact) or mentally (in love, league)
2. Bind (up), (make a) conspire (-acy, -ator), join together, knit, stronger
3. Work (treason). to bind, tie, bind together, league together, conspire
4. To bind, confine, to league together, conspire
a. To be bound, be bound up
b. To bind onto, bind fast to, bind, tie to, bind to oneself
c. Robust, vigorous (participle), to conspire

When souls are knitted, there is an actual tying together that occurs. This knitting girds like a belt and is robust and vigorous in nature. The soul tie is conspiring to be strong where people are locked together such that they love and uphold one another as one soul. SHIFT!

- ***Ecclesiastes 4:9-12*** *Two are better than one, because they have a good [more satisfying] reward for their labor; For if they fall, the one will lift up his fellow. But woe to him who is alone when he falls and has not another to lift him up! Again, if two lie down together, then they have warmth; but how can one be warm alone? And though a man might prevail against him who is alone, two will withstand him. A threefold cord is not quickly broken. (AMP)*

A threefold cord is equated to a covenant agreement between parties. The concept that a threefold cord is not quickly broken confirms that there is a binding together that can occur between two or more people or between two people and God that can be so strong that it is not easy to break. It is unifying that is so strong, it can literally hold the weight of a person up within the relationship. The threefold cord asserts that each person can be sustained, empowered, built up, and held up by the other person and by God within the relationship; that even in the weakness of one person, the cord can pull that person up just by the mere vigorous power of the binding cord that connects their souls, hearts, spirits, and lives together.

The word *fall* is *nasal* in Hebrew and means:
1. To fall, lie, be cast down, fail, to fall (of violent death)
2. To fall prostrate, prostrate oneself before, to fall upon, attack, desert
3. Fall away to, go away too, fall into the hand of, to fall short, fail, fall out
4. Turn out, result, to settle, waste away, be offered, be inferior to, to lie, lie prostrate

As we consider the power of a knitted cord between two or more people, it will take more than just the separation of the relationship to break it.

The word *together* in Hebrew is *săkab* and means:
1. A primitive root - to lie down (for rest, sexual connection, decease, or any other purpose)
2. At all, cast down, ((lover-)) lay (self) (down)
3. (make to) lie (down, down to sleep, still with), lodge, ravish, take rest, sleep, stay

Heat in Hebrew is *hâmam* and means:
1. A primitive root - to be hot (literally or figuratively)
2. Enflame self, get (have) heat, be (wax) hot, (be, wax) warm (self, at)
3. To become aroused, inflame oneself with, passioned, to be or grow warm

Prevails in Hebrew is *taqap* and means, *"to prevail over or against, overcome, overpower."* Within our physical bodies are mechanisms in our metabolism and hormone levels that produce natural heat as two people lie together to keep warm. This same heat is possible as our souls are knitted in friendship and in companionship. Because friendships and companionships are knitted through our hearts, souls, emotions, and spirits, the knitting is even more infused as these areas responding to the laws of the spirit and the soulish realm and the principles of God that he established in the earth when he created it. The heat automatically leaves when our physical bodies depart, but the heat remains when our hearts, souls, emotions, and spirits are knitted. Your body walks away, but the other parts of you are still knitted by the prevailing power of the soul tie that was formed in the soulish and spiritual realm.

- *Matthew 18:19 Again I say unto you, That if two of you shall agree on earth as touching anything that they shall ask, it shall be done for them of my Father which is in heaven.*

  - ✓ When we touch, we are saying we are giving an account regarding that person, place, or thing.
  - ✓ We are giving our approval that we want the knitting or manifestation that is taking place.

- ✓ We are giving our agreement that we want covenant or prevailing with that person, place, or thing.

<u>Marriage Soul ties</u> – When people get married, their lives are knitted in covenant with their spouse and they become one with one another. They are no longer individuals, but the two become one when married.

- ***Genesis 2:24*** *Therefore shall a man leave his father and his mother, and shall cleave unto his wife: and they shall be one flesh.*

- ***Matthew 19:5*** *And said, For this cause shall a man leave father and mother, and shall cleave to his wife: and they twain shall be one flesh?*

<u>Cleave is *dâbaq* Hebrew and means:</u>
1. A primitive root; properly, to impinge, i.e. cling or adhere
2. Figuratively, to catch by pursuit
3. Abide fast, cleave (fast together), follow close (hard after)
4. Be joined (together), keep (fast), overtake, pursue hard, stick, take

<u>Cleave is *proskollao* in Greek and means:</u>
1. to glue to, i.e. (figuratively) to adhere
2. cleave, join (self), cleave oneself to, stick to

The cleaving of godly covenant marriage bonds a couple together like glue. When two people are not married but operate as married or engage in marital relations, their words, life posture, and soul are leaving and cleaving. This is an illegal leaving and cleaving, but everything about their life becomes one soul with that one another, and the sexual relations make the cleaving even stronger.

<u>Ungodly Soul ties</u> – An ungodly soul tie is any knitting of a person with a person, place, or thing that is not of God or that is not God's will and plan for their lives. God will not have a person bond to sin, idolatry, unhealthiness, unfruitfulness, or bondage. He will not have a person engage or remain in a relationship that is a transgression against his word, will, and plan for their lives. God will not have a person tied to something that is going to deplete them rather than build them in him and in their identity, purpose, and destiny.

- ***1Corinthians 6:16*** *What? know ye not that he which is joined (Hebrew word Kollao meaning glue, cement, fasting) to a harlot is one body? for two, saith he, shall be one flesh.*

- ***Genesis 34:1-3*** *And Dinah the daughter of Leah, which she bare unto Jacob went out to see the daughters of the land. And when Shechem the son of Hamor the Hivite, prince of* *the country, saw her, he took her, and lay with her, and defiled her. And his soul clave unto Dinah the daughter of Jacob, and he loved the damsel, and spake kindly unto the damsel. Verse 8 And Hamor communed with them, saying the soul of my son Shechem longeth for your daughter: I pray you give her him to wife. Sexual involvement can form such entangling tentacles of soul ties that it is extremely hard to break off the relationship.*

- ***Proverbs 5:20-24*** *And why wilt thou, my son, be ravished with a strange woman, and embrace the bosom of a stranger? For the ways of man are before the eyes of the Lord, and he pondereth all his goings. His own iniquities shall take the wicked himself, and he shall be holden with the cords of his sins. He shall die without instruction; and in the greatness of his folly he shall go astray.*

- ***Psalm 1:1*** *Blessed is the man that walketh not in the counsel of the ungodly, nor standeth in the way of sinners, nor sitteth in the seat of the scornful*

- ***2Corinthians 6:14-18*** *Be ye not unequally yoked together with unbelievers: for what fellowship hath righteousness with unrighteousness? and what communion hath light with darkness? And what concord hath Christ with Belial? or what part hath he that believeth with an infidel? And what agreement hath the temple of God with idols? for ye are the temple of the living God; as God hath said, I will dwell in them, and walk in them; and I will be their God, and they shall be my people. Wherefore come out from among them, and be ye separate, saith the Lord, and touch not the unclean thing; and I will receive you, And will be a Father unto you, and ye shall be my sons and daughters, saith the Lord Almighty.*

<u>Soul ties With A Place</u> – A person can be tied to a place, and it can become a high place in their life, where they do not want to leave it or cannot leave it. In the scripture, a high place is referring to a place of idolatrous worship. A high place can be any place that has exalted itself above God in a person's life. A person can be tied to a place where God has brought them out of, but the tie keeps pulling them back in. Spiritually the person is free, but their soul is bound to it. Lot's wife had a soul tie with Sodom and Gomorrah. God was destroying the city because of perversion, idolatry, lewdness, and lawlessness. God only allowed so many to live and allowed them time to get out of the city before he destroyed it. As they were walking out, Lot's wife looked back and turned into a pillar of salt.

- ***Genesis 19:23-26*** *Then the Lord rained upon Sodom and upon Gomorrah brimstone and fire from the Lord out of heaven; And he overthrew those cities, and all the plain, and all the inhabitants of the cities, and that which grew upon the ground. But his wife looked back from behind him, and she became a pillar of salt.*

Even though God had graced Lot's wife with deliverance, her eyes and heart had regard for what she was leaving behind. Because her soul was still knitted to Sodom and Gomorrah, God caused her to perish with it. Being tied to something that God is freeing the person from will deplete their life and even bring destruction upon them.

Agreement with God's will for the relationship along with healthiness is important in a Godly Soultie.

- *Amos 3:3 Can two walk together, except they be agreed?*
- *Do two people walk hand in hand if they aren't going to the same place? (MSG)*

When the agreement is unhealthy, it makes for an ungodly soul tie. Regardless to whether the person agrees or not, if a soul tie is formed, it has to be broken in order for them to be free of whatever was knitted and transferred through that tie. This is vital, as rape, incest, abuse, mind control, religious sects, erred beliefs, etc. are ties that form without their agreement, out of ignorance, fear, or lack of knowledge, depending on the circumstance. When they are not broken, whatever the offender deposited lives in the person. Some people result in manifesting the traits of their offender, while others live in the false identity of what was deposited. You or others you minister to may require counseling to identify traits that have been transferred from the offender. Be open to entering this process of deliverance so you can be free of false identities, demonic spirits, and deposits that SHIFTED in through these experiences.

When a person experiences divorce, it is best to break soul ties with the now ex-spouse. Many people have a difficult time moving forward because their souls are still tied to their ex-spouse. The covenant of marriage must be repented for and broken in the spirit realm, and soul ties must be cleansed and broken so the person can be free from all that was deposited and shared while married.

Teach yourself and others the following regarding breaking soul ties:
- Spend time before the Lord identifying every ungodly soul tie you have in your life.
- Confessing and repenting for your role in the soul tie, even if it was just giving in to the lies and false identity of your offender.
- Forgive those you had a soul tie with and forgive yourself for engaging in the soul tie.
- Break and remove the soul ties. Address and call out every person's name you have a soul tie with; go through these steps, and break and remove each tie.
- Using the blood of Jesus and the fire of God to cleanse all ungodly deposits, and command any parts of your soul, heart, mind, and identity to be restored back to God's identity and wellness.
- Occasionally spend time cleansing any unhealthiness in your Godly soul tie relationships, and any deposits that may have come from misunderstandings,

miscommunication, taking one another for granted, being more to one another than God was saying, or becoming lax, fleshy, or imbalanced in your interactions.

DEMONIC SPIRITS ABORT PROGRESS

During intense seasons where it is important to remain focused, disciplined, enduring, and persevering, the enemy will unleash demonic assignments sent to distract and abort progress. People yield to these demonic spirits and their actions due to a need to prove defend, protect, and assert their own justice. Rather than staying the course with God and trusting what he says, they get into carnal wards that cause discord, confusion, drama, lashing, affliction, weariness, and drainage. The ultimate goals of these attacks is to cause people to abort their progress and to even yield to spiritual and sometimes literal death of their destiny, calling, and/or lives. Below is a apostolic watch revelation that God gave me for the body of Christ during a pivotal time of SHIFTING. I want to add it to this encyclopedia because I believe this word and the revealing of these demonic spirits will be a lifesaver for some people during significant seasons of their destiny journey.

Apostolic Watch 2022
This is the season to be bold and fierce against the enemy. Even as you are bold and fierce, it is important to be disciplined and focused in your stance concerning me, what I have spoken, and what I have called you to do says the Lord. The enemy will attempt to distract and frustrate you, especially with petty warfare and old pesty familiar attacks that I have already judged and delivered you from. It is important to know that no weapon formed against you is prospering and to assert your right to judge, dislodge, and thwart every weapon of the enemy.

Proverbs 19:21 *Many are the plans in a man's heart, but it is the Lord's purpose that prevails.*

Isaiah 54:17 *No weapon that is formed against thee shall prosper; and every tongue that shall rise against thee in judgment thou shalt condemn. This is the heritage of the servants of the LORD, and their righteousness is of me, saith the LORD.*

Please know that as the enemy will use people, your fight is not against flesh and blood. Do not get into flesh and blood wars. They will drain you of your time, attention, and power. They are blood drainers being sent to snuff out your literal breath and life so that you cannot fight the true battle that is spiritual. And so that you will not know that this fight is not even your fight. It is a distraction so that you won't fight the true spiritual fight.

- ✓ Use wisdom and discernment and stay focused.
- ✓ Use wisdom and discernment and do not yield to operating in your flesh where you become carnal and where you fight a flesh and blood war that is really a demonic distraction to the real battle.

The real battle is not old petty warfare or pests that would try to draw you into a territorial fight or into defending yourself or your name. The real battle is not a judgment that I did not bring to you. The real battle is not the thing that is trying to be a thorn in your side or the tracking spirit that sounds like me but really is the devil's voice trying to make you feel some kind of way about me, some kind of way about you, some kind of way about what I am saying and doing regarding you, your life, and destiny. This is not the real battle. Staff focused so you can remain in my might regarding the real battle and defeat the trickery of the enemy.

Below is a list of demonic spirits to be mindful of and not yield to in this season. Proactively pray to cancel their assignments before and as they would attempt to operate. Be mindful not to yield to their tactics. Be discerning. Engage from your spirit and through spiritual warfare and stay the course with God. I keep hearing Holy Spirit say bait and switch - these spirits will appear to be real issues and of God but they are frauds. When you react it release and act to hook you as they use the tactic of bait and switch on you.

Petty Warfare Spirits draws you into fighting in your flesh or yielding to carnality. These spirits want you to be distracted and tied up in flesh and blood contentions, or wasting your time defending yourself when the true battle in the spiritual realms is advancing and overtaking you. If not discerning, this battle will weary you, mock you, and drain you quickly of strength and focus. It will come to hit quickly so you cannot discern its carnality, while mistaking it for a spiritual battle.

Spirits of Distraction releases familiar and old fights, wars, and issues, that God has already delivered you from. You will be focused on delivering yourself unnecessarily. Your relent to this spirit will open the door for these issues and wars to have a foothold in your life. You giving it attention and time will cause a legal right to be activated as this attack is being sent to hook and bewitch you into a battle or bondage that is not yours, yet it becomes yours as you take the bait.

Spirit of Frustration & Discouragement will seek to cause you to doubt God and be frustrated where you question him and his ability to bless, protect, deliver, and follow through with his promises and prophecies.

Spirit of Divination will come as a tracking spirit. This demonic spirit will follow you around like the girl who followed Apostle Paul around in the book of ***Acts 16***. This spirit will say the right thing but have the wrong spirit. The spirit will twist God's words, use scriptures and the name of the Lord to make it sound like God, will speak false warnings, judgments, and even require conditions, payments, and recompense that God is not saying or requiring. It will be a self absorb, deceitful, prideful, and operate with ill intent. Its motive of operation behind is to judge, reprove, and destroy you, while validating its own assignment, competition, and malice with and towards you.

This spirit is seeking to kill revival, growth, expansion, purpose, and destiny. Its intent is to create space for you to fall, while acting like it is for you, it knows you, it is with you, and is has your best interest at heart. But the bait and switch is their ready to deplete and destroy you.

Malice is defined as *"a desire to inflict injury, harm, or suffering on another, either because of a hostile impulse or out of deep-seated meanness."*

Proverbs 26:24-28 *He who hates pretends with his lips, but stores up deceit within himself. When he speaks kindly, do not trust him, for seven abominations are in his heart. Though his hatred covers itself with guile, his wickedness shall be shown openly before the assembly. Whoever digs a pit [for another man's feet] shall fall into it himself, and he who rolls a stone [up a height to do mischief], it will return upon him. A lying tongue hates those it wounds and crushes, and a flattering mouth works ruin.*

The Message Bible *Your enemy shakes hands and greets you like an old friend, all the while conniving against you. When he speaks warmly to you, don't believe him for a minute; he's just waiting for the chance to rip you off. No matter how cunningly he conceals his malice, eventually his evil will be exposed in public. Malice backfires; spite boomerangs. Liars hate their victims; flatterers sabotage trust.*

Psalm 41:4-13 *Mine enemies speak evil of me, When shall he die, and his name perish? And if he come to see me, he speaketh vanity: his heart gathereth iniquity to itself; when he goeth abroad, he telleth it. All that hate me whisper together against me: against me do they devise my hurt. An evil disease, say they, cleaveth fast unto him: and now that he lieth he shall rise up no more. Yea, mine own familiar friend, in whom I trusted, which did eat of my bread, hath lifted up his heel against me. But thou, O LORD, be merciful unto me, and raise me up, that I may requite them. By this I know that thou favourest me, because mine enemy doth not triumph over me. And as for me, thou upholdest me in mine integrity, and settest me before thy face for ever. Blessed be the LORD God of Israel from everlasting, and to everlasting. Amen, and Amen.*

You will want to give the person being used maliciously the benefit of the doubt because of your compassionate heart and because the state they are in, but it will be essential to discern their fruit for the malice is stored within them. Until they are delivered, you have to trust what God is revealing to you less you be hooked into their deceit, and overtaken by the way the enemy is using them to hook you.

Luke 6:45-46 *A good man brings good things out of the good stored up in his heart, and an evil man brings evil things out of the evil stored up in his heart. For the mouth speaks what the heart is full of. "Why do you call me, 'Lord, Lord,' and do not do what I say?*

DEMONIC SPIRITS THAT ATTACK IDENTITY

The world would say that identity is being one's authentic self. I define healthy identity as, "being who God created us to be." Biblically, identity means, "being created in the likeness and image of God," as *identity* began in the garden with Adam and Eve.

Genesis 1:26 *And God said, Let us make man in our image, after our likeness: and let them have dominion over the fish of the sea, and over the fowl of the air, and over the cattle, and over all the earth, and over every creeping thing that creepeth upon the earth. God spoke: "Let us make human beings in our image, make them reflecting our nature So they can be responsible for the fish in the sea, the birds in the air, the cattle, And, yes, Earth itself, and every animal that moves on the face of Earth." (MSG)*

Image is *selem* in Hebrew and means:
1. To shade; a phantom, i.e. (figuratively) illusion, resemblance
2. Hence, a representative figure, especially an idol
3. Image, vain show

Likeness in Hebrew is *dmut* and means:
1. Resemblance; concretely, model, shape; adverbially, like
2. Fashion, like (-ness, as), manner, similitude

Dictionary.com defines *likeness* as:
1. A representation, picture, or image, especially a portrait
2. The state or fact of being like
3. The semblance or appearance of something; guise
4. Correspondence in appearance; something that corresponds

Dictionary.com defines *identity* as:
1. The state or fact of remaining the same one or ones, as under varying aspects or conditions
2. The condition of being oneself or itself, and not another
3. Condition or character as to who a person or what a thing is
4. The state or fact of being the same one as described
5. The sense of self, provides sameness and continuity in personality over time and sometimes disturbed in mental illnesses, such as schizophrenia
6. Exact likeness in nature or qualities
7. An instance or point of sameness or likeness

No matter how much we redefine, reinvent, distort, reject, our true selves, we cannot have a true identity apart from God. True God-identity requires having a relationship with him and evolving in who he has created us to be as a progressive lifestyle.

When we are not secure in our identity or take on an alternate identity, it opens the doors to flesh and demonic spirits dictating who we are and how we engage in life and relationships. Often times this causes us to engage in demonic or unhealthy characteristics and behaviors that are not of God. Such operations strive to take precedent in our lives and even who God is to be to us. It also causes us to glory in our own will, perceptions, and ideologies, which is a sin against God.

1Corinthians 1:29 contends *'that no flesh should glory in his presence."*

The flesh can entail sin issues but is also anything that is carnal or not in the nature or character of God.

In this particular scripture, the word *glory* means to *"boast or become vain"* and the word *presence* means *"to be in the face of or to come into sight."*

The false identity is not manifesting as if it is our true identity, however, it is really what is being revealed as we seek to illuminate something that is not the truth of who God is nor who he created us to be. In an effort to regard people's free will, the laws of the land, and a host of other mental and psychological factors as it relates to those struggling with erred, distorted, or rejected identity, we have succumbed to demons oppressing and overtaking people's identity. Daily we engage with people who do not know who they are and are oppressed by spirits that dictate to them and us who they are. As a deliverer, it will be important to identify these demonizations and how they operate, while also seeking God for the strategy of how to help set people free. Strategy is vital in this area so please make sure you seek God for it. He will aid you in how to transform yourself into his likeness, and aid others in wanting his identity over anything they, the world, or demons could shape themselves into.

Let's explore some demonic characteristics and/or spirits that attack our God-identity.

- *Shyness* is a form of fear that manifests as being bashful, easily frightened away; timid, suspicious; distrustful, reluctant; guarded, deficient, not bearing or breeding freely (producing or reproducing freely). Though it is natural to be nervous as this shows our dependence on God, we should not be shy or fearful. The scriptures let us know that fear, shyness, timidity, etc., is a demonic spirit. *2Timothy 1:7* states *"For God hath not given us the spirit of fear (timidity, fearfulness, cowardice); but of power, and of love, and of a sound mind."*

  Shyness can be crippling and yields that the person feels that they will not be accepted, will not be understood, and/or has a fear of failing. Shyness tends to be a self-centered state, as the person is really revealing that in their hearts, they are desperately seeking approval from others; but when around or before people, they strive to hide within themselves, hide in the floor by starring at the ground, or hide in the presence by staring in the sky, hide off in space by staring past the people, for fear of not receiving the approval they so desperately desire.

- *Fear* is a distressing emotion, concern, or anxiety aroused by impending danger, evil, pain, sweating, rejection, etc., whether the threat is real or imagined; it is the feeling or condition of being afraid. When fear boasts in the presence of God it displays our thoughts of not feeling capable, equipped, valued, secure, trusted, disciplined, controlled, and whole. It is basically displaying that there is something in our personality and character that requires deliverance and healing. When fear manifests in the dance, it appears as anxiety, panic; we may exhibit wide eyes and as if we are frightened and just want to run from before the people. Our emotions, thoughts, and behaviors may appear disheveled or frenzied. Fear can also manifest with such a grip that the person will be stiff and barely presentable as fear will be wrapped around the person or has a hold of the person's heart and soul, where they are restricted in life and their decision making.

- *Condemnation* means to give judgment against, to judge worthy of punishment, and/or to feel and operate as if others have judged even though a sentence may not have been passed yet. Condemnation causes us to operate in guilt and shame.

    Guilt insinuates that we have committed or feel responsible for an offense, crime, violation, or wrong.

    Shame is a painful feeling arising from the consciousness of something dishonorable, improper, ridiculous, etc., done by oneself or another. It is also a feeling of disgrace or regret.

    When we operate in life with issues of shame and guilt, we attempt to become faceless before the people. We do not want to be judged so we become downtrodden and faceless in an effort not to be condemned. We enter in a disposition of shame and guilt where pain, emotionalism, or even little to no emotion or movement, is displayed in our lives and actions. We are just stuck in the self-offense and the victimization of what happened to us or what we opened ourselves up to.

    For example, a person can be bound to the point where he or she hides within themselves and no emotion is displayed in their facial expression, no thoughts or opinions or drive to make important decisions, or in knowing who they are. It is almost as if the person is lethargic and motionless as they fear being judged or they have already judged themselves so they are not free to be themselves.

    Often the person who experiences condemnation can only express emotion related to trauma, pain, or hurt, and even in these instances, the ministry is more erratic and overly emotional than expressing balanced emotion and thoughts that display the identity of God that is upon their lives. What the person is exuding is often in an attempt to compensate and pay the debt for judgment that has them bound. Their lives become more about their trauma than who they are and what they are to be on earth.

- **_Inadequacy, Insecurity, & Low Self-Esteem_** - I would define inadequacy as, *"having a feeling of deficiency, feeling incomplete or insufficient regarding life or for a position, task or duty."*

    Dictionary.com defines *inadequate* as:
    1. not adequate or sufficient; inept or unsuitable
    2. psychiatry: ineffectual in response to emotional, social, intellectual, and physical demands in the absence of any obvious mental or physical deficiency

In collaboration with Dictionary.com, I would define *insecurity* as, *"a lack of confidence or assurance; self-doubt, instability, inferiority, low self-esteem, fear of what others will think, timidity, shyness, embarrassment, self-consciousness, uncertainty."*

I would define *low self-esteem* as *"having a generally negative overall opinion of oneself, judging or evaluating oneself negatively, and placing a general negative value on oneself as a person."*

A person who is insecure, inadequate, or of low self-esteem will attempt to hide within themselves or behind others, they engage in life. They often do not are restricted and insecure in their body movement, their interactions, their abilities, their appearance, their disposition, God, and his uniqueness in them.

- They lack personality even though they are full of unique traits and abilities.
- Their lives may mimic others who they want to be like.
- Their lives may also be bland and ineffective due to having no personal identity and character regarding who they are in God and his purpose and call upon their lives.

<u>Rejection</u> means to throw away, as anything useless or vile, to cast off; to forsake, to refuse to receive; to slight; to despise.

Because a person is dealing with issues of rejection, they are already in a place of separation before they even engage people or life. They have already ostracized and separated themselves and have decided that no one wants to be bothered with or value who they are and their purpose on earth. This is because they lack the ability to connect or fear connecting, so they self-reject to protect themselves from being rejected.

Therefore the rejected person attempts to get their needs met for approval and belonging through their abilities and what they can do for you. They are seeking to buy love and approval with their talents and the sacrificing of themselves. The person tends to waver in operating in pride or superiority due to presenting as having a high or inordinate opinion of themselves. Yet they really are not prideful or haughty. Truthfully, they are insecure but are masking it with the false confidence of self.

This person will do things to be seen and will take the credit for any public success to receive approval, applause, or accolades. Their actions tend to be attention-seeking, overly dramatic, and distracting, as they seek to receive the approval and accolades to feed the void of wanting to be validated, wanting to belong, wanting to be loved, wanting to feel good about themselves, wanting others to help them feel good about themselves, wanting others to prove that they value them even though they do not value themselves. It will be about them and not about you or the situation at hand. You may benefit, but it is all about them feeding their rejection.

The rejection puts a void in a person's heart and soul. Such persons can be draining because the void is like an empty pocket with a hole in it. The more you fill it, the more to demand validation from you. They become passive-aggressive and even abusive when you seek to put boundaries in place or decide not to feed a void that can only be filled through their self-acceptance and being healed of root issues of rejection. They may not intentionally abuse or become passive-aggressive towards you the spirit of rejection controls their identity. They find it difficult to operate or sustain in their wellness because the minute they do not feel validated, even if it is misperceived or perceived, that potential to regress to operating in rejection is right there knocking on the door of their heart and soul. They need to be healed of self-hate and learn how to love themselves, who God is, and who God has created them to be before they can truly journey in wellness as a lifestyle. Though this may not always be the case, it has been my experience that such persons need ongoing counseling to sustain wellness. They need constant support from a professional therapist that can maintain boundaries with them and hold them accountable to remain rooted and grounded in their God-identity.

- _Pride_ means a high or inordinate opinion of one's own dignity, importance, merit, or superiority, whether as cherished in the mind or as displayed in capabilities, character, conduct, etc.

   The prideful person may present as if they are better than everyone else, everyone needs who they are and what they have, the world revolves around them, and even as if they are God. They may exude a "me, myself, and I," complex. They may lack humility, have a difficult time being a team player, and tend to dictate and order others rather than being open to exploring options that benefit everyone.

- ***Lust*** manifests as very sensual, wooing, sexy, and physically and emotionally seductive. One of the challenges with lust is that it causes others to stumble. It is a spirit that tempts or entices by tapping into the vulnerable and unhealed areas of a person's challenges and plants inordinate seeds and thoughts to trigger blatant sin. Lust tends to mesmerize the souls, hearts, emotions, and flesh of people rather than pierce the spirit where people can be transformed.

   Matthew 5:28 But I say unto you, That whosoever looketh on a woman to lust after her hath committed adultery with her already in his heart. And if thy right eye offend thee, pluck it out, and cast it from thee: for it is profitable for thee that one of thy members should perish, and not that thy whole body should be cast into hell.

The Amplified Version *But I say to you that everyone who so much as looks at a woman with evil desire for her has already committed adultery with her in his heart. If your right eye serves as a trap to ensnare you or is an occasion for you to stumble and sin, pluck it out and throw it away. It is better that you lose one of your members than that your whole body be cast into hell (Gehenna).*

Lust means *"to desire to have a thing or to covet."* It means *"to desire wrongfully, inordinately, or without due regard for the rights of others."*

Dictionary.com defines *lust* as:
1. Intense sexual desire or appetite
2. Uncontrolled or illicit sexual desire or appetite; lecherousness
3. A passionate or overmastering desire or craving

We are quick to say "*I was just looking or I was just thinking but I did not touch*" however, Jesus warns us that the operation of lust is so subtle that even looking at a woman and desiring or thinking of her past a place of admiration is a sin. Because we are constantly being tempted by the world, media, and the enemy in an effort to draw us into things that are not beneficial to us, or to gluten for, or illegally obtain more of what is beneficial to us (e.g. Food, clothes, sex, idolatry), as ministers we should always be cleansing out lust even if we are not in blatant sin. We could be housing lust and not even know it, or be so comfortable with lusting and being enticed to things in a covetous nature that we are desensitized to the presence of lust within us.

Though we cannot control how a person lusts after us, we can control what is in us so that people encounter the virtuous power of God and not lust. Lust will manifest in our body language, conversation, our dress, movement, and our actions. Lust also manifests as spooky spiritual or bewitching. It has a texture, presentation, and movement that draws a person to it rather than to a posture of admiration, honor, and regard, or to the spirit of God. As lust draws, it provokes lustful thoughts that draw a person into sin if they do not cast them down **(2Corinthians 10:5).**

Even as you seek to not allow lust to glory in you, be mindful not to be drawn away and enticed by the lust of others.

1Corinthians 6:18-19 *What? know ye not that your body is the temple of the Holy Ghost which is in you, which ye have of God, and ye are not your own? For ye are bought with a price: therefore glorify God in your body, and in your spirit, which are God's.*

<u>Glorify</u> in Greek is *doxazō* and means:
1. To render (or esteem) glorious (in a wide application): — (make) glorify(-ious), full of (have) glory, honor
2. To think, suppose, be of opinion, to praise, extol, magnify, celebrate to honor, do honor to, hold in honor, to make glorious
3. Adorn with luster, clothe with splendor, to impart glory to something, render it excellent to make renowned, render illustrious
4. To cause the dignity and worth of some person or thing to become manifest and acknowledged

We glorify God in our bodies by seeking to be pure vessels where he can fully dwell. Some ways I keep my body pure is that I spend time washing and purging my body, soul, mind, emotions, appetite, and thought life, in the blood of Jesus, then I soak myself in the virtue, purity, righteousness, holiness, and glory of God. There are also times when I will use the holy fire of God to burn out ungodly roots, demonic impartations, and imprints, demonic, soulish, or emotional fruits, warfare darts, and words coming from people and the enemy. I do this:

- After I minister, I cleanse myself of anything that may have transferred from the atmosphere, region, and/or people that I ministered too
- After work or after I have been around people where carnality, compromise, or sin dwelled, or when being in a situation that has been trying, perverted, lustful, full of witchcraft or idolatry, etc. Because the world is so infiltrated such places could be as simple as going to the mall, out to dinner with friends or family, visiting family and friends, etc.
- I guard what I watch, listen to, and what I expose myself to. At times when I have watched things on TV that are full of lust, sin, perversion, idolatry, blood, and gore, I spend time repenting and cleansing myself with the blood of Jesus, the fire of God, and glory of God. Sometimes things pop up in the commercials, kid shows, etc. Be mindful to consistently cleanse and wash yourself of lust and any other demonic or ungodly deposits.
- I cleanse myself after scrolling on social media, the internet, as many videos, pictures, articles that are full of mess; I, therefore, strive to restore myself in holiness unto the Lord.

The more you cleanse yourself, the keener you will be in discerning what is not like the Holy Spirit, and the more God's power and authority can live and work through you for his glory.

The devil is an identity thief. Let me list some ways he and his kingdom totally seeks to steal our God-identity. From my manual, "*Kingdom Wellness Counseling & Mentoring Manual Volume I.*"

Identity Theft - Identity theft is when a person's identity has totally been stolen and used by someone who is not who they portray themselves to be. The enemy steals a person's uniqueness when he causes confusion, distortion, brokenness, idolatry, delays, immaturity, stagnation, etc., within a person's identity. *John 10:10* says, "*The thief cometh not, but for to steal, and to kill, and to destroy: I have come that they might have life, and that they might have it more abundantly.*"

Identity Confusion - The person's identity has been confused and contaminated and they waver between who God says they are, who they want to be, and/or who people, society, or the demonic forces desire them to be. The person is tormented and/or frustrated by who they believe they are to be and who they want to be, or who others want them to be or say they are. The person's identity is unclear, indistinct, and confounded. Their identity is blurred between two or three belief systems that compete and battle for hierarchy in their lives and often cause disorder in their relationships and interactions. Though not always the case, their identity can also affect their education, job duties, and relating in society. This is because confusion, conflicts, misunderstandings, and drama seem to follow them. Some of them can become aggressive and manipulative in efforts to assert justice for themselves. Moreover, there are instances where they are the victims or perceive themselves as the victims. Because of continual conflicts surrounding identity confusion, they feel that no one understands them and that people are against them. Truly, it can be difficult to describe, understand, and engage the person because they fail to properly distinguish who they are and there is a perplexity about them that is bewildering. A biblical example is, how frequently the Israelites were challenged with identity confusion.

Distorted Identity - The person's identity tends to be false or untrue and is more rooted in fantasy, lies, or misrepresentations than in truths.

Twisting of Truth - These people tend to embellish stories, tell lies, or present facts that are not true and do not align with their life experiences, abilities, or presentation of who they are. These facts do not represent what loved ones and/or the Counselor knows about the person or what they present regarding themselves. The person's identity can appear twisted and confusing because it is mixed with lies and truths or misperceptions.

These people can also perceive, feel, or believe themselves to be one way but in reality, it is another way. For example, body image struggles to cause a person to feel fat when, in reality, they are slender. They experience gender distortion and see themselves as the victim while operating as an offender. They see their lives as hopeless when, in reality, it is hopeful.

Fantasy Life - These people tend to live and operate within twisted truths, fantasies, and/or false realities. They are challenged with accepting the reality of who they are because the perceptions, feelings, and thoughts of the distorted identity can be tormenting to the point that they begin to favor the distorted reality over the truth. The fantasy life can be seducing, risk-taking, enjoyable, and, in some ways, more fulfilling than their true identity. A person begins to favor the distorted identity over their true identity. Sometimes the distorted identity can cause people to hate and reject their true identity. They resist and reject acknowledging and accepting their true selves and the changes they need to make within themselves and within their lives that would enable them to enjoy, love, and value, their true selves.

Sometimes these people have become so engulfed in their fantasy life that they do not know what is real or true about themselves anymore. This can cause great torment in the person's soul, heart, and mind. It can also cause challenges in the person's relationships and societal interactions. They will have a difficult time engaging people and life situations and find it difficult feeling loved or as if they belong.

Shun Responsibility - Sometimes the shunned person does not want to take responsibility for life decisions or for change. Therefore, they will live in a fantasy world, and act as if the responsibilities do not exist. Procrastination, stagnation, self-sabotage tends to steal their progress and success. They tend to do just enough to survive but not enough to make changes that progress their lives. Because of the interference and interaction of the fantasy world, sometimes, it will take them years to accomplish what they are capable of accomplishing in a few weeks or months.

Twisted Morals & Values - There are instances where the person with a distorted reality will know right from wrong but will depart from the right, normal, or usual, course of their lives or of what they have been taught or know is right. They will know the truth or what is morally correct but will deviate from those truths and morals.

- Often this is to satisfy voids and needs for love and belonging as they are seeking self-fulfillment even if it is temporary fulfillment.
- Sometimes, it is because they are operating through their distorted identity where morals and values are blurred or mixed with misperceptions.
- Sometimes, they have become mentally unstable or have a lapse in their mental state because they are living in the distorted reality that makes them feel they do not have any consequences to their actions or what they are doing is okay or justifiable.

Identity Deformity - These people have lived in a distorted personality for so long that their identity becomes deformed and has thus taken on the form of that false identity. The natural shape of their identity has become disfigured and they begin to completely identify and identify themselves through the distorted identity. The distortion causes the person to behave and even look like an entirely different person than who God created them to be. This deformity is often warped, strange, and odd. The person appears and behaves crippled, contorted, and mangled in their identity, as there is a misshaping of their true selves. They are attempting to transform their nature in order to birth forth their desired identity. This is impossible to do because the nature of who a person is can never be changed. Many people, who experience a confused identity, strive to change their entire lives based upon what they feel or believe about themselves and ultimately SHIFT to living through a deformed identity.

Broken Identity - The person's identity has been fractured, breached, split, compromised, or mishandled by some challenging experiences. Because of the experience, the person has a difficult time:

- Accepting who they are to be,
- Dealing with the pain and challenges surrounding who they are to be or having to become, due to that experience,
- Pain, rejection, and or rebellion is now ruling the identity and the person begins to operate through different personalities of who they are and who they have become rather than a healthy identity.
- Biblical Examples: Tamar, Moses.

Undeveloped Identity - The person becomes stuck at a certain age or developmental state. Multiple studies have proven that a person who is incarcerated becomes stuck in the age-relevant to their conviction as opportunity is lacking for normal social development. When a person is imprisoned mentally, emotionally, or spiritually, the same paradigm applies.

Erikson's psychosocial theory of development considers the impact of external factors, parents, and society on personality development from childhood to adulthood.

According to Erikson's theory, every person must pass through a series of eight interrelated stages over the entire life cycle.

Diagram 15.0 Erik Erikson: Stages of Psychosocial Development

\<Erikson's Stage Theory in its Final Version\>			
Age	Conflict	Resolution or "Virtue"	Culmination in old age
Infancy (0-1 year)	Basic trust vs. mistrust	Hope	Appreciation of interdependence and relatedness
Early childhood (1-3 years)	Autonomy vs. shame	Will	Acceptance of the cycle of life, from integration to disintegration
Play age (3-6 years)	Initiative vs. guilt	Purpose	Humor; empathy; resilience
School age (6-12 years)	Industry vs. Inferiority	Competence	Humility; acceptance of the course of one's life and unfulfilled hopes
Adolescence (12-19 years)	Identity vs. Confusion	Fidelity	Sense of complexity of life; merging of sensory, logical and aesthetic perception
Early adulthood (20-25 years)	Intimacy vs. Isolation	Love	Sense of the complexity of relationships; value of tenderness and loving freely
Adulthood (26-64 years)	Generativity vs. stagnation	Care	Caritas, caring for others, and agape, empathy and concern
Old age (65-death)	Integrity vs. Despair	Wisdom	Existential identity; a sense of integrity strong enough to withstand physical disintegration

Source: Google images, 2019

These eight stages, spanning from birth to death, are split into general age ranges. Sometimes (not always the case), we can recognize when people are experiencing an undeveloped identity when their personalities fluctuate between identity stages. For example, an adult may act like a child at times, even to the point of throwing tantrums, or an adult may behave like a teenager who is just learning how to be responsible for life choices. The person will fluctuate between being an adult and being a kid or teen. Parts of their personality may be stuck at a specific age or due to a split in their personality. They go back and forth between their true age and being a child or teen. When exploring what needs the person is striving to have met based on Erikson's chart, you as a counselor, can most often discern what age a person is operating in.

Moreover, you can ask that person if they had a challenging experience in childhood or adolescence and can discern what parts of their personality are stuck or underdeveloped, based on the time of that experience.

The reason I say sometimes is because sometimes a person can revert to an age where they attempted to deal with an experience. The actual experience may have happened in childhood; however, the person may be stuck in their teen years where they tried to deal with that childhood trauma. It is therefore best not to make assumptions, but ask lots of questions. It is also essential to seek God for knowledge and revelation on what the person is dealing with. This may be exceptionally true when dealing with a client who has experienced childhood sexual trauma.

1Corinthians 3:11 *When I was a child, I spoke as a child, I understood as a child, I thought as a child: but when I became a man, I put away childish things.*

<u>*Seasonal (Time) Identity Challenges*</u> - Experiences that happen at different times in a person's life can cause an underdeveloped or non-progressing identity.

- If it was a good season, the person may fear moving on and even failing, so they can remain stuck in that place.
- If it was a bad season, the person has some unhealed pain or root issues that need to be dealt with. These challenges are hindering them from maturing in their identity
- Society, people, or life itself, has changed but the person -
    - Is stuck in a time warp,
    - Is rebelling against changing with the times,
    - Fears moving with the times (may think they will lose memories, fulfillment, or comfortability), or
    - Lacks the knowledge to move with the times resulting in stagnation.

Ecclesiastes 3:1 *To everything there is a season, and a time to every purpose under the heaven.*

<u>*Situational or Needs-Based Identity Challenges*</u> - An underdeveloped identity can also be caused by a lack of life's needs being met. According to Abraham Maslow, we all have basic needs that must be met in order for us to develop properly into healthy functioning individuals who can self-actualize in life. *Self-actualization* is the attainment of a person's complete potential or capability through creativity, independence, spontaneity, and achievements, as they seek to conquer their life's destiny. Maslow believes we must develop and receive these basic needs before we can become self-actualized. Though I do not agree with how some people and/or societies meet these needs as my belief standards are based on biblical principles, I do agree that most of these needs are essential to people having a healthy identity. People need to eat, drink, have shelter, sleep, have sex if they are married, feel safe, have a support system, a sense of belonging, etc.

Diagram 15.1 Maslow's Expanded Needs Hierarchy

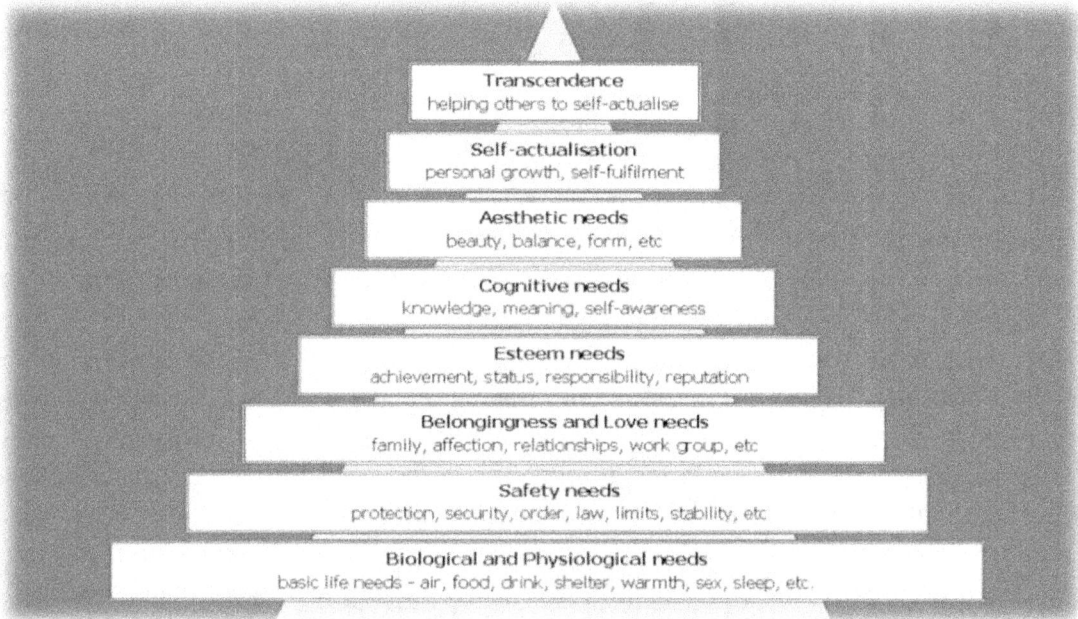

Source: Google images, 2019

James 1:27 *Pure religion and undefiled before God and the Father is this, To visit the fatherless and widows in their affliction, and to keep himself unspotted from the world.*

Many times, in the church, we either want people to deny these needs, sacrifice them, or we may only want to meet them one time and call it a testimony of how we evangelized and helped people. We do not want to provide avenues where people can be fulfilled and sustained in these needs so we can assist them with maturing in their identity.

We also have the challenge of wanting to strip people of their identity, especially if many of their needs are being met in an unhealthy manner. However, we do not provide pathways or we do not process people to wholeness where their identity is built through:

- God's provisional means,
- Who God says they are to be,
- Healthy relationships and interactions,
- Destiny oriented successes,
- Skills and training that sustain personal and generational success and inheritance.

We expect people to accomplish this independently and without adequate counseling, mentoring, and equipping. This is the main reason people return to sin habits, cycling patterns of deliverance, and backsliding or think that God and the church have no power to deliver and heal.

Philippians 2:3-5 *Do nothing from factional motives [through contentiousness, strife, selfishness, or for unworthy ends] or prompted by conceit and empty arrogance. Instead, in the true spirit of humility (lowliness of mind) let each regard the others as better than and superior to himself [thinking more highly of one another than you do of yourselves].*

Let each of you esteem and look upon and be concerned for not [merely] his own interests, but also each for the interests of others. Let this same attitude and purpose and [humble] mind be in you which was in Christ Jesus: [Let Him be your example in humility:] (AMP)

Ephesians 4:11-16 *And he gave some, apostles; and some, prophets; and some, evangelists; and some, pastors and teachers; For the perfecting of the saints, for the work of the ministry, for the edifying of the body of Christ: Till we all come in the unity of the faith, and of the knowledge of the Son of God, unto a perfect man, unto the measure of the stature of the fulness of Christ: That we henceforth be no more children, tossed to and fro, and carried about with every wind of doctrine, by the sleight of men, and cunning craftiness, whereby they lie in wait to deceive; But speaking the truth in love, may grow up into him in all things, which is the head, even Christ: From whom the whole body fitly joined together and compacted by that which every joint supplieth, according to the effectual working in the measure of every part, maketh increase of the body unto the edifying of itself in love.*

Perfecting is *katartismos* in the Geek and means to "*completely furnish or equip.*" This means the church is responsible for building up the entire person's identity. Not just parts of it that benefit our churches, our agendas, or our egos.

Identity Inferiority - This is where the person feels inadequate about who they are and either undercompensate or overcompensate in their behaviors in an effort to define and assert their identity. The person fluctuates between these two extreme personalities due to a lack of self-esteem, thoughts, and feelings of self-security or self-sufficiency, or due to a lack of self-confidence. One minute they are prideful and haughty, and the next they are inferior and helpless. Psychiatry calls this an identity or inferiority complex. Biblical Example: Saul

Rejection. Individuals who struggle with having an inferiority complex struggle to find a place to "fit in." Over time, the result is a pattern of rejection that builds a defense system of rejection. These individuals often struggle to maintain friendships or relationships because they have internalized a need to reject others before experiencing the rejection they feel is inevitably coming. They will sabotage relationships without having a clear understanding of why they are taking that course which embeds the identity inferiority even deeper.

Humor. It is not uncommon to find that comedians or individuals who are known for their humor are struggling with identity inferiority. The humor becomes a mask to wear for their performance of gaining approval from others, yet there is always the dark undercurrent of wondering if they are "enough." Many will think that they are merely struggling with depression or anxiety, but those diagnoses are not reaching the core of the issue that is driving the humorous personality.

Idolatrous Identity - The person thinks they are God or desires to be God. The person tends to worship creation rather than the Creator. The worship tends to be of themselves, their ideas and perceptions, or an idol god. It may seem farfetched, but there are religious practices that construct an altar of worship in the person's mind and invite various deities to come and worship. The deity that comes is the one that also becomes that person's identity.

Though this is not always the case, sometimes a person with an idolatrous identity, may not know they have become their own idol or that they are requiring others to idolize them. They may become upset if God or a person suggests this to them, yet, a person with an idolatrous identity tends to be right in their own eyes. They have a difficult time accepting constructive criticism, rebuking, and acknowledging ungodly or unhealthy behaviors.

Some people with idolatrous identities can be narcissistic. Narcists have an obsessive, grandiose, erotic, absorbed interest, and focus on themselves. Most, if not all, of their decisions, are rooted in self-centered benefits. Even when they perform good acts, there is an ulterior motive of personal benefit. They gain pleasure, gratification, and even arousal (for some) from how their actions, whether positive or negative, impact others. They may feel entitled to use and abuse people for their personal pleasure and gain.

Narcissists have a profound impact on people with a confused or inferior identity. They can control these types of people by isolating them, and further stealing and stripping them of their identity. Biblical Examples: Jezebel, Athaliah, Satan

Spirit of Jealousy Envy, & Division That Attack God Identity – Seeks to attack mantles and callings. Even though David did nothing to promote himself, in *1Samuel 18:7*, we find a group of women singing of how David killed tens of thousands while Saul killed thousands.

And the women sang to one another as they played, and said, Saul, has slain his thousands, and David his ten thousands.

This song caused a spirit of jealousy, envy, and division to operate between David and his leader Saul.

Jealousy is when a person harbors resentment, ill will, ill intent, against a rival, someone they do not like or want to be like. Envy is when a person is discontent within themselves – their own life and identity – and thus, covet someone else's abilities, capabilities, life, success, destiny. Such a person can release an all-out assault on their rival. The rival is often someone who has not done anything. However, their very existence and disposition incite jealousy in the person. Jealousy is often rooted in rejection, rebellion, insecurity, inadequacy, inferiority, and self-hatred. The person will create drama and scenarios to make their rival look bad in the eyes of others; or to highlight their weaknesses or mishaps in an effort to make themselves look important, the rescuer and fixer of the person's mistakes, or better than that person. This person will use the situations they create to strengthen their attack and reproach of their prey. They seek to destroy and annihilate them and make it their life's mission to murder who they covet in that person. In many ways, the jealous person is seeking to destroy that person so they do not have to be reminded of who they are not, what they do not want to work to achieve and eliminate what they consider to be their competition to being viewed as the best or "God" in everyone's eyes.

These demonic spirits were allowed to enter because Saul battled with personal insecurity and inadequacy. This caused Saul to be immature in being able to handle David's anointing and success, so rather than empower him, he sought to kill the destiny and gifting that was upon David's life. We see this a lot in ministry in general,

Demonic & Manmade Or Man Directed Armor – Such demonic spirits or people will encourage a person to put on the armor of the devil or the armor of other people. It will have a person operating in weapons, armor, gifts, and callings, that God did not direct or ordain. When David was preparing to fight Goliath, King Saul attempts to dress David in his armor.

1Samuel 17:38-40 And Saul armed David with his armour, and he put an helmet of brass upon his head; also he armed him with a coat of mail. And David girded his sword upon his armour, and he assayed to go; for he had not proved it. And David said unto Saul, I cannot go with these; for I have not proved them. And David put them off him. And he took his staff in his hand, and chose him five smooth stones out of the brook, and put them in a shepherd's bag which he had, even in a scrip; and his sling was in his hand: and he drew near to the Philistine.

Armor in this passage of scripture means *"garment, judgment, raiment, clothes, or stature."* David refused to wear Saul's armor because he had not proven it. This meant that he had not tested the armor. This was interesting because David had been anointed king in *1Samuel 16:11-13*, and had a chance to wear the king's garments in war, but he recognized that he was not ready for the mantle and armor of a king, and had not achieved such qualification and prestige.

In the secular world, there are clothing styles and apparel that one person may be able to wear, yet it may not look as well on another person. The clothes we choose may also have to do with our age, financial status, culture, region, nation, trends, creativity, and taste. However, to God, clothing encompasses more than these attributes. Clothing represents our armor in the spirit and as we consider the definition of *armor*, they also are given to us based on judgment, our ability to judge, our stature, and authority in the spirit realm.

Oftentimes, we will seek to wear, borrow, or mimic the armor, gifts, callings, visions of others. This results in looking like copycats, rather than originals of ourselves and our own unique gifting and calling.

Dictionary.com defines *stature* as, *"degree of development attained, level of achievement."* If David would have worn Saul's armor, he would have come under the level of achievement and development of Saul, and what had been obtained through Saul's armor, rather than his own development and achievements. David's developments and achievements were destined and designed to exceed that of Saul's stature and authority. Therefore, if he had worn his armor, David would have come under a limited capacity and ability. Whose authority and stature have you subjected yourself to by wearing their armor rather than being an original version of who God ordained you to be and how he chooses to dress you in the spirit?

In *1Samuel 17:2-10*, we find the army of Saul afraid to come out and face Goliath.

And Saul and the men of Israel were gathered together, and pitched by the valley of Elah, and set the battle in array against the Philistines. And the Philistines stood on a mountain on the one side, and Israel stood on a mountain on the other side: and there was a valley between them. And there went out a champion out of the camp of the Philistines, named Goliath, of Gath, whose height was six cubits and a span.

And he had a helmet of brass upon his head, and he was armed with a coat of mail; and the weight of the coat was five thousand shekels of brass. And he had greaves of brass upon his legs, and a target of brass between his shoulders. And the staff of his spear was like a weaver's beam; and his spear's head weighed six hundred shekels of iron: and one bearing a shield went before him.

And he stood and cried unto the armies of Israel, and said unto them, Why are ye come out to set your battle in array? am not I a Philistine, and ye servants to Saul? choose you a man for you, and let him come down to me. If he be able to fight with me, and to kill me, then will we be your servants: but if I prevail against him, and kill him, then shall ye be our servants, and serve us. And the Philistine said, I defy the armies of Israel this day; give me a man, that we may fight together. When Saul and all Israel heard those words of the Philistine, they were dismayed and greatly afraid.

Verse 26 And David spake to the men that stood by him, saying, What shall be done to the man that killeth this Philistine, and taketh away the reproach from Israel? for who is this uncircumcised Philistine, that he should defy the armies of the living God?

David was the only person who felt that he could defeat Goliath.   Everyone else was scared, insecure, and fearful. The scripture describes them, including Saul, as terrified and deeply shaken. Even though he was still positioned as king, Saul was not confident in his armor, stature, authority, or his ability to judge and overthrow Goliath. He was insecure in his spiritual and natural armor, and did not believe he was equipped to defeat Goliath. Had David fought with that armor, he would have been fighting through the well of fear, insecurity, terror, and defeat, as all of this was enmeshed in Saul's armor. You are only as strong as the armor you put on. This is why we are told to put on the armor of the Lord as that is the best and most complete armor we can wear (***Ephesians 6:11-12***).

At this point of fighting Goliath, God had already rejected Saul and David was anointed as the new king.

1Samuel 13:13-14 And Samuel said to Saul, Thou hast done foolishly: thou hast not kept the commandment of the LORD thy God, which he commanded thee: for now would the LORD have established thy kingdom upon Israel forever. But now thy kingdom shall not continue: the LORD hath sought him a man after his own heart, and the LORD hath commanded him to be captain over his people, because thou hast not kept that which the LORD commanded thee.

1Samuel 16:1 And the LORD said unto Samuel, How long wilt thou mourn for Saul, seeing I have rejected him from reigning over Israel? fill thine horn with oil, and go, I will send thee to Jesse the Bethlehemite: for I have provided me a king among his sons.

Verse 11-13 And Samuel said unto Jesse, Are here all thy children? And he said, There remaineth yet the youngest, and, behold, he keepeth the sheep. And Samuel said unto Jesse, Send and fetch him: for we will not sit down till he come hither. And he sent, and brought him in. Now he was ruddy, and withal of a beautiful countenance, and goodly to look to. And the Lord said, Arise, anoint him: for this is he. Then Samuel took the horn of oil, and anointed him in the midst of his brethren: and the Spirit of the Lord came upon David from that day forward. So Samuel rose up, and went to Ramah.

Had David fought with Saul's armor, he would have been fighting through the judgment of God that was upon Saul and fighting with rejected armor. He would have contended he was fighting in the name of the Lord, but God would not have shown up. God had left Saul. David would have been fighting confused, as to how can the accepted king fight under the covering of the rejected king? This is the reason David fought in the name of the Lord. He was not fighting under Saul as Saul was rejected but under the covering of the Lord who had all authority over him and who he was as king.

1Samuel 17:45 Then said David to the Philistine, Thou comest to me with a sword, and with a spear, and with a shield: but I come to thee in the name of the Lord of hosts, the God of the armies of Israel, whom thou hast defied.

Aside from David's brothers, the people were not aware of what had transpired in secret, and that Saul was no longer the king and the leader of the people in the Lord's eyes. Therefore, when Goliath, the regional principality, came to war against Israel, Saul did not have the authority to defeat him. Saul no longer had any authority in that region nor in the spirit realm. Had David fought with Saul's armor, he would have had no authority as God had already judged Saul, rejected him and stripped him of his armor and stature.

<u>Clones & Copycat Spirits</u> - David refused to be a clone – a copycat. A clone or copycat is an organism that is a genetically identical copy of something or someone else. It is a person that duplicates, imitates, or closely resembles another in appearance, function, performance, or style. God considers clones to be idols. God hates idolatry because it dilutes, steals, kills, and destroys his authenticity in people. He is not allowed to be uniquely and authentically represented in that person.

Exodus 20:3-4 *Thou shalt have no other gods before me. Thou shalt not make unto thee any graven image or any likeness of anything that is in heaven above, or that is in the earth beneath, or that is in the water under the earth.*

Leviticus 26:1 *Ye shall make you no idols nor graven image, neither rear you up a standing image, neither shall ye set up [any] image of stone in your land, to bow down unto it: for I [am] the LORD your God.*

When you become a copycat of someone else, you have not only become a clone but an idol. If you clone others to be like you, you have actually formed (carved and shaped) an idol. And though you think you are unique in God- identity and your life and works are fashioned in him, you are actually a representation and a worshipper of the idol you fashioned, and you have sacrificed those who are cloned in your likeness to that idol.

2Timothy 3:1-3 *This know also, that in the last days perilous times shall come. For men shall be lovers of their own selves, covetous, boasters, proud, blasphemers, disobedient to parents, unthankful, unholy, Without natural affection, trucebreakers, false accusers, incontinent, fierce, despisers of those that are good, Traitors, heady, highminded, lovers of pleasures more than lovers of God; Having a form of godliness, but denying the power thereof: from such turn away.*

David was confident that God would deliver him, therefore, he was not concerned whether his armor was sufficient. When you are a clone, people will be blessed but lives will not be changed by who you are, as the enemy you were meant to conquer, remains in a position of the conqueror. You went to war, but you did not win the fight.

You were no challenge to the enemy because you are operating from a counterfeit and under a grace that is not your own.

If you have lost your uniqueness and creativity due to becoming a clone, repent and ask God to restore your mantle and identity in his likeness.

If you have cultivated a group of clones, repent and ask God to show you the mantle, purpose, and calling of those you are called to, how to train them under the anointing that is on your life while helping to individually cultivate who they are in the earth.

Today we apply the blood of Jesus to cleanse and break free from any spiritual armor and cloning, that we have on that is not God's original armor and identity for our lives.

Today we embrace our unique giftings and callings. We SHIFT before God so that the Holy Spirit can teach us how to operate in the armor and purpose that is upon our lives. SHIFT!

DEMONIC SPIRITS THAT ATTACK GOD'S WORD

By: Taquetta Baker & Minister Reenita Keys of Kingdom Shifters Ministries
From my book, *"Discerning The Voice Of God."*

These demonic spirits attack a person's ability to hear God, stand in God, be faithful to God, his covenant, his word, and His purpose for their lives. These demonic spirits come for the character, nature, fruit, identity, uniqueness, and greatness of who a person is. They are counterfeit spirits. They want to be God, his word, and purpose in people's lives.

<u>**Diviners, Sorcerers, High Priest, Witches, Warlocks**</u> - Can hear from the 3rd heaven, but they operate from the 2nd heaven. Many of them are falling prophets who still possess the gift and mantle but do not have their heavenly authority. They, therefore, can access words that have already been released from the third heaven and are on the frequencies and airwaves of the 1st, 2nd, and 3rd heaven.

Romans 11:29 *For the gifts and calling of God are without repentance.*

<u>**Unbelief and Doubt**</u> – Speak distrust and doubt to cause a person to question, be suspicious of, fear, or reject the true word of God. Many of the interjections are due to a lack of faith and sometimes sound reasonable, but lack faith and trust in God. Inability to walk by faith or journey in faith until substance manifests. Will want you to reject God until manifestation prevails.

Hebrews 11:1 *Now faith is the substance of things hoped for, the evidence of things not seen.*

<u>**Naysayers**</u> – Habitually express negative or pessimistic views about God, his body, and his word. Constantly speak unhopeful, joyless, doom-type words to cast doubt and gloom on the true word of God. Do not want people to believe in prophecy or anything about God that does not have what they consider physically tangible evidence (***Study Exodus 3-4***). Naysayers will also try to publicly embarrass you for believing a word of God. They will get you before people and then speak of your prophecy and ridicule, drill, and question what God has spoken. Their purpose is to get you to reject what God is speaking and to scorn you for holding fast to the prophetic word.

Matthew 10:18-20 (English Standard Bible) *And you will be dragged before governors and kings for my sake, to bear witness before them and the Gentiles. When they deliver you over, do not be anxious about how you are to speak or what you are to say, for what you are to say will be given to you in that hour. For it is not you who speak, but the Spirit of your Father speaking through you.*

<u>Debaters</u> – Cause to debate, test, and prove the word based on doctrine and ideologies that oppose the true word and prophetic authority and power of God (Study Noah). The quarreling is more for entertainment purposes as they mock your belief and stance than truly wanting to learn, change and understand what God has spoken or will do in your life. Strive to get you out of character so they can prove that you are not godly and neither are your beliefs.

Titus 3:9 - *But avoid foolish questions, and genealogies, and contentions, and strivings about the law; for they are unprofitable and vain.*

<u>Mockers & Scorners</u> – Laughs and pock fun for standing on God's prophecies. Will cause psychological warfare of fear in making you believe you will fail or that God is not going to show up and fulfill his promises for you. Jeremiah had mockers. They were mocking and beckoning God to follow through with releasing wrath upon them. People mock Jesus' return. Sigh!!!!!

Jeremiah 17:15 *Listen to what they are saying to me. They are saying, "Where are the things the LORD threatens us with? Come on! Let's see them happen!"*

Psalm 1:1 *Blessed is the man that walketh not in the counsel of the ungodly, nor standeth in the way of sinners, nor sitteth in the seat of the scornful.*

2Peter 3:3-4 *Knowing this first, that there shall come in the last days scoffers, walking after their own lusts, And saying, Where is the promise of his coming? for since the fathers fell asleep, all things continue as they were from the beginning of the creation.*

Deuteronomy 31:6 *Be strong and of a good courage, fear not, nor be afraid of them: for the LORD thy God, he it is that doth go with thee; he will not fail thee, nor forsake thee.*

<u>Psychological Warfare</u> (Study the story of Nehemiah) – Derives from territorial spirits, powers, spells and word curses, and witchcraft sent from witches, warlocks, and demonic chatter from demons, ungodly, foolish, or ignorant, people. Words live on airways and demons pick them up, especially the negative ones then speak them back to you to distract, weary, and kill your progress or stance in God. This warfare causes anxiety, insecurity, wrestling, and questioning of God's word. Break the powers of wrestling and questioning. Blatantly muzzle and silence demonic voices by telling them to SHUT UP! Break the powers of spells, soothsaying, psychic powers, and telepathy being sent against you. Use the blood of Jesus to cleanse airways and frequencies of ungodly, negative, and demonic words that have been spoken about you.

Ezekiel 8:12 *Then He said to me, "Son of man, do you see what the elders of the house of Israel are committing in the dark, each man in the room of his carved images? For they say, 'The LORD does not see us; the LORD has forsaken the land.*

Ephesians 6:12 *For our struggle is not against flesh and blood, but against the rulers, against the powers, against the world forces of this darkness, against the spiritual forces of wickedness in the heavenly places.*

False Prophecy – Prophetic words that contradict the true word of God. They cause confusion, double-mindedness, spiritual schizophrenia, and false hope. Makes it difficult for people to discern God's word from lies. They lead people to the truth and cause them to believe and trust in lies.

Matthew 7:15-16 *Beware of the false prophets, who come to you in sheep's clothing, but inwardly are ravenous wolves. "You will know them by their fruits. Grapes are not gathered from thorn bushes nor figs from thistles, are they?*

Jeremiah 28:15 *Then Jeremiah the prophet said to Hananiah the prophet, "Listen now, Hananiah, the LORD has not sent you, and you have made this people trust in a lie.*

Spirit Of Error - Twist prophetic scriptures and cause misinterpretation and misinterpretation of what God is saying. Picking and choosing what is deemed "valid' and misrepresenting or mishandling the message God was speaking.

Mark 12:24 *Jesus said to them, "Is this not the reason you are mistaken, that you do not understand the Scriptures or the power of God?*

1John 4:6 *We are from God; he who knows God listens to us; he who is not from God does not listen to us By this we know the spirit of truth and the spirit of error.*

Idolatry - Comes to entice and trick people into listening to, serving, worshipping, and offering up sacrifices unto another god so they will abort the word of the true and living God.

Spirit of Oppression & Depression – While people are holding fast to the prophetic word, this spirit causes them to be depressed and melancholy and will cause them to experience withdrawal, tiredness, weightiness, pressure, hopelessness, helplessness, and suicidal thoughts, making it difficult with having to trust, work, or wait on the word to come to pass.

Mark 4:18-19 *Still others, like seed sown among thorns, hear the word; 19 but the worries of this life, the deceitfulness of wealth and the desires for other things come in and choke the word, making it unfruitful.*

Spirits of the Past – Stifles the prophetic word by bringing up the past, especially past failures, or challenging experiences. Often comes through familiar family spirits, close relatives and friends who do not have a strong relationship with the Lord, lack of faith or a true understanding of living by the word of God, and jealous people who want others to fail.

Philippians 3:13-14 *Brothers, I do not consider that I have made it my own. But one thing I do: forgetting what lies behind and straining forward to what lies ahead, I press on toward the goal for the prize of the upward call of God in Christ Jesus.*

Isaiah 43:18-19 *Remember not the former things, nor consider the things of old. Behold, I am doing a new thing; now it springs forth, do you not perceive it? I will make a way in the wilderness and rivers in the desert.*

2Corinthians 5:17 *Therefore, if anyone is in Christ, he is a new creation. The old has passed away; behold, the new has come.*

<u>**Orphan Spirit**</u> - Wars against prophetic words. Paints ungodly imaginations and instills lies filled with inadequacy and unworthiness regarding what God is speaking. Causes an abortion of true sonship. When not aligned with true sonship it is easy to believe words will not come to pass, the word was for someone else, or feel undeserving of the word. Causes warfare against identity where a person cannot connect and embrace the prophetic words. Orphan spirit often tag teams with the spirit of rejection and the vagabond spirit.

Romans 8:15 The Amplified Bible *For [the Spirit which] you have now received [is] not a spirit of slavery to put you once more in bondage to fear, but you have received the Spirit of adoption [the Spirit producing sonship] in [the bliss of] which we cry, Abba (Father)! Father!*

<u>**Spirit of Pride**</u> – Puffed up, vain, ego-tripping, self-exalted, conceited, haughty, stubborn, rebellious, haughty in heart, aggressive, easily enraged, self-righteous in one's character. Not willing to be corrected when in error concerning a word. Does not care about the character or nature to which a word is released, how it impacts people and ministries or how it represents God.

Proverbs 16:18 *Pride goeth before destruction, and an haughty spirit before a fall.*

<u>**Spirit of Rebellion**</u> – Provokes people to be anti-submissive to the word of God and receive the word of God. Provokes prophets and prophetic people to be anti-submissive and nonconforming to leadership and to God. Tend to be flighty, renegade, aggressive, defensive, and resistant in releasing the word of God without any regard to order, protocol, or submitting their gift to accountability. Postures the prophetic inside the 1st and 2nd heaven where it becomes witchcraft and divination due to being rooted in self-focused, self-willed, selfish, and prideful motives.

1Samuel 15:23 For rebellion is as the sin of witchcraft, and stubbornness is as iniquity and idolatry. Because thou hast rejected the word of the Lord, he hath also rejected thee from being king.

Proverbs 17:11 Evil people are eager for rebellion, but they will be severely punished.

<u>*Spirit of Vagabond*</u> – Wander from place to place receiving words, but never settling in God to see them come to pass. Drain prophets and prophetic people by constantly receiving the same word with minimal to no activation of what is being spoken. Lives life postured in rejection, self-rejection, and fear of rejection, ostracism, and false hope – empty and because of unresolved issues, there is an inability to maintain and sustain the substance of God's truth and creative words.

Genesis 4:14 Behold, thou hast driven me out this day from the face of the earth; and from thy face shall I be hid; and I shall be a fugitive and a vagabond in the earth; and it shall come to pass, that every one that findeth me shall slay me.

Psalm 109:10 Let his children be continually vagabonds, and beg: let them seek their bread also out of their desolate places.

<u>*Spirit of Rejection*</u> – Causes people to reject the word of God, the prophetic gift, prophetic office, and those being used to release God's word. Causes prophets and prophetic people to fear being rejected so they coward by releasing words.

Matthew 10:14 And whosoever shall not receive you, nor hear your words, when ye depart out of that house or city, shake off the dust of your feet.

<u>*Spirit of Mammon*</u> - Fights the prosperity, fruit, multiplication, and legacy of prophetic words. Uses words of God for financial gain. Attaches prophecies and words of God to money, material gain, and success so people will think ill of them, view them as divination and worldliness, and not want to receive them. Manipulate and seduce people out of their money by charging them for words of God. Make them feel they will not succeed, progress, or be cared for if they do not give. Have people focused on the lust of the eyes, lust of the flesh, and the pride of life rather than the kingdom and covenant of God? Attempts to get people to serve the god of money rather than the true and living God.

Matthew 6:24 No one can serve two masters; for either he will hate the one and love the other, or else he will be loyal to the one and despise the other. You cannot serve God and mammon.

Matthew 6:19-21 Do not lay up for yourselves treasures on earth, where moth and rust destroy and where thieves break in and steal; but lay up for yourselves treasures in heaven, where neither moth nor rust destroys and where thieves do not break in and steal. For where your treasure is, there your heart will be also.

Spirit of Dissatisfaction & Gluttony - Become familiar with the voice of God. Cause the receiver to believe their word was not that big of a deal and there is a much "bigger word" they can get from God. Provokes comparison, envy, lust, overindulgence, and compulsiveness, where the person is dull to the fruit and substance of the word. Rather than activate it, constant thirst and feasting for words manifest. This is one of the reasons why certain people keep going back and forth into prophetic lines getting all the words they can. This spirit creates unsatisfaction, where the person is always receiving and seeking, yet never being fulfilled or postured to receive the fulfillment of what God is speaking for their lives.

Deuteronomy 21:20 *They shall say to the elders, "This son of ours is stubborn and rebellious. He will not obey us. He is a glutton and a drunkard."*

Philippians 3:19 *Their destiny is destruction, their god is their stomach, and their glory is in their shame. Their mind is set on earthly things.*

Spirit of Python - Restricts and squeezes out the word of God. Restricts the prophetic word from going forth in ministries and prophetic people. Attacks prophets with the attempt to suffocate the prophetic voice of God. Sales the prophetic word for gain. Attempts to fit in with those who have the true word of God so it can snuff out God's prophetic word with ungodly words. Tied to the spirit of death and necromancy. Uses spirits of the dead to speak familiar words while making people believe these words are from the Lord.

Acts 16:16-18 *Once when we were going to the place of prayer, we were met by a female slave who had a spirit by which she predicted the future. She earned a great deal of money for her owners by fortune-telling. She followed Paul and the rest of us, shouting, "These men are servants of the Most High God, who are telling you the way to be saved." She kept this up for many days. Finally, Paul became so annoyed that he turned around and said to the spirit, "In the name of Jesus Christ I command you to come out of her!" At that moment the spirit left her.*

Spirit of Leviathan - Twists and causes confusion in communicating God's word accurately.

Job 41:1 *Can you draw out Leviathan with a fishhook? Or press down his tongue with a cord? "Can you put a rope in his nose Or pierce his jaw with a hook? "Will he make many supplications to you, Or will he speak to you soft words?*

Spirit of Jezebel (Study Story of Elijah) - Seduces, manipulates and controls with lustful, enticing, flattering, and false words.

Revelation 2:20 *Notwithstanding I have a few things against thee, because thou sufferest that woman Jezebel, which calleth herself a prophetess, to teach and to seduce my servants to commit fornication, and to eat things sacrificed unto idols.*

DESTINY KILLING SPIRITS

From my manual, "*Sustaining The Vision Workbook.*'

It is important to understand that when you commit to destiny and to producing your entrepreneurial vision on earth, you will be faced with even greater demonic opposition than what you already experienced as a child of God. This is to be expected as **Matthew 11:12** contends: *And from the days of John the Baptist until now, the Kingdom of Heaven suffereth violence, and the violent take it by force.* We must take destiny by force, and we must implement God's purpose and plans into the earth by force. That word *force* means to *seize*. Our destiny and entrepreneurial vision are not a negotiation. It is not a compromise. We are not striving to share a destiny with devils. Please know the enemy is not trying to negotiate, compromise, or share space. He is roaming about seeking whom he may devour (*1Peter 5:8*). We have the legal authority to possess dominion in the earth by whatever spiritual force necessary.

Ephesians 6:12-13 *For we wrestle not against flesh and blood, but against principalities, against powers, against the rulers of the darkness of this world, against spiritual wickedness in high places.*

Much of your destiny contending is in the spiritual realms with real demons who do not want to give up their ranks and only want to lay hold of what is rightfully yours. You can act like devils do not exist, they do not fight against you, you can just praise your way through, but none of this prevents the enemy from attacking you. It just makes it easier to attack you and makes it easier for him to lay claim of everything you refuse to seize. You should embrace warfare as part of your destiny lifestyle. But even as you embrace it, you do not have to tolerate it. Though some reject warfare, many folks like to brag about the warfare they endure. They deem it as a badge of honor of how anointed they are. While they are boasting about their anointing, the enemy is beating them up and wreaking havoc in their lives. We should always be seeking God for how to tower over the enemy. There is always a strategy for dismantling the works of darkness. The more we assert authority over the enemy, the easier it is to tower in destiny.

2Corinthians 10:4-5 *For the weapons of our warfare are not carnal, but mighty through God to the pulling down of strong holds; Casting down imaginations, and every high thing that exalteth itself against the knowledge of God, and bringing into captivity every thought to the obedience of Christ.*

As we assert our authority over the darkness that beset us, we bring it into obedience where it is subject to God's word and purpose in our lives. What used to control us is now under our control. We bring low everything that thinks it is above God's will and purpose for our lives. I could give you countless warfare strategies to help you tower in destiny. But it will be important to seek God for yourself, so he can give you correct weaponry for each season and situation in your life. Your weapons will change and may not even be what you would consider a weapon or effective strategy. But God's ways are not like ours and they are not like the devils. His weapons are not carnal as even his weapon of love, joy, praise, etc. can annihilate the enemy.

1John 4:18 There is no fear in love; but perfect love casteth out fear: because fear hath torment. He that feareth is not made perfect in love.

Isaiah 61:3 To appoint unto them that mourn in Zion, to give unto them beauty for ashes, the oil of joy for mourning, the garment of praise for the spirit of heaviness; that they might be called trees of righteousness, the planting of the Lord, that he might be glorified.

The Lord's very presence – his glory – can be a weapon against the enemy.

Psalm 84:11 For the LORD God is a sun and shield: the LORD will give grace and glory: no good thing will he withhold from them that walk uprightly.

Psalm 91:1-2 Whoever dwells in the shelter of the Most High will rest in the shadow of the Almighty. I will say of the Lord, "He is my refuge and my fortress, my God, in whom I trust.

The Lord may have you enter into warfare with the enemy as a stealth bomber. A stealth bomber goes in subtle and undetected then - blasts the enemy, so you will be subtle and unassuming. As the Holy Spirit leads, you SHIFT and begin to blast the enemy with warfare strategy.

Psalm 18:28-29 For thou wilt light my candle: the Lord my God will enlighten my darkness. For by thee I have run through a troop; and by my God have I leaped over a wall.

I did not share those to give you warfare strategies, but so you could understand the fullness of God's word when he says his weapons are not carnal. His word is full of strategies and weapons to defeat the enemy, and he can reveal what weapons, keys, and strategies you need to deal with the warfare of your destiny and life's vision. Depending on what your calling is and the vision you are releasing in the earth, you can experience warfare from:

<u>**High Ranking Demons**</u> - Principalities, territorial spirits, and powers from your region and spheres of influence.

<u>**Familiar Spirits & Bondages**</u> **-** Generational strongholds within your family line.

<u>**Destiny Killing Spirits**</u> - Generational or personal curses and spirits assigned to thwart your destiny.

Monitoring Spirits - Demonic spirits that operate with destiny-killing spirits and demonic systems, witchcraft practitioners and their witchcraft systems, to track, monitor, oppress, possess, depress, influence, torment, and attack people. The purpose of the monitoring is to bind, control, intimidate, seduce, distress, stress, discombobulate, traumatize, insight fear afflict, steal, kill, and destroy a person's hope, faith, purpose, will, plan, and calling on their lives. People will pay witches, warlocks, demonic priests to cast spells to monitor people's lives. Spells will be cast and demons will be unleashed to attach to their foods, medicines, clothing, etc. for the purposes of monitoring and causing oppression, possession, demonic influence, and interference. Sometimes these spirits track and attack in the dream realm or operate as literal physical devices phone people's bodies where they will attack different organs and parts of the body and cause affliction, torment, pain, blockages, etc. It is nothing for people to state that they feel like a spirit is attached to their brains, backs, hooked around their neck, limbs, sexual organs. Identifying root issues and closing doors will be key to dismantling this demonic spirit and its workings.

Spirits Of The Thief - Thieving, depleting, illegal spirits, and people that come to steal your seeds, fruit, harvest, momentum, progress, vision *Proverbs 6:31*.

Vampire Spirits - Come to drain your energy, giftings, and suck the life out of you so you cannot work & sustain in the vision.

Python Spirits - Come to slowly squeeze the life out of you and the vision. This spirit comes as depression, heaviness, financial hardship, subtle drainage of an area/s of your life and vision- google and study this spirit so you can combat it.

Serpent Spirits - Do not commune with snakes. They slither up to you and offer you fame, power, money, and enlightenment that is ahead of the timing of God or not the will of God. God has foundational laws and boundaries. Though he changes, the foundation of who he is never changed. Be careful of people and opportunities that strive to get you to go against something God commanded you not to do or that is against God's character and nature; see *Genesis 2:16-17, Genesis 3:4-8*.

Mammon, Poverty, & Spirits of Lack - Attacks your mindset & perceptions about money as it relates to life and the vision, and attacks your finances, resources, and connections; can cause frivolous spending, poor financial decision making, focus on money rather than the vision, fear of sowing and being a cheerful giver.

Leviathan Spirit - This is a haughty, strong, stubborn, prideful spirit. It works through a boastful arrogance of superiority and draws people into negativity by attacking communication, dialogue, and frequencies between people and systems, cause confusion as you are speaking, and you are striving to communicate with people or your audience; can work with zapping spirit, the spirit of darkness, stuttering spirit to cause forgetfulness, slurred and staggered speech intended to cause unnecessary stress, frustration, and drama. This spirit tends to find an open door for those dealing with pride or false pride that is underlying insecurity. Once it finds its prey or airway, it wreaks havoc. It also works with the whispering spirit to cause murmuring, discontentment, mocking, and confusion. Leviathan can attack as a principality depending on the region or sphere of influence it is over. It is also known to attack at night, by sending haughty taunts, threats, bewitchment, telepathic gestures to get people to prove themselves while yielding to prideful and self-glory behavior. *Psalm 104:25-26, Ezekiel 29:3-5, Psalm 74:13-14, Isaiah 27:1*.

Spirit Of The Hydra - This is a serpent spirit with many heads to which you cut the head off and it just grows back with extra heads. Cannot just cut the head off this spirit, but cut the tail off, as cutting this, cuts off its ability to restore itself. This spirit comes to weary and wears you out and have you dealing with the same issue over and over again with increased intensity each time you strive to resolve the matter by dealing with the head or symptoms, rather than the root of the matter. Deal with the foundation and the root, cut off it is seed supply and you kill its regeneration process.

Spirit Of The Crab - This spirit moves sideways and never forward. It attempts to get you to do this as well. It uses its claws to pull you down or off the correct path with God every time you gain some progress and momentum in God. It pulls you to a place of sidetracking, backsliding, regression, or to stifle your success and advancement where you are working on the same thing over and over again, while never progressing or moving past a certain point in your life. Break this spirit's legs, as it uses its claws of words, belittlement, error, obligation, plan B, sin, poverty, and low-level mindsets and behaviors, etc., to snatch you back down to its downgraded level or a level beneath God's will for your life.

Spirits of Control & Jezebel - Come to control, manipulate, alter, and even steal the word and plan of God for the vision.

Spirit Of Rebellion - This spirit is a disobedient, anti-submissive, self-absorbed, self-willed, self-driven, covetous demon that will have a person seeking the validation of praises of man while implementing plans and purposes that are contrary to God. As the person is disobedient via rebellion, it will cause God to reject them, strip them of your purpose, and the personal and generational blessings, authority, and sphere of influence they were supposed to succeed in as a called one in the earth. Study the life of King Saul in the Bible.

1Samual 15:23 For rebellion is as the sin of witchcraft, and stubbornness is as iniquity and idolatry. Because thou hast rejected the word of the LORD, he hath also rejected thee from being king.

Spirits Of Sabotage - Self sabotage, sabotage from the enemy & people.

Spirit Of The Waster - Cause you to waste finances, resources, time, gifts, energy, on things that are not a part of the vision or come to steal your focus in consistently working the vision.

Spirit of Radon - Attacks communications systems such as microphones, speakers, music and technical equipment, phones, computers, where they do not function properly and even break; can work with leviathan and spirits of confusion.

Time Stealing Spirits - Procrastination, Stagnation, Sluggardness, Laziness.

Blocking Spirits - Hinder you from getting started, progressing, having destiny moments, finishing assignments, and/or fully bringing a vision to pass.

Spirit Of Assumptions - Spirits and mindsets that keep you bound in assumptions about people, situations, etc., rather than seeking God specifically for his will regarding the vision.

Spirits of Distraction - Spirits, mindsets, and situations that come to steal your focus and zeal.

Spirits of Harassment - Hounds of hell that come at specific times to harass and cower you into thwarting the vision.

Witchcraft - Witches and warlocks who pray and cast spells against God's kingdom and his people.

Bewitching Spirits - Steal or bind your mind, so you cannot receive revelation, guidance, or strategies for bringing the vision to past; these spirits also cast spells, so you become double minded, mentally challenged, and hopeless, regarding the vision and about the things of the Lord.

Time Release Curses - Generational or personal curses sent or established at specific times of the year and seasons to thwart your destiny.

Friendly Fire - Challenges, contention, conflict, drama, betrayal, neglect, from those who should support you, once supported you, or those within the body of Christ.

Psychological Warfare - Psychological and mental strongholds and demons who have set themselves as vain imaginations against the word of God for your life and destiny.

Religion & Tradition - Religious and traditional spirits and systems who want to oppose your unique destiny and vision.

Babylon - The world's system and worldly people who do not want God's kingdom established on earth.

<u>For the Gospel Sake</u> - Persecution comes from preaching and proclaiming the gospel of Jesus Christ.

<u>Spirit Of The Hater</u> - Jealous people, stupid people, ignorant people who are open doors for demons to use against you.

<u>Fleshly Laws Causing Wars Within Your Members</u> - Your flesh, unhealed wounds, and inner man that has to be sacrificed and subjected to your spirit in order to submit to your destiny and entrepreneurial vision process **Romans 7:23**.

<u>Prides Of Life</u> - Through your circumstances sent to confound and stress your life and relationships.

Sometimes warfare battles can manifest as the following:
- Where you are sieged and closed in on every side
- A psychological and mental battle that comes to steal your truth, your emotional balance, and your mind
- Oppression where it is laying on top of you, burdensome, restrained, weighty, troubled, subdued, suppressed, crushed, pressed against
- Possession where something has entered your soul, heart, mind, body, home, life, ministry, circumstance
- Infestation where you feel contaminated, impure, slimed by the roots, fruits, and injections of demons, darkness, witchcraft, worldliness, perversion, evil
- Depression where you experience gloom, sullenness, dejection, demoted, low in spirit, dispirited, low in value, weak, loss of energy, loss of stamina, dull, hopelessness, helplessness, suicidal; feel pressed down
- Blocked where a literal wall or demonic force is erected in your path; this barrier can be physical or spiritual. Sometimes it makes the spirit realm look black or dark because you are looking at a wall. It can also make God and heaven seem far away due to the barrier erected between you and God. May feel blocked in going forward in destiny or the entrepreneurial vision
- Blinded or bound in the mind. This often feels like something is spiritually wrapped around your head or over your eyes where you cannot see. It can feel like a vice grip on the head of a demonic headpiece. Sometimes it can be an octopus spirit, squid spirit, or python spirit. Sometimes it can be a demonic device. It can also feel like it is wrapped around the brain
- Suffocated where you feel like a demonic yoke is binding you, choking you, suffocating you, and strangling you
- Anxious where you feel consistently worried, anxious, restless, unable to sleep, rest, believe God

- Fearful and panicked where you feel nervous, scared, terrorized like something is following you or after you fear going to sleep, experience night terrors, night attacks, and nightmares in your sleep; may experience literal panic attacks
- The distraction that comes to steal your focus, strength, drains you of your stamina and progress. Draining spirits also attack, especially through people who suck the life out of you, deplete you, steal your strength and virtue
- Caged, snared, incantation, boxed in. Witchcraft spells, hexes, and vexes often have this effect. Also, when the enemy attempts to imprison us or our goods, we can feel this way
- Perversion is such that you have floods of sexual and vile thoughts and images that are not your own. You did not watch anything or engage in anything. Sometimes we experience this when we are picking up strongholds in the atmosphere. Sometimes the enemy sends these attacks to shame us or to get us to open a door to lust, perversion, adultery, fornication, masturbation, inordinacy, etc.
- Demonic visitations, demonic dreams, dream manipulators, agents, & importers who attack while you are sleeping
- Spirit realm attacks during sleep or when being translated in the spirit to engage in warfare, intercession, or kingdom work

It does not matter how the enemy comes, know God can give you strategies and weapons to defeat him. Ask God to teach you how to be a skilled warrior (***Psalm 18:34, Psalm 144:1***). Also, be mindful to be full of God's word and Holy Spirit as these weapons alone can enable you to stand against the enemy.

SPIRITS THAT ATTACK CHILDREN

From my book entitled, *"Cultivating Destiny From The Womb."*

<u>*Spirits of Child Abuse*</u> - Child abuse negates the blessing of children and the inheritance of who they are in our lives and family lineage. Children are guiltless and innocent in God's eyes. To abuse them – to provoke them to anger and trauma – is an abomination in God's eyes an incite of his judgment.

Ephesians 6:4 *And, ye fathers, provoke not your children to wrath: but bring them up in the nurture and admonition of the Lord.*

Mark 9:42 *And whosoever shall offend one of [these] little ones that believe in me, it is better for him that a millstone were hanged about his neck, and he were cast into the sea.*

Exodus 21:22 *If men strive, and hurt a woman with child, so that her fruit depart [from her], and yet no mischief follow: he shall be surely punished, according as the woman's husband will lay upon him; and he shall pay as the judges [determine].*

Exodus 23:7 *Keep thee far from a false matter; and the innocent and righteous slay thou not: for I will not justify the wicked.*

Deuteronomy 2:25 *Cursed be he that taketh reward to slay an innocent person. And all the people shall say, Amen.*

Colossians 3:21 *Fathers, provoke not your children [to anger], lest they be discouraged.*

According to childhelp.org, child abuse is defined as *"when a parent or caregiver, whether through action or failing to act, causes injury, death, emotional harm or risk of serious harm to a child. There are many forms of child maltreatment, including neglect, physical abuse, sexual abuse, exploitation, and emotional abuse."*

Depending on the type of abuse, it can strip children of their identity and cause them to be stunted in their spiritual, physical, and natural growth. Abuse can cause them to develop a complex and live on to reinforce generational cycles of abuse and brokenness.

Abuse often can even strip children from their families. Children who are placed in the foster care system are then dependent on strangers to define who they are and what their identity is when truly they were born into those specific family lines for a reason. Abuse can kill the kingdom heir – the bloodline breaker - before they ever take their place in restoring the blessings of the Lord back into the family. Instead of focusing on identity development and destiny, abused children spend their lives trying to get basic needs of love, safety, and acceptance met. It is a destiny thief and killer.

Next to aborting one's destiny, abusing, misusing, trafficking, and neglecting a child's destiny can stifle them to the point where they do not even desire God's blueprint but are stuck in a lifelong cycle of trauma and crisis. Abuse and trauma open the door to a gateway to other destiny-killing spirits where the child was once fighting to overcome abuse and healing are now more susceptible to all of these other destiny-killing spirits attached to their trauma. The spirits of rejection, abandonment, fear, inadequacy, etc., all work together to dismantle the child's identity before they can develop into destiny.

Children who were subjected to emotional, physical, or sexual abuse, are more likely to suffer from re-victimization as adults, physical health problems, mental health challenges, suicidal ideations, drug and alcohol addiction, obesity and eating disorders, homelessness, becoming generational abusers, criminal & high-risk behavior, and the list go on.

Trafficking Spirits - Sex trafficking and child labor is a displacement of children from the alignment and will of God. It is the action or practice of illegally transporting children from one country or area to another, typically for the purposes of forced labor, marriage, prostitution, sexual exploitation, and organ removal. When a child is exploited, they are used or utilized for profit or someone else's gain, needs, or pleasure.

The International Labor Organization (ILO) estimates that 1.2 million children are trafficked each year. This number is increasing at alarming rates. Most sex trafficking victims are women and girls, though men, boys, trans, intersex, and nonbinary individuals can be victims as well. According to the International Labor Organization report, more than 70% of sex trafficking victims were located in Asia and the Pacific, compared with 14% in Europe and Central Asia and 4% in the Americas.

In illicit massage parlors in the U.S., the vast majority of reported trafficking victims are from China, with a notable number from the Fujian province in southeastern China. South Korea forms the second highest group.

As we consider this topic, we can explore the possibility that abortion and sex trafficking in the natural realm is the spirit of Molech running rampant in our society.

Leviticus 18:21 *And thou shalt not let any of thy seed pass through the fire to Molech, neither shalt thou profane the name of thy God: I am the LORD.*

2Kings 16:3 *But he walked in the way of the kings of Israel; indeed he made his son pass through the fire, according to the abominations of the nations whom the LORD had cast out from before the children of Israel.*

Ezekiel 23:36-39 *The Lord said moreover unto me; Son of man, wilt thou judge Aholah and Aholibah? yea, declare unto them their abominations; That they have committed adultery, and* *blood is in their hands, and with their idols have they committed adultery, and have also caused their sons, whom they bare unto me, to pass for them through the fire, to devour them. Moreover this they have done unto me: they have defiled my sanctuary in the same day, and have profaned my sabbaths. For when they had slain their children to their idols, then they came the same day into my sanctuary to profane it; and, lo, thus have they done in the midst of mine house.*

When the people offered sacrifices to their idol god – Molech - they would put the child in the fire as a sacrifice of purification. How did they see this as a sacrifice of purification exceeds anything most of us can grasp, but this is how idolatry will twist your thinking into believing right is wrong and wrong is right. And in this case, having some operating in such a wretched evil act and them thinking it is benefiting their lives and is an honor to a demon god.

When children are trafficked, they are sacrificed as if their lives and destinies have no value. They are no more than a commodity, objects, slaves, labor. Their innocence, identity, and childhood are stolen at the expense of someone else's perversion, sin, or transgression.

Some parents are selling their children into trafficking for money. The child is sold all together or is someone's slave while money is sent to their parents to help pay bills. All types of things happen to these children as they are stripped of their innocence, childhood, and identity for the sake of their families. Some parents who have lots of children will sell their children into child labor or sex trafficking, so they do not have to care for them. If parents and traffickers regarded the value of life, understood godly purpose, and had a revelation that children are destined for greatness from the womb, these activities would not be as prevalent. We must start advocating for the godly value of our children. We must change the mindset of how they are viewed so that they will be regarded and even begin to live their destiny and purpose from the womb.

Spirits of Idolatry & Witchcraft - These spirits cause children to become idol worshipers, witches, and warlocks. They engage in blood sacrifices, vows, and covenants with their peers, do rituals to make bonds and pacts in their relationships, engage in self-inflicting cutting behaviors to numb pain, offer sacrifices to idols and demons, do spells on people. They may learn this behavior from parents, caregivers, peers, or from cartoons, TV shows, social media, and the internet. Such open doors cause them to be fascinated with magic, astrology, horoscopes, wizards, witches, divination, spells, the spirit world, spirits of the dead, Halloween, pagan practices, Yoga, Karate, martial arts, Ouija boards, witchcraft games, minds craft games, bloodthirst games and activities, occultism, and satanism *(Exodus 711, 12, Exodus 20:3-6, Daniel 4:7, Psalm 135:15-18, Isaiah 2:8, Ezekiel 18:14-17, Romans 120, Galatians 5:22-23, Colossians 1:15, 1John 5:21).*

2Chronicles 33:1-8 Manasseh was twelve years old when he began to reign, and he reigned fifty and five years in Jerusalem: But did that which was evil in the sight of the Lord, like unto the abominations of the heathen, whom the Lord had cast out before the children of Israel. For he built again the high places which Hezekiah his father had broken down, and he reared up altars for Baalim, and made groves, and worshipped all the host of heaven, and served them. Also, he built altars in the house of the Lord, whereof the Lord had said, In Jerusalem shall my name be forever.

And he built altars for all the host of heaven in the two courts of the house of the Lord. And he caused his children to pass through the fire in the valley of the son of Hinnom: also he observed times, and used enchantments, and used witchcraft, and dealt with a familiar spirit, and with wizards: he wrought much evil in the sight of the Lord, to provoke him to anger. And he set a carved image, the idol which he had made, in the house of God, of which God had said to David and to Solomon his son, In this house, and in Jerusalem, which I have chosen before all the tribes of Israel, will I put my name forever.

When children are not cultivated in destiny, they can end up walking in their calling, but using their purpose for evil. In this passage of scripture, we see Manasseh begin to reign as king at age 12. But he did not know the Lord. He was not cultivated in godly destiny. He, therefore, reigned 55 years in Jerusalem while leading the people in idolatry. He rebuilt high places that were torn down. He had no fear or reverence for the Lord as he built a high place inside the house of the Lord. He sacrificed his children and engaged in all types of idolatrous witchcraft practices.

Manasseh was basically a childhood warlock who groomed his nation to be witches and warlocks. We have a lot of childhood witches and warlocks in society today. Some are taught by their parents and others ignorantly become witches and warlocks through the cultural trends released in society. We have a lot of children engaging in idolatrous witchcraft practices today because they are not cultivated in destiny, nor are they taught to serve the Lord. They are exposed to witchcraft at an early age through cartoons, TV shows and movies, books, social media, peers, etc. Prayer has been taken out of school, while witchcraft has crept into the school through yoga and other meditation new age practices that are perceived as harmless. Many parents do not attend church or serve God themselves. Many children have been given more leeway by parents to dictate what is good for them so many children do not attend church even if their parents go. Children are dictating what type of clothing is appropriate for them, what peer group is best for them, what sex and gender they want to be, etc. Laws are being put in place to allow children to make these choices, thus further stripping the voice and the rights of parents to effectively govern their households. A lack of true God identity is causing children to be depressed and suicidal if they are not allowed to change their sex and/or gender. Fears of losing children to mental illness and/or death further bind the hands of parents and lawmakers. As a result, definitions like the ones below are institutionalized to help re-identify children and people who want to be classified in different sex or gender other than the one they one born as.

- **Gender Confusion** - Individual's feeling of not identifying with his or her assigned gender.
- **Neutral Genealogy** - Not wanting to be defined by a specific gender, even the gender one was born in.
- **Gender Genocide** - the systematic killing of the origin of gender that specifically defines and separates us as male and female.

The culture and gender epidemic we are experiencing with children wanting to change their sex and people not wanting to be identified by gender derives from a lack of governing:

- God's standard of him and his biblical principles being the foundation of our lives and families, where his ordained will, purpose, and destinies for our lives is active and flourishing all down through our generations.
- God's innate purpose for procreation.
- God's innate purpose for family.
- The woman's honor and position as a birther - creator - a womb bearer.
- The man's honor as head and carrier of God's family legacy on earth.
- Our seed and egg even before procreation.
- The womb as children is incubated during pregnancy.
- DNA and personality interruptions and interferences due to what is being put into a child's body through foods, beverages, medicines, medical procedures, and vaccinations.

No one in the bible ever created themselves. God is the author of all creation. To decide you are going to change your identity is to decide that you are your own God and creator. The bible warns us of this.

Romans 1:21-27 *Because that, when they knew God, they glorified him not as God, neither were thankful; but became vain in their imaginations, and their foolish heart was darkened. Professing themselves to be wise, they became fools, And changed the glory of the uncorruptible God into an image made like to corruptible man, and to birds, and fourfooted beasts, and creeping things.*

Wherefore God also gave them up to uncleanness through the lusts of their own hearts, to dishonor their own bodies between themselves: Who changed the truth of God into a lie, and worshipped and served the creature more than the Creator, who is blessed for ever. Amen. For this cause God gave them up unto vile affections: for even their women did change the natural use into that which is against nature: And likewise also the men, leaving the natural use of the woman, burned in their lust one toward another; men with men working that which is unseemly, and receiving in themselves that recompense of their error which was meet.

When our households do not worship and serve God, and when we and our children are not cultivated in God's identity and his purpose for our lives, we risk being influenced by the demonic realm, culture and trends, the world's system, generational curses, and propensities, and by our ideology of what we believe is right or wrong. For a time, God convicts us and tries to turn us back to him. But the more we succumb to vain imaginations, God turns us over to serve what we have created. We think it's right because we lack conviction. We do not realize that we have become reprobates.

Genesis 1:26-28 *God said, Let Us [Father, Son, and Holy Spirit] make mankind in Our image, after Our likeness, and let them have complete authority over the fish of the sea, the birds of the air, the [tame] beasts, and over all of the earth, and over everything that creeps upon the earth. So God created man in His own image, in the image and likeness of God He created him; male and female He created them. And God blessed them and said to them, Be fruitful, multiply, and fill the earth, and subdue it [using all its vast resources in the service of God and man]; and have dominion over the fish of the sea, the birds of the air, and over every living creature that moves upon the earth.*

We are made in the image (physical likeness-representation of God) and likeness (spiritual likeness-act like God) - reflecting his identity and nature. Gender is part of the foundation of our identity in God. God created us this way because he is about replication, procreation, multiplication, fruitfulness, advancement, and mankind being responsible and accountable over what they produce and reproduce. This is the reason he gave male and female dominion over the earth.

Dominion means to assert governmental rule and reign in every sphere of our lives. We cannot properly reign in our God-ordained image and likeness when we reject our gender, as it provides a significant distinction of how we are to have dominion in the earth.

- Male - dress it and to keep - serve as a laborer, work, worship, care for, provide, be a watchman, guard, protect
- Female - help meet - help, relief, relieve, aid, assist

To reject our gender is to reject his image - the likeness to which he created us and identified us as his. To reject our gender SHIFTS us into a role of God's likeness that he did not ordain for us; we, therefore, cannot properly function on earth. When we do not properly govern in the dominion of our gender, we cannot govern properly in our God-ordained identity. Our God-ordained identity entails who and what God uniquely created us to be and do on earth.

As we lived through our God-ordained identity, we must also govern over our seed. Our seed is what we are to produce and reproduce in the earth, particularly children. The seed also entail:

- Life and resources water - fish of the sea
- lands, regions, and airways - fouls of the air
- Animals - creepy things

When we go about living life without governing through the authority God has given us, we give way for the enemy to creep in and establish his kingdom, principles, wickedness, and strongholds in our midst. Especially in regard to our children. They are the ultimate seed that keeps life going and that carries the image, likeness, and dominion of God from generation to generation.

Spirit of Molech - Spirit of Abortion - Wants to kill a child before they are born. Wants children to return to heaven; wants children to be offered up as sacrifices to the devil *(Psalm 82:3-4, Exodus 21:22-25, Leviticus 18:21, 1Kings 11:7, 2Kings 23:10, Ezekiel 16:21).*

Spirits of Premature Death - Wants to kill a child while in the womb or before they have had time to live and fulfill destiny *(Exodus 15:11, Exodus 12:29, Exodus 12, Luke 17-19 John 4:46-52, Luke 8:49-55, Matthew 9:23-25, Mark 5:38-43).*

Spirits of Suicide - Wants to coerce a child to take their own life. Spirit will often come as a familiar spirit that serves as a playmate, spiritual guide, and/or friend to a child. Will use unfavorable situations such as bullying, low self-esteem, lack of friends, and fitting into peer groups to talk the child in feeling hopeless about life and living, while considering suicide as a coping mechanism. The challenge is that suicide is a final act. You cannot come back from suicide as it is not a coping mechanism but murder of self *(Psalm 55:22, Jeremiah 29:11, John 10:10).*

Spirits of Sabotage - Wants a child to engage in activities and behaviors to sabotage his destiny or creates life scenarios to sabotage the progress, growth, life, and/or destiny of a child *(Judges 16).*

Spirits of Rebellion - Causes a child to rebel against parents, teachers, authority figures, and/God; the child may be self-willed, selfish, stubborn, controlling, vengeful, vindictive, bitter, aggressive, violent, lawless; they can be unruly, anti-submissive, uncontrollable, intolerable, while resisting, rejecting or defying rules, regulations, boundaries, laws, and standards that would keep them in order, safe, and regarding the rights of organization, society, and other people. *(Proverbs 13:24, Proverbs 20:11, Proverbs 22:15, 1Samuel 15:23-25, Ephesians 6:1-3)*

Orphan Spirit - Causes parents to give up or leave a child for other parents, people, communities, society, or organizational systems to care for, nurture, raise, develop, train, and equip for life and destiny. Such experience can cause a child to feel void, wounded, rejected, unloved, devalued, disregarded, unwanted, displaced in their identity, life, worth, and destiny. The child can have difficulty in bonding or feeling attached or connected to others or if they have a place in life. It is important for new parents and/or caregivers to understand that when they take a child in or adopt a child, they now have legal and spiritual authority over that child's life and destiny. That child SHIFTS under their care and governmental rulership and they can break generational and life curses off that child, cast demonic spirits out of them, and SHIFT them under the blessings, identity, and blessings of Jesus Christ. It is therefore important for that parent or caregiver to consciously bond with adopted children and spend time praying over them, while literally and spiritually connecting them in mind, heart, soul, body, identity, to them personally, to the family, and under their covering as parents *(Exodus 2:1-10, Psalm 27:10-14)*.

Spirits of Abandonment - Causes a parent to abandon a child. The child can be left at birth or at some point in their life. Such an experience can cause a child to feel deserted, unwanted, outcast, displaced, and forsaken. The child is left with wounds in their soul, heart, and identity. If not healed can battle fears of abandonment throughout life and have difficulty attaching or trusting others due to abandonment issues *(Psalm 27:10-14)*.

Spirit of the Vagabond - Causes the life course of a child to drift or take a direction where the child is wandering, drifting, or feeling helpless about life and his or her destiny. This can happen if a parent moves around a lot while the child is growing up if the child does not experience a stable and safe home life while growing up if the child is orphaned, abandoned, displaced at any time in childhood. The child can have difficulty sitting still, being quiet and attentive, staying focused, or settling into a stable environment or relationship. The child can become a drifting wandering adult that is always trying to find his or her place, identity, and destiny; can have trouble committing, settling, and being rooted and grounded in life, success, or relationships. The spirit of vagabond can sometimes be due to a curse *(Genesis 4:12-14, Proverbs 6:11, Psalm 109:10, Jeremiah 48:12, Acts 19:13-20)*.

Outcast Spirits - Cause children to feel like they do not fit in or belong. A child feels and believes they are always on the outskirts of peer groups and life situations or that they are not accepted or good enough for particular peer groups, organizations, activities, projects, social settings, experiences, or assignments *(Isaiah 56:7-8, Isaiah 16:3, Jeremiah 30:17, Psalm 147:2)*.

Spirits of Rejection - Creates situations that cause wounds in a child's soul so they will reject themselves, reject their identity, reject destiny, reject their lives, reject progressing healthy or successful in life, and fear rejection from others. Many orphans, abandoned, displaced, outcasts, and bullied children experience rejection. If these wounds are not healed, it opens the door for a spirit of rejection to come in and form a personality of rejection in the child. This spirit of rejection rules their identity and cause them to constantly be victimized through rejected experiences, and to victimize themselves by creating situations where they are rejecting others, rejecting truth, rejecting themselves and blaming it on others, or by experiencing rejection from people, life, and society *(Genesis 37:2-36, 2Kings 17, Hosea 4:6, Luke 9:22).*

Spirit of Self-Hatred - Causes a child to hate themselves. They may want to be someone else other than themselves; will constantly speak negatively of themselves. Deem themselves invisible, worthless, unimportant, not measuring up to others; feel empty most of the time; dread living and dreading their life even when things are going well. Have difficulty receiving compliments and accolades. Will tear down what someone speaks about them. Have difficulty receiving love and affection. Wants it and longs for it but rejects it, cringes, and is guarded when it is given.

Spirit of the Victim - Causes spirits to enter a child's life through unresolved issues, pain, and wounds. Causes the child to constantly view themselves as a victim and to relive and rehearse hurts of the past. A child cannot receive love and happiness due to being stuck in a victim mentality. The child will create situations where they are the victim. The child will sabotage victories so they can prove that life will always be full of pain, dread, and victimization. Drowns in sorrow and wants others to live there with them. Children views correction as punishment as if they are the victim rather than taking responsibility for actions and changing life for the better.

Spirits of Deception & Trickery - Causes children to engage in lying, haughtiness, deceptive, manipulative, trickery behavior for self-gain, self-will, craftiness, cunningness. Behavior can range from petty to treacherous shrewdness. Causes the child to Infringe on the rights of others and violates the person's space, boundaries, morals, standards, virtue, with no regard to that person; will cause the child to discard or disregard the person after they have deceived, abused, and used the person *(2Samuel 13).*

Spirits of Anti-Submissiveness & Disobedience - Cause children to defy and reject authority; they disregard rules, regulations, boundaries, and standards that authority figures out in place to keep them safe, lawful, honorable, honoring, and respecting the rights of others *(Proverbs 29:15, Proverbs 22:15, Mark 12:30, Colossians 3:20, Ephesians 6:1-3).*

Spirit of Absalom - Cause children to usurp and betray their parents, caregivers, and/or authority figures. They will create and cause discontentment and strife between them and their parents, authority figures, etc., or between their parents and other people. They will gossip and spread lies and rumors, win the favor of others by exposing secrets, sins, and information, create scenarios to put them in a favorable light while putting the parent, etc., in a negative light, set traps and snares to cause challenges for their parents, etc., gather others and information to strengthen their attack against their parents, etc., release an alternative vision that is more in favor of them than the parent or authority figure, set plans to literally kill their parents, caregivers, authority figures…*(2Samuel 15).*

Spirits of Death and Hell - Spirits sent to kill steal and destroy the life and destiny of a child. These spirits tend to follow the child from birth while releasing terror, tragedy, and/or hardship upon the child to stifle, delay, wound, afflict, murder the child's hope, and outlook on their life and future, and/or to literally take their lives so they will not fulfill their life's purpose *(Matthew 9:18, Matthew 9:23-25, Mark 5:22-24, Mark 5"38-43, Luke 8:41-55).*

Spirits of Fear - Cause a child to be fearful of the dark, going outside, being alone, going to sleep, attending school, engaging, building relationships, embarking upon life, trying new things, fear of engaging society. Spirits can grow up with children and cause them to become fearful panicky, anxious, stressful adults. Spirits will hide in children's rooms, under their beds, in their closets, in their mirrors, in and around their windows, and terrorize them at night. Uses the child to disrupt the peace and sleeping patterns of parents and family members in the home. Spirits of fear must be dealt with as can create an open door to mental illness, infirmities, and phobias *(Psalm 91, 2Timothy 1:7, 1John 4:18).*

Spirits of False Identity - These spirits create experiences, use experiences, hardships, word curses, generational curses, to release confusion, distortion, misperceptions, brokenness, and breaks in a child's identity. These alterations cause parents and children to mold and shape children in an identity that is not the child's identity *(Deuteronomy 11:19, 2Timothy 3:5-7, 2Timothy 3:14-18, Psalm 8:2, Psalm 139, Isaiah 54:13 John 12:36).*

Spirits of Jezebel - Cause children to be controlling, manipulative, seductive, intimidating, overbearing, and overpowering towards, parents, siblings, family members, peers, teachers, etc. Such children are often prophets and leaders of God. This spirit likes to snatch them up early so that they become witches, warlocks, and prophets of the idol god Baal *(1Kings 16-22).*

Spirits of Ahab - Cause children to be controlled by Jezebel's parents, siblings, family members, peers, and peer groups. Children grow up passive, cowering, manipulated and slaves to Jezebel and bullies, fearing and dreading confrontation, having no voice, victims, and with a victim mentality that often becomes rooted in their adult personality, while ruling their identity *(1Kings 16-22).*

Spirits of Athaliah - This spirit identifies and seeks to murder the royal seed - the chosen leaders in the family line. This spirit is ruthless towards grandchildren and extended seeds in the family line as it wants to rule in its stead. It is willing to stifle the blessings and growth of the family line by killing the seed so that it can reign. This spirit is vicious with words and releases abusive actions to kill the hope, identity, and life of its own grandchildren. Be careful leaving your children with bitter, no-loving family members. Listen to your children when they state that they do not like spending the night or being around certain family members and when they are sharing words and actions that are demeaning, condemning, and abusive in nature. Your child is probably revealing Athaliah who is murdering your child so that they can reign in their stead *(2Kings 11)*.

Spirits of Goliath - Bullying Spirits - This spirit mocks, belittles, brown eats, intimidated, cowers, physically and emotionally abuse children, shaping them to simulate Ahab, making them suicidal, making them live in the trenches of life in fear, rather than coming out and confronting life itself, wars, life challenges, and wanting to live and progress in life. These are your school and neighborhood bullies. They are vindictive and often unrepented. They get joy from beating and asserting power and fear over others. These children may have been taught this behavior by bullying parents or may be bound by a generational curse of Goliath. These children can appear friendly and helpful around authority figures then strike and attack in secret, in and among peers. This spirit will browbeat and abuse you to the point when a child will feel suicide is the only option to being free from this spirit. It is important for parents to protect their children from Goliaths, expose and deal with children with these spirits, instill God's identity in their child so they will know they have authority over Goliath *(Proverbs 22:10, 1Samuel 17)*.

Spirits of Jealous, Envy, & Comparison - Cause children to be jealous, resentful, begrudging, and covetous of others. Cause children to ridicule, stifle, reject, make light of, belittle, and sabotage the advancement of others due to wanting to be them, being jealous of them, hating the favor that is on the child's life, hating that the child is better than them *(Genesis 4, Genesis 25:19-34, Genesis 37, 1Samuel 17)*.

Spirits that Mock - These spirits cause children to tease, taunt, laugh at, embarrass, scorn, ridicule, disrespect, terrorize, and poke fun at others to the point of cruelty, verbal abuse, and tormenting. *(2Kings 2:23-24)*.

Spirit of Saul - Causes a child to engage in behaviors of rivalry, competition, antagonism, ambition, strife, emulation, contention, pride, driving, striving, argument, pride, ego, strife, jealousy, envy, ambition. The child may even engage in vicious and murderous acts to stifle, wound, afflict or kill their competition so that they are the reigning competitor even if the person is nice to the child, they are so driven by a rivalry that they will have bouts of wanting to harm and prove they are better than the person *(1Samuel 18-19, James 4:1-2)*.

Spirit of the People Pleaser - Causes a child to seek to please others at the expense of their own identity, integrity, and worship. Sacrifices their needs, desires, and value to be accepted and validated by others. Will even allow others to use them, abuse them, and take advantage of them so they can feel love like they belong, and value *(Psalm 118:8, Ephesians 6:7)*.

Spirits of Worldliness - Cause a child to be carnal, fleshy, sinful, sensual, prideful, vain, materialistic, greedy; It causes a child to succumb to the spirit of the age rather than the will, plan, and purpose of God. The child succumbs to the mixture and/or the world's ways while negating and defying the ways of God and his kingdom. These spirits will cause a child to use their gifts and callings for the world and for Satan for personal gain, wealth, and success. The focus is more on prosperity, awards, accolades, and personal advancement rather than glorifying God and advancing his kingdom. Many children get caught up in this system when their parents and caregivers are not submitted to God and are not seeking God for their destiny. Children result in living through the world systems and when they do come into an understanding of God and their identity, they are having to be deprogrammed to fight their way out of the world's system, into God's system *(1Corinthians 2:12, Ephesians 2:1-3, Luke 11:15-32, 1John 2:16)*.

Spirits of Peer Pressure - Cause a child to yield to the pressures of peers, society, and culture in order to be valued, validated, fit in, or accepted. These pressures tend to draw a child into ungodliness, unholiness, and worldliness. They can also cause the child to be drawn away from God's identity and destiny for their lives *(Exodus 23:2, Proverbs 1:10, Daniel 3, Daniel 6, Romans 12:2, Ephesians 5:11)*.

Spirits of Perversion - Causes a child to engage in twisted and perverted thinking and interactions; draws children into sexual curiosity before they are old enough to understand it and before they are grown and married. Sets up situations for children to succumb to the horrors of incest, molestation, rape, trafficking, masturbation, sodomy; homosexuality, lesbianism, pornography, uncleanness. These spirits can also cause children to experience gender confusion, sexual confusion, be attracted to the same sex, reject their gender and their sex. Preys on the purity, naivety, and innocence of children by stealing and killing their virtue through perverse acts and experiences. Will also pervert children and use them to pervert other children *(1Samuel 2:12-36, 2Samuel 13), Matthew 17:17, Acts 2:40)*.

Spirit of Lust - Cause a child to be drawn away from God through the lust of the eyes, the lust of the flesh, and prides of life *(Numbers 11, Proverbs 6:25-26, Psalm 119:9-10, Ezekiel 23, Mark 7:20-23, 1John 2:16, 1Corinthians 1Thessalonians 3:4-5, 2Timothy 2:22, James 1:14-15)*.

Spirits of Incubus and Succubus - These spirits prey on children through dreams and while they are asleep by entering their dreams and sleep realms and engaging them in perverted sexual acts. They will fondle children, masturbate them, rape them. These experiences awaken children's sexual appetite before the proper time and further draw them into sexual sin and secret sin when they are awake *(Genesis 6:1-22, Jude 16-7, Ephesians 6:12)*.

Spirits of Mare - The spirits cause children to have night terrors, nightmares, fear of going to sleep, fear of sleeping in their room, fear of the dark. These spirits attack in the dream realm or hide in children's rooms at night and instill fear in them. The child is scared and often in panic and terror due to the constant attacks from this spirit. It is important to listen to your children, pray over them, and their rooms in generally but especially when they have nightmares, speak of invisible playmates, or when they are scared of the night and experiences occurring around their night and dream realms *(Job 4:13-16, Proverbs 3:24, Psalm 4:8, Psalm 91- terror by night)*.

Spirits of Mental Illness - These spirits attack children's minds, emotions, and/or identity and cause severe and/or altered mental instability, split personalities, and extreme inability to cope in life, learn in life, advance in life. Spirits of mental illness can through a generational curse, attack when a child is in the womb, in the initial developmental stages of a child's life, when they start attending school, or in their preteen and teenage years. It is important to pray against generational curses in this area, govern your child's development, break word curses off their lives from authority figures and peers build them up in God identity'. It is important to be active in their school development and progression where you are engaging with teachers and even teaching teachers how to aide your child in learning, coping and growing as they develop and learn and grow in destiny. Teach your children healthy coping, communication, conflict resolution, relational, and social skills so they can practice them daily and be helping in how they engage life and experiences *(Matthew 17:14-18, Mark 7:24-30, Mark 9:17-27)*.

Spirit of Insanity - Causes a child to have fits of being out of control, out of their mind, beside themselves. Children will display madness, confusion, impaired thinking, lunacy, mania, delirium, psychosis, derangement for no apparent reason or when they become stressed, threatened, upset, or challenged.

Spirit of Rage - Cause children to lend to fits of rage, anger, fury, retaliation, murderous words and actions, tantrums, wrath, passion, raving, blind rage, burning rage, and uncontrollable rage. These children may even physically and verbally abuse their parents, caregivers, authority figures, and peers during these episodes *(Proverbs 14:7, Proverbs 29:22, Ephesians 4:26, Ephesians 4:32, James 1:19-20)*.

Spirits of Restlessness & Anxiety - These spirits create situations and cause children to be stressed, apprehensive, tense, worry, dread, fear, be nervous, panic, be restlessness, uneasy, fretful, and inconsolable regarding life issues. These spirits can children to experience hyperactivity or attention deficit and even be diagnosed with these disorders. Such labels open the door for children to be diagnosed with other mental disorders as other spirits come and bind and alter the personality and mental faculties of the child.

Death & Dumb Spirits - Cause children to be mute physically and spiritually where they may not be able to hear or speak. This spirit may also cloud a child's mind and mental faculties where they are unable to comprehend clearly, have trouble learning, have trouble communicating their needs, desires, thoughts, and feelings ***(Mark 9:17-27, 2Timothy 3:7).***

Spirits of Cutting & Self-Harm - These spirits may cause children to bang their heads, cut themselves, pick at wounds that should be healing, create wounds then pick at them, deliberately hurt themselves for attention, bruise or break bones, pull their hair out, etc. These acts can be done to escape the pains of life, numb pain, release stress and anxiety, relieve feelings of hopelessness or helplessness, assert a sense of power over one's choices. These spirits and acts can sometimes be tied to witchcraft, idolatry, the spirit of Jezebel, and be a form of Baal worship. Jezebel and the idol god Baal require their worshippers to cut themselves and offer their blood as sacrifices to them. ***(Deuteronomy 14:1-2, 1Kings 18:24, Leviticus 19:28, Psalm 34:18m Mark 5:2-5, 1Corinthians 6:12, 1Corinthians 6:19).***

Spirit of Arrested Development - These spirits cause trauma through some experience in childhood or find a way to imprison the child's development in order to hinder them from growing into adulthood. The child's personality is not fully developed as parts of it is stuck at the age of trauma and/or arrested development. A spirit of the little girl and /or little may enter through this door and intertwine in the personality. They operate through a split identity where they are the arrested age one minute and their current age the next. The little girl and/or little boy spirit is literally seen in operation through them as they manifest tantrums, rage, passive aggressiveness, immaturity, foolishness, infantile, and juvenile delinquent behavior. The child will have delivered from trauma, the little girl/boy spirit will have to be cast out. Their personality will need to be prayed for so deliverance and healing can manifest and commanding the personality to grow up to their current age will have to be done where full mending and healing comes to the child's identity. If the little girl/boy spirit was intertwined in their personality, they will have to learn new healthy ways of behaving to fully mature in their personality and identity.

Attention Seeking Spirits - Cause children to do things to seek, demand, and command attention. Causes them to draw attention to themselves; thrive on any attention even negative attention as long as they are center stage. Will cause the child to be envious and compete with others for attention.

Spirit of Shyness - Rejection, self-consciousness, timidity, fear, hesitation, fear of rejection, withdrawal, apprehension, nervousness, bashfulness, low self-esteem.

Spirit of Low Self-Worth - Causes children to think in low and poor regard and self-image about themselves. Causes them to doubt their abilities, capabilities, value, and worth. Works with self-hatred and rejection of self and keeps the person for embodying their full worth.

Spirits of Infirmity - These spirits afflict, and infirm children with sickness, diseases, viruses, allergies, infections, to stifle their growth, development, and destiny. These attacks can come in the womb or while the child is growing up. Some children can battle long-term affliction and infirmity by these spirits. Some children can even be bedridden or bound to the home, where they cannot go outside and play or attend school. These spirits can attack through generational curses, sins of parents and others in the home, and because of a child's destiny and calling **(Psalm 34:19, Luke 9:38-43, Luke 7:11-15, John 4:46-52)**.

Spirit of Anorexia Nervosa - cause eating disorders in children. Causes them to starve themselves even unto severe sickness and death. Makes the child think they are fat, fear becoming fat; will provoke compulsive dieting and starvation to maintain the desired weight. Usually hides in the eye gates as no matter how skinny the child is, they think they are fat and need to lose more weight. A child will self- reject, be depressed, anxious, panicky; and isolate themself to hide issues of starvation and obsession with weight.

Spirit of Bulimia Nervosa - Cause a child to binge eat and gorge lots of food then use methods to regurgitate or eliminate it from their bodies in order to lose weight and maintain weight. This spirit may work with spirits of lust, gluttony, pride, control. This spirit may be lodge in the eyes as the child is gripped with psychological warfare of body distortion; they have a poor image of their body battle thoughts and feelings of guilt or shame regarding eating, and their body image.

RELATIONSHIP DESTROYING DEMONS

From my manual entitled, *"Kingdom Keys To Governing Relationships."*

The demonic spirits listed in this chapter drain people and relationships. They are fruit stealers and relationship killers. Decreeing complete deliverance from them personally and generationally. Decreeing every root is plucked up as you are enlightened concerning their works and break their powers off your life and relationships.

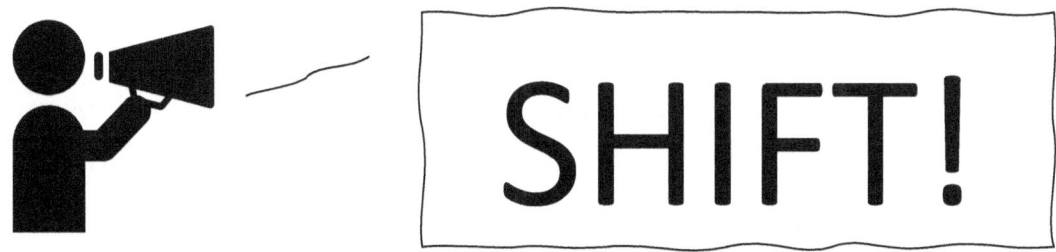

Try just yelling that out as you drive or wherever you are, "SHIFT!" I promise you will feel better! Now, let's get down to business and bust up some relationship-destroying demons!

Spirit of Victimization - This spirit postures the person as the victim where they generally view themselves as the victim, even when they are wrong. The person usually operates through resolved wounds where they have been victimized. Repeated offenses disable their ability to see themselves in any other light or to operate from any other role than being the victim. As this spirit uses those wounds as an open door, the person will create drama and experiences to be victimized or to strengthen their victim mentality. They often carry an air that draws offenders and manipulators, such that they are continuously bound by victimizing experiences. This air is really the seed and fruit of victimization that has oppressed them, where other offending spirits or mentalities can connect and further rape these people of hope and thrive for life.

Spirit of Sabotage - This spirit works through people and situations to sabotage relationships. It usually does not want the person to be joyful, loved, or fulfilled in life; or the person is not able to embrace joy, love, fulfillment. It seeks to find and open door to instill fear, suspicion, hopelessness, drama so that there is a lack of trust in the person or the relationship. It also pursues an opportune time to strike and ruin the relationship. This is a destiny-killing spirit and a relationship-killing spirit. It does not play fair and is not justified in how it operates. It is seeking to kill anything good and godly. This spirit will set traps and create drama-filled situations, so that murder of the relationship can happen.

Spirit of Passive Aggression - Passive-aggressive spirit is in operation when a person displays a pattern of indirectly expressing their true thoughts and feelings towards someone or a situation. The person is negative, pessimistic when displaying their behavior. They are internally angry but do not initially or blatantly display it. The person pretends to be pleasant or unbothered while seething with anger. They engage in other passive or non-overt behavior to demonstrate their anger. This behavior is in an effort to punish, retaliate, intimidate, control, and express rage and anger without admitting or acknowledging one's feelings, thoughts, and concerns. The person may deny they are being passive-aggressive when confronted or being made accountable for their actions. They will use jokes, flattery, accolades, gifts, help, in an effort to cover up their indirect aggression. This spirit whips the person with internal psychological and mental warfare, even as it is whipping you with delayed aggression. This spirit will have the person making excuses for their actions and justifying the reason it is okay to whip you. Often this behavior further sabotages the progress of relationships and the ability to resolve conflict in a swift healthy manner. The spirit in them is dominating and is generally abusive even to the person. It is important to place boundaries in your relationships with passive-aggressive people. And whether they are capable of changing or not, do not allow false loyalties and obligations to remain bound to their abuse. Assert your right to be treated with honor and regard. You are not a slave and do not deserve to be constantly whipped by someone who claims to have your best interest at heart.

Spirit of Leviathan - This spirit is rooted in pride and haughtiness. This spirit interrupts and distorts communication between the speaker and the listener, between God and the person/ministry, and within atmospheres. Its' effort is to sow offense, discord, irritation, anger, misunderstanding, faultfinding, ungodly judging, mistrust, and suspicion. Job speaks of how Leviathan operates in *Job 41:26-32*. This spirit was in operation between him and his friends who were striving to understand why God allowed the enemy to bring havoc upon his life. This spirit also distorted Job's views where he could not receive wise counsel from God during this time of trial with the Lord. This spirit will enter when life and relationships are under heavy warfare, experiencing challenges, and/or when they are transitioning to new dimensions in life and in their covenant interaction. It wants to cause an operation of vain haughtiness that distorts communication and creates layers of challenges, where people and the relationship cannot tower or SHIFT forward in life, life situations, and/or in their relationship. Quick repentance and forgiveness is the easiest way to combat the leviathan. The unity and love of Christ will dismantle and displace this spirit.

Deaf and Dumb Spirit - This spirit lays like a blanket of clouds over a person's mind so that information cannot get in or be retained. It is a mind immobilizing spirit where the person feels like they are talking to a mute person. The person is saying they understand, and they are even engaging in dialog at times, but they are not retaining anything to a degree where change will occur. Or it is like talking to a person who is watching a movie. They appear engrossed - appear to be grasping all that is occurring. They may appear to be starring as if they are listening and comprehending, but nothing is getting past the death and dumb helmet that is locked upon their brain. Those oppressed by this spirit will come back and ask the same questions that were just explained or ask for the information shared again with the same detail to which it was just downloaded to them. They will be able to share and dialog about what was discussed, however, when proceeding to implement it, the information is zapped out or frozen in their minds. This spirit as well causes people to talk themselves out of the information where they are so confused, they do not remember what was said to them or the purpose that it has on their lives. This can be so challenging when setting goals, boundaries, and expectations in relationships. The person will constantly receive clear vision but cannot activate it due to a lack of retention. The relationship will feel like you are sharing the same information over and over and doing more teaching and parenting than walking alongside the person.

Spirits of the Fear of Receiving, Giving Love - This spirit cause panic, extreme anxiety, and paranoia as it relates to being vulnerable, and being able to be and give love. The person harbors a fear of being hurt or that the love will be stripped away. This spirit causes them to withhold love for fear of not getting it in return or being taken advantage of. They are constantly fearing the worse and tend to speak a lot of doom and death into the relationship. They are often guarded and on edge. Due to the grip of this spirit, it takes a lot of time and patience to convince them that they are safe and will be hurt in the relationship. Receiving love can overwhelm them, and spiral them into a panic, where they operate from flight mode. They either run or want to run from the relationship. They do a lot of connecting and disconnecting in the relationship.

Spirits of Rejection - Rejecting love, fear of not being loved, fear of being hurt. This spirit makes the person feel or believe they are a reject. No matter how much they are told or shown that they are accepted, they are unable to receive it. They self- reject for fear of being rejected. They self-reject then become passive-aggressive by blaming the other person for rejecting them even though it was them that were self-rejected due to fear of being rejected. The rejection creates a bottomless pit in their souls and their hearts where no matter how much love, attention, acceptance, approval, they receive, they still feel rejected. As they are like a bottomless pit that can never be fed. The more they receive the more they want and sometimes they become enraged and vindictive even passively if a person attempts to be balanced and healthy in their interactions with themselves.

This spirit will cause people to be jealous and envious of the love, healthy relationships, and success others have. They will strive to connect with these types of people. Sometimes they will strive to live secretly through them while taking on parts of their identity in an effort to feel loved, accepted, and successful. They will be living through fantasy or false reality in their minds as it relates to this person. They will tend to be inordinate and sensual in how they perceive and give love. In friendships, mentorships, or spiritual relationships, it will at times feel sexual and sensual in nature; the interactions and fellowship become one of a lover more so than the roles the person is supposed to have in one's life. In dating and married-type relationships, the person will engage as constantly needy, possessive, moody, insecure. This spirit causes them to feed off the drive for drama and conflict, then makeup in a passionate manner, as this feeds their love for attention and the need for people to perform as a demonstration of love and acceptance. The relationship will be full of inordinate lustful passion due to the person being so overly emotional and needing their emotions and identity constantly fed. When fed, the person tends to respond as intensely loving, sexual, and passionate. This seems great for a time but is draining due to it being centered around continuous drama, and then needing to be habitually validated in their identity and regarding approval of them.

Spirit of Jezebel & Narcissism – It is worth doing a personal study on this spirit as what I will share is only a glimpse of how this spirit operates. This spirit is dominating, rebellious, idolatrous, narcissistic, and operates in witchcraft. This spirit will cause people to control the life and relationship of others. It is a bewitching, tangling, and webbing-type spirit. Jezebel wants to wear the pants in the relationship. This spirit is not interested in an agreement, walking together in godly covenant, and only tends to give and consider the person in an effort to gain control over them so that it can release its future needs and desires of governing over the person. This spirit seduces and manipulates its' way into setting up rulership and authority in a person's life or the relationship. Its aim is to be the main controlling voice in a person's life. It will use the person to the web itself into every area of one's life, where they feel helpless without the person, yet entrapped by the person. The Jezebel spirit can operate very cunning, seducing, and deceiving initially. The person with this spirit will even be very loving initially but once they have gripped their prey, their true motives, and personality manifest.

The study of Jezebel is its own book; however, you can read about this evil queen beginning in I Kings 16:31. Jezebel is historically a real person, but she is also representative of a dynamic that can corrupt a person's character. The Jezebel characteristics can be in any gender.

- Jezebel is clever, devious, dishonest, and out for personal gain. Jezebel will act like he or she is your new best friend or the lover you always wanted; however, they are seducing you into trusting them.
- Jezebel will lavish you with gifts, provide financial support to your life endeavors, offer to pay for things you need and desire.

- Jezebel is wise by nature. She is also very intelligent and smart. Jezebel will display natural alluring wisdom and will seek out answers so he or she can gain superiority as the voice to lean on in your life.
- Jezebel watches your life, actions, and interactions so he or she can fulfill voids, make up for your flaws, and insert suspicion to people or things they feel are competition to her isolating you unto herself, and so they can use the information to further lure you or against you when you reject him or her.
- Jezebel will appear very dependable and insert himself or herself into your life to present as loyal support, yet he or she is really seeking to control you. They are also aspiring to use the fact that they are your most loyal support later when you try to bring balance to your interactions with her or him. They will demand repayment of what they have done for you and will often want this debt paid by demanding compliance.
- Once Jezebel has you in his or her grasp, they will make it be your fault that you are no longer happy in the relationship. They will punish you by not being what they initially were to you, and demand you perform to receive that.
- Jezebel will withhold love, attention, encouragement, accolades, time, sex, support, to get you to submit to their controlling ways. This passive-aggressive behavior can be draining, confusing, perverted, and oppressing. You will eventually develop perceptions about yourself that are not true as it plays on your identity and self-worth.
- Jezebel can also be verbally, physically, and sexually abusive. This spirit will cause people to have anger and rage outbursts, engage in property destruction, use intimidation, and threats to control others. They will throw tantrums and cause public scenes due to hideous behaviors.
- Jezebel will rally others against you and sow seeds of discord to get others to be suspicious or mistrusting of you. Because they have become intertwined in your life, they will sow seeds of discord where others betray you or give the impression you are betraying others. The end game is to end your relationships, to punish you, or control you into being subject to their authority.

Many people who operate through a Jezebel spirit do not know they have this spirit, and often do not want to search for themselves when it is pointed out to them. The spirit deceives the person into thinking they are perfect and that everyone else is the problem and not them. This spirit is also very prideful and reprobate. It is not easily repented, is anti-god, and anti-transformation. Especially in relation to relinquishing its place of authority in one's life and life in general and relinquishing the benefits it receives from ruling over people and the relationship.

Spirit of Ahab – This spirit works with Jezebel. This spirit often marries or is friended by Jezebel and works with Jezebel so it can accomplish its purpose in lives and relationships. The spirit of Ahab causes people to fear confrontation, likes it better when it is dominated where others can make decisions for them. This spirit causes the person to be insecure, weak, live from a failure state, is irresponsible, lack assertiveness, and unable to rule in areas that he or she should succeed. The person with this spirit is afraid of rejection, tends to expect those bad things will happen, is passive in putting up with Jezebel or unhealthy behaviors and actions of others. This spirit causes the person to be clingy, needy, helpless. They have a need for love and belonging, fear abandonment, and will relinquish their power and authority to others to feel validated, loved, and worthy. They can appear excessively nice but generally have an ulterior motive or it's because they desire love, attention, and honor. The person will be passive-aggressive in that when it becomes angry it will get Jezebel to intervene and punish the person for hurting them or get Jezebel to fulfill his or her desires and to bring joy to their lives. It is also a passively angry, pouting, tantrum-throwing spirit. The person with this spirit may have a little girl or little boy spirit, where they at times act like a child due to part of their personality being stuck in some childhood or teenage year of their life.

Spirit of Narcissism – This spirit causes a person to have an inflated, grandiose, sense of self-importance. The person tends to be prideful, haughty, overly confident, boastful, self-absorbed, has a deep sense or need for excessive attention and admiration. They believe they are superior to others and possess an extreme brilliance, power, and ability for success. They may be very beautiful, handsome, and very seductive. They feel entitled to be treated in high regard and can be aggressive and abusive when they feel they are being treated beneath their standards. They lack empathy for others, do not have the compassion to be consistent, are unable to care for the hearts, purposes, and lives of others, and can only have relationships if it is centered around them. Most conversations and activities within the relationship are centered around them. They make them seem so important that the other person does not realize that their entire lives are being drawn into a world of narcissism. What they use to like, dislike, the thing was fun, good, bad, etc., no longer matter whether is a distant memory because the narcissist has made them believe that only the things that benefit them are important.

The person with this spirit is NOT CAPABLE of giving and receiving love in a healthy manner; anything they give is for personal gain. Everything is about them, even other people. This can be confusing because such people are very charismatic, alluring, captivating, initially loving, and giving; they appear to have a caring nature. But somewhere the root of this charm reveals itself and usually baffles and confuses its binding victims. Victims are often left stripped of their own identity because it has been lost or entangled inside the identity of the narcissist. The narcissist tends to passive-aggressively compete with the person they are in a relationship. This is because they are jealous, envious, NEED TO MAKE SURE they are always the focus of attention. Therefore, they use negative jabs, belittling comments, verbal abuse, play on words regarding the person's flaws and weaknesses, and subtle suggestions of what the person should change, to make the person feel insecure, uneasy, and confused in their identity and self-worth. Their aim is to strip the person where they do not know who they are apart from the narcissist or feel they are a nobody apart from the narcissist. They use gaslighting behaviors to manipulate, cause doubt and questioning, confuse, dismantle, discombobulate, and drain their victim's identity and strength so they rely on them, and their truth about what the person's life should be, what life is, what occurred during their interactions, conversations, and experiences, and how that person's life should feed theirs. They get bored quickly so they have a lot of people and projects they are maneuvering to keep their ego fed and empowered. Many victims need time to put their lives back together because the narcissist absorbs their life so they have to find themselves again.

Spirit of Abuse – This spirit causes people to be physically, emotionally, and psychologically abusive. This spirit can be accompanied by a personal or generational curse. They tend to be very offending, while using mistreatment, torment, criticism, cursing, exploitation, perversion, hurt to control, punish and bind their victims. They treat people as if they are beneath them and worthless. These spirits can have no regard for how they impact others. Nor may they have any regard for the life and property of others. They tend to be hateful, bitter, unforgiving, resentful, easily angered and enraged, and can explode or strike unwarrantedly.

- Sexual abuse (rape, incest, molestation, sex trafficking, prostitution, sadomasochism),
- Mental abuse (mind control, mind blinding, mind binding, mind games, domination, telepathy),
- Physical abuse (beatings, pushing, shoving, slapping, bruising, cruelty, imprisonment, property destruction),
- Religious abuse (legalism, control, guilt, shame, condemnation, cults, using scriptures to bind people; succumbing to false religious obligation),
- Emotional abuse (hurt, deep hurt, wounds, manipulation of emotions to control the victim, manipulating through crying and mood swings).

Offender Spirit - The person with this spirit may be easily offended. They become up by the simplest of matters. People around them tend to walk on eggshells because they never know when this person is going to become upset. There can be instances where the offense is true, yet the person will contend they are not offended, while passively aggressively punishing those who hurt them. These people have a difficult time communicating, resolving conflict, or expressing their thoughts and feelings in a healthy manner. They are usually bitter, pessimistic, and constantly interject negativity into the atmosphere, situations, conversations, and interactions. Some other ways this spirit operates through people is as followed:

- Miscommunication & misperception - where the person continually misunderstands what is being said and communicated with them.
- Unhealed issues of the past where they have been abused, ridiculed, bullied, and truly offended, but they are harboring this offense and reflecting it upon you when you say something that reminds them and takes them back to this offense.
- Triggers - words and actions that remind them of things that happened in the past that take them back to reliving the past offenses. Insecurities, inadequacies, and low self-esteem that has come in through past offenses, experiences, abuse
- The Victim's spirit – they deem themselves the victim and create situations where they become the victim.

An offender spirit also tends to operate through those who seek to take advantage of others. This often applies to rapists, pedophiles, traffickers, abusers, controllers, and narcissistic personalities. Individuals with an offender spirit carry the ability to transfer their seed into others. This is the reason that many who are victimized by them have some form of an offender spirit, whether it be becoming a rapist, molestation, trafficker, abuser, etc., having some propensity for these attributes, or engaging in lesser perversions or adverse behaviors of these characteristics, e.g. a woman who has been raped become promiscuous; a child that has been molested growing up to be sneaky in their actions; someone that has been freed from sex trafficking struggles with sexual seduction behaviors. The offender spirit seeks to recycle and procreate itself. Psychological theories support this concept of unhealed victims using the same sort of abuse with others as an unconscious mechanism to reclaim the personal power that was stripped from them. Therefore, it is important that if you have experienced an offending spirit, cast out this spirit, while also being healed from the root issues of your experience.

Spirit of Division - This spirit comes for the unity of a relationship. It prevents people from agreeing and walking together as one or in unison with one another. It constantly causes conflicts that are often rooted in pride, a self-focus, and a person being more focused on their agenda, needs, and desires, rather than caring about the other person or the fullness of the relationship

Spirit of Divorce - This spirit attacks the covenant union of a relationship. This spirit can operate as a generational curse or a personal curse upon a person. People can also send curses that release this spirit into their relationships or interject situations that cause open doors to divorce. This spirit also operates by causing a person to be disloyal, untrustworthy, unfaithful vow, and goal breaker. The person is unable to keep their word - their agreement - their vow - therefore constantly breaching the covenant of the relationship. The more breaching there is, the more the foundation and walls of the relationship crumble, causing exposure to separation, destruction, and divorce.

Spirit of Singleness - Whether friendships or marriage, this spirit wants people to be alone. It does not want people to have partners, covenants, or reliable people they can walk within a relationship. This spirit can be a generational curse brought upon the family line through sin, especially perversion, adultery, fornication, idolatry, and witchcraft. It can also be a curse released due to a vow a person has made due to hurtful experiences in relationships. A person can also be bewitched by someone speaking this spell/hex upon them and until it is broken it blocks them from being able to have successful relationships or to be married. When people claim us as mates in the spirit, this can block our ordained mates from seeing us. This is the reason it is important to break vows with old lovers, boyfriends, and girlfriends and those that may be potential mates but not "the one." In this day, it is even important to cast down vows that people make as they would fellowship with us on social media. People are quick to inbox someone and claim they are their husbands and wives. These witchcraft claims can lock us down into spirits of singleness and hinder marriage and healthy sustaining relationships to enter our lives. This spirit can also operate as a spirit of barrenness present with a spirit of barrenness where it is blocking the ability for a person to be positioned to bear children. It can also operate as sickness against the person's reproductive organs where they cannot procreate, have a difficult time procreating, or lose the child if they do procreate.

Spirit of Trauma - Trauma is due to a deeply disturbing, overwhelming, appalling, distressful experience. These situations can occur in relationships or life in general. When these experiences occur, they can lodge shock and awe in our hearts, souls, and minds. Many people literally feel this shock as numbness, pain, panic, or blockages in their bodies. When these experiences are not dealt with, the enemy uses them as an open door to release a spirit of trauma into our lives. Usually, that spirit is lodged where we are experiencing the literal manifestation of shock and awe and sometimes can enter our lives immediately upon the impact of that experience. The spirit of trauma and any spirits that accompanied it must be cast out, along with being deliverance and healing of the trauma that experienced before complete wholeness can manifest. Otherwise, the person will still be triggered by the impact, thoughts, and feelings of the experience and have a difficult time engaging, trusting, resting in, and feeling safe in a relationship. They will have walls up, constant anxiety and fears, and a bounty of connecting and disconnecting from the person and the relationship.

Bewitchment - This spirit or witchcraft act is done through the casting of a spell by releasing words, hexes, vexes, incantations, upon a person such that they are bound to a person or that relationship. Or where they are bound in life and cannot operate in the free will to choose their path and to be successful. The bewitchment can be done by a person within the relationship with or they may solicit the help of an outside source that does witchcraft. A very controlling or manipulative person can use verbal abuse and overbearing words to bewitch a person. The bewitched person may experience hallucinations, delusions, constant negative thoughts, confusion, mind binding, mind blinding, depression, mood swings, doom, gloom, fear, uncontrollable drawing, or reliance on the person that bewitched them. They may feel they need to get out of the relationship but may not have any willpower to do so. Or if they do, they will feel fearful, often like something is after them, or as if they are going to die if they do not return to the relationship. This is because some of the curses accompany death spells and so spirits of doom and gloom work with bewitchment to keep the person scared and bound to the relationship. These doom and gloom spirits have also been known to cause affliction, hardship, and tragedy when a person leaves a person who has bewitched them.

Sometimes sex is used to bewitch a person and keep the person bewitched. When we have sex with someone our souls become tied to one another. If that person is a witch, warlock, operating in witchcraft, they will use the soul tie through sex to lock their partner into the relationship. Until the soul tie is broken, that bewitched person will be drawn to that person and to have continual intercourse with that person. The bewitched person will feel addicted to the person and to having sex with them. They will also feel controlled and manipulated but will feel helpless to get out of the relationship.

Bewitching relationships are often tumultuous and draining. There will be constant drama, tension, psychological games and play on words, entrapment through words and situations, suspicion, and confusion. The bewitched person will constantly feel like life and blood are being sucked out of them as they are being controlled seduced and manipulated by the other person.

Sometimes spells are placed jewelry, trinkets, and other items and are given to partners to keep them bound to the person and the relationship. These items will be thrown away to help break the spell.

SPIRITS THAT DEAL DEATH

From my manual entitled, "*Processing Through Grief & Loss.*"

Death & Hell - Spirits that are unleashed from hell that gang up on a person or vision to unleash hell, terror, wrath, and fury.

Spirits of Sheol – Sheol is Hades or the world of the dead; it can consist of the grave, hell, pit, and the underworld. This is a place where demonic spirits, wicked people, and unbelievers are and will be exiled. Demonic spirits can oppress us, causing our soul to SHIFT down to this exiled place. The person literally feels as though they have died and are operating in a zombie-like state, although they are still alive.

Psalm 86:13 For great is thy mercy toward me: and thou hast delivered my soul from the lowest hell.

Psalm 16:10 For You will not abandon my soul to Sheol; Nor will You allow Your Holy One to undergo decay.

Psalm 30:3 O LORD, You have brought up my soul from Sheol; You have kept me alive, that I would not go down to the pit.

Psalm 56:13 For You have delivered my soul from death, Indeed my feet from stumbling, So that I may walk before God In the light of the living.

Spirit of The Coffin – Spirits or witchcraft can oppress and incarnate a person where they have succumbed to a literal coffin or grave. It is important to be mindful of your words, actions, vows when loved ones die. People will try to get in the coffin or grave with the deceased because of grieving or they will make statements saying they wished they'd died with their loved one. These comments can open the door to the operation of coffin spirits. A person can be so grieved that the grief itself incarnates them to the point of feeling as if they are in a coffin or grave and cannot get out. Sometimes witches and warlocks will release incantation spells on a person and they will succumb to this spirit. We see incantation spells a lot in movies that have circles with candles around them.

Death Siege - Spirits that trap or enclose a person or vision in an effort to cause death upon a person or vision. Attacks appear to come from everywhere - on every side to cause tragedy, murder, annihilation, destruction. Principalities, territorial spirits, powers, rulers of darkness, spiritual wickedness in high places, usually aid in creating this death siege - *Ephesians 6:12*.

Spirits of Doom & Gloom – These spirits hover over the person's life and take up residents in their atmosphere causing darkness, depression, and heaviness to reside there. There can be a literal dark presence in and around the person that follows the person wherever they go. It tends to dwell on their own or in any place where they have been released or have experienced heavy grief. The person may even look dark in their appearance as if they are lifeless or dying. People will feel the presence of doom and gloom whenever the person is around.

Spirit of Grief – This spirit will take advantage of a person who is grieving and keep them stuck in the grief stages. The person will constantly manifest stages of grief and live much of their days and nights grieving. This spirit will open the door to spirits of anger, rage, unforgiveness, loss, strife, division, discord, depression, fear, denial, suicide, infirmity, premature death, etc. They will be inconsolable and will reject being consoled. The person will experience consistent, agonizing grief and will feel guilty during moments of enjoying or moving forward in life or living. Sometimes this spirit convinces the person that this is how they should live and then the person will reject anything or anyone who would attempt to bestow comfort, support, love, joy, and a willingness to live upon them.

Spirit of Loss – This spirit will cause the person to feel and experience an extreme sense of loss. The person is stuck in who and what they lose. No matter how much they succeed, who comes into their lives, or what they gain, they are stuck in what they lose, by way of a person's death or other factor happening in their lives. This spirit opens the door to doom and gloom, pessimism, and hopelessness. The person lives through the doom of what might happen and views life and circumstances through a dark and gloomy lens. They are unable to discern or embrace the good due to the void that the spirit of loss has created in their heart, mind, soul, and will.

Spirit of Abortion - Seeks to abort the vision while it is being cultivated in the womb before it is fully birthed forth.

Spirit of Murder - Killing spirits; attempts to kill the person and their life's vision.

Spirit of Onan - Seed spilling spirit; refuses to connect or procreate so that the will, purposes, and vision of God can birth forth. Withdraws seed because it wants pleasure but not a relationship, covenant, procreation, or responsibility; is illegal and not a true heir, is careless, wasteful, neglectful with the seed - **Genesis 38**.

Spirit of Barrenness - Fruit stealer; Not producing results, infertile, fruitless. Barren means simply a lack of blessing. We can be barren in our wombs, health, heart, home, finances, and lives.

Hemorrhaging Spirits - Spirits that cause blood loss or drain the blood out of a person or vision that is in the womb. Things in the spiritual womb that are not in alignment with God or are not working with God and the Carrier, so they begin to afflict the Carrier causing affliction and rupture to the womb.

Spirit Of The Thief - Steals the seed, vision, will, purposes of God for a person's life, destiny, and ministry.

Spirit Of The Destroyer - Seeks to totally annihilate people, generations, the vision, destiny, and blueprint of a person's life.

Hindering **Spirits** - Causes walls, blockages, barriers, tumors, afflictions that hinder or cause challenges to things birthing forth on time, in time, without pain, torment, in healthiness, in joy, in the true salvation and purposes of God - **1Thessalonians 2:19**.

Spirit of Delay - Delays, stifles, postpones, suspension, detention, withholding the promises and prophecies of God. Causes lingering and setbacks to impede the process or progress of what is due or on the horizon. Spirit of delay works with the spirit of suicide, hope deferred weariness, and sabotage.

Spirit Of Suicide - Causes a person to kill themselves, kill their destiny due to hopelessness, helplessness, and weariness.

Hope Deferred - Causes a person to become disappointed, hopeless, helpless, afflicted, and sick due to delay - **Proverbs 13:12**.

Spirit Of Weariness - Causes continual toiling and laboring so the person and vision will become faint, weary, tired, frustrated, such that a quoting occurs - **Isaiah 40:31**.

Spirit of Sabotage - Causes a person to implement an alternate plan or sabotage their God-ordained progress due to immaturity, unhealthiness, unresolved issues, sin issues, backsliding and cycling tendencies, carelessness, ignorance, not being equipped to sustain in their success or progress, restlessness with waiting, not being fully committed to God and his will and purposes, being strong-willed and self-absorbed in one's own desires, listening and following unwise counsel.

Spirits of Necromancy & Sorcery - Spirits that witches, warlocks, wicked, and ignorant people conjure from the dead to confuse, spook, haunt and attack people, places, and things. Witches, warlocks, etc., also use demons to assist their works of casting spells, hexes, vexes, and incantations of death, murder, tragedy, suicide, on people.

Spirit of Laban - Makes a person constantly work for what is rightfully theirs, what God has already said is theirs, what they have already worked hard for; tricks the person into believing they have to keep on working to receive what rightfully belongs to them - *Genesis 24:29-60*.

Spirit of Judas - Causes betrayal to abort covenant, and kill the fruit, progress, and success of a relationship, covenant, the vision, promises, and prophecies; Spirit will cause people to sell you for money or to sell out for something that is easier or less than what they are to have with you or with the vision - *Matthew 26:15, Matthew 27:10*.

Spirit & Systems of Jezebel - Wants to control the person and the vision and if it cannot control it, will put out a hit to kill the person and/or the vision - *1Kings 19:2, Revelations 2:20*.

Spirit of Python - Restricts and seeks to kill by wrapping around its prey, while squeezing and sucking the life out of the person and the vision: draws people away from God, His people, and the vision rather than to Him - *1Chronicles 10:13, Acts 16:16-21*.

Spirit Of Leviathan - Wants the person to serve self and vision via pride and haughtiness, through self-idolatry, so God can judge and kill the person and the vision - *Proverbs 6:16*.

Pandemics, Plagues, Pestilences, Wasters, Calamities - Spirits that cause oppression, disease, and tragedies upon people, visions, communities, and nations so they are distracted, infirmed, afflicted, traumatized, weak, impoverished, and unable to live in the full life and light of God - *Psalm 91, Joel 1-2, 1Kings 8, 2Chronicles 7:14*.

Dream Realm Spirits - Spirits of death attack in the dream realm to incite fear or to get the person to agree that death will occur so that it has an open door to attack with tragedy. Works with familiar spirits and shape-shifting demons in dreams so the person's guard will be down; Causes them to view the particles in the dream as safe and then attack with terror and death as the dream proceeds to its original intent.

Counterattacking Death Spirits
Counterattack these spirits using the deliverance and inner healing revelation in the previous chapter to breakthrough, while implementing the following strategy:

- Repent for any vows, dedications, or covenants you made with death, or the person that is dying, even those made under duress -*Proverbs 20:5, Provers 18:7, Numbers 30:20*.

- Restore yourself unto salvation and right covenant with God.

- Bind and cast these spirits out of your life, generational, home, the sphere of influence, and vision; deal with them territorially as it relates to the community and region you were born in, live in, are releasing the vision in, and govern over - *Matthew 16:19, Matthew 18:18, Ephesians 6:12.*

- Break soul ties with death and hell, Sheol, coffin spirits, words you spoke related to death and dying - *Hebrew 4:12.*

- Examine how these spirits have attacked your life, mental health, destiny, and vision. Close the doorways, gateways, pathways, to their actions, and discern how they will try to return as your life and vision progresses – *James 4:7, 1Peter 5:8, Isaiah 59:19,*

- Spend time decreeing eternal life and salvation over yourself - *John 3:16.*

- Spend time decreeing the abundant life of God over yourself - *John 10:10.*

- Spend time receiving and declaring that the promises and prophecies of God are true for your life *Habakkuk 2:3, Malachi 3:16-18, Hebrews 5:14.*

- Seek God for further revelation of how to stay well and free from these death bondages. Be obedient to what God is telling you to do - *James 1-22, John 14:23, 1John 2:17, Mathew 7:14, Proverbs 10:17.*

- Spend time commanding and expecting life and miracles to SHIFT into your life. Stand in faith as God produces new oil through His life and wellness SHIFTING into your life - *John 14:12, Matthew 10:8, Mark 16:17, Acts 3:16.*

DISMANTLING SEXUAL ACTS & DEMONS

Many of the definitions from this chapter are from dictionary.com or they are my general synopsis of what the word means.

<u>*Sexual Intercourse*</u> - To have genital contact, especially the insertion of the penis into the vagina followed by orgasm; coitus; copulation.

<u>*Sex*</u> - Sexual relations or activity, especially sexual intercourse.

Some people believe that sex only counts as sex if a penis enters the vagina, however, we can detect from the definition of sex that any activity of a sexually relational nature is **SEX**. Different types of sex include:

- Vaginal Sex (penis-in-vagina intercourse)
- Oral Sex (mouth-to-genital contact)
- Anal Sex (penis-in-butt intercourse)
- Fingering or Hand Jobs (hand-to-genital contact)
- Dry Humping, Genital Rubbing, Clothes Burning (stimulating arousal and release by rubbing bodies together)
- Masturbation (touching yourself)

To God, any sexual act is considered sex. Moreover, sexual acts outside the boundaries of marriage and outside the boundaries of what God has deemed proper and lawful, even in marriage, are considered unclean, covetous, filthy, and even perverse.

Let's explore revelation on the ***undefiled bed*** from my book entitled, "*Crushing Warlock Opposition*," so we can be clear about what the Bible says. This will aid in helping us to realize that we are becoming prey to the subtle religious jargon and scriptures used to manipulate us into thinking that all sexual practices are proper and lawful in marriage. And that has us believe, that what is a violation outside of marriage is a **YES LORD** in the marriage bed.

Hebrews 13:14 *Marriage is honourable in all, and the bed undefiled: but whoremongers and adulterers God will judge.*

The Amplified Bible *Let marriage be held in honor (esteemed worthy, precious, of great price, and especially dear) in all things. And thus let the marriage bed be undefiled (kept undishonored); for God will judge and punish the unchaste [all guilty of sexual vice] and adulterous.*

Undefiled is *amiantos* in Greek and means:
1. Unsoiled, i.e. (figuratively) pure: — undefiled
2. Not defiled, free from that by which the nature of a thing is deformed and debased, or its force and vigor impaired

Dictionary.com defines *undishonored* as:
1. Lack or loss of honor; disgraceful or dishonest character or conduct
2. Disgrace; ignominy; shame
3. An indignity; insult
4. A cause of shame or disgrace
5. To deprive of honor; disgrace; bring reproach or shame on
6. To rape or seduce

We'd like to think an undefiled bed means we can do what we desire because we are married or are in a relationship that has the potential for marriage. But if there is sexual interaction outside of wedlock or, if there are acts that bring shame, dishonor, reproach, and disgrace upon a partner and upon God, then the bed is subject to defilement. If we are making our partners engage in acts that they are uncomfortable with, especially if there are areas of their soul and identity that need to be healed regarding intimacy, we could be defiling the marriage bed. When we enter into areas of our imagination that cross over into deviant, lascivious, perverted acts, we are SHIFTING into the defilement of ourselves, our spouses, and our covenant with God. As we examine the definitions, some acts could be considered rape when there is seduction in the form of manipulation and control rather than in the form of *Eros love* and a desire to romanticize your mate. Thus, we could be subjecting the marriage bed to defilement.

When defilement enters the marriage bed or a relationship, we are operating in *Aheb love* rather than *Eros love*.

- *Aheb love* can be an inordinate love rooted in physical attraction, lust, ungodly cravings, perversion, vain imaginations, demonization, and erred doctrine, where the person is engaging in relationship interactions and sexual acts that are sinful, wicked, rooted in man's flesh, or that disregard the boundaries of God.

- *Eros love* is romantic love, admiration, esteem, passion, and attraction between a woman and a man. It is the love a man or a woman has for a partner of the opposite sex that they romantically admire and would desire to marry. Eros love is often misconstrued and even tainted with lust. Even though it is a healthy innate love, if Eros love is not properly governed or filtered through a pure mind, heart, and soul, it can cause people to fall into fornication, adultery, inappropriate sexual or lustful behaviors. This type of love is intended for marriage and should not be intricately engaged or ignited outside of matrimony. After marriage, Eros love can be fully awakened and is essential for the wellness of sexual intimacy, and the strengthening of the relationship bond within the marriage covenant.

Aheb love will have us succumbing to a love that is driven more by perversion than the innate desires of sex and intimacy that God instilled in us.

Many people believe purity means abstaining and self-control, but purity means sanctification.

1Thessalonians 4:3-4 *For this is the will of God, even your sanctification, that ye should abstain from fornication: That every one of you should know how to possess his vessel in sanctification and honour.*

<u>Sanctification in Greek is *hagiasmos* and means:</u>
1. Purification, i.e. (the state) purity
2. Concretely (by hebraism) a purifier
3. Holiness, sanctification, consecration
4. The effect of consecration
5. Sanctification of heart and life

Sanctification is about being restored in innocence, holiness, and purity according to the standard and will of God.

Sanctification is a state of separation from God. As we are separated from God, we are able to abstain.

All believers enter into an initial state of sanctification when they are born of God. Sanctification is not possible outside of God's presence, relationship, and will, as a person cannot purify themselves. Neither is there anything apart from God that can make a person acceptable unto Him. A person must continue to glory in His presence and in covenant with Him if they are to continue to evolve in sanctification with Him.

1Corinthians 1:29-31 *That no flesh should glory in his presence. But of him are ye in Christ Jesus, who of God is made unto us wisdom, and righteousness, and sanctification, and redemption: That, according as it is written, He that glorieth, let him glory in the Lord.*

Jesus did not come to save our flesh, but to save our spirit. There must be a relinquishing of flesh to produce sanctification. When having to give up sin for sanctification, our flesh will always war for gratification – it wars against the spirit of God in us.

The flesh is going to be flesh; it will never be happy about having to die inside God's presence, not being able to be fed by what it desires. It will only want sanctification when it has died inside of God and has risen in resurrection power by being crucified unto Christ Jesus.

Galatians 5:17 For the flesh lusteth against the Spirit, and the Spirit against the flesh: and these are contrary the one to the other: so that ye cannot do the things that ye would.

Romans. 7:15-23 For that which I do I allow not: for what I would, that do I not; but what I hate, that do I. If then I do that which I would not, I consent unto the law that it is good. Now then it is no more I that do it, but sin that dwelleth in me. For I know that in me (that is, in my flesh,) dwelleth no good thing: for to will is present with me; but how to perform that which is good I find not. For the good that I would I do not: but the evil which I would not, that I do. Now if I do that I would not, it is no more I that do it, but sin that dwelleth in me. I find then a law, that, when I would do good, evil is present with me. For I delight in the law of God after the inward man: But I see another law in my members, warring against the law of my mind, and bringing me into captivity to the law of sin which is in my members

When our flesh wars against our spirit, it feels as if we're being punished and as if being saved is a drag, rather than viewing sanctification as a needful blessing that demonstrates God's love and likeness.

2Thessalonians 2:13 But we ought always to thank God for you, brothers and sisters loved by the Lord, because God chose you as firstfruits to be saved through the sanctifying work of the Spirit and through belief in the truth.

2Timothy 2:21 Those who cleanse themselves from the latter will be instruments for special purposes, made holy, useful to the Master and prepared to do any good work.

Galatians 2:20 I have been crucified with Christ and I no longer live, but Christ lives in me. The life I now live in the body, I live by faith in the Son of God, who loved me and gave himself for me.

Hebrews 9:14 How much more, then, will the blood of Christ, who through the eternal Spirit offered himself unblemished to God, cleanse our consciences from acts that lead to death, so that we may serve the living God!

Sanctification provides discipline, self-control, temperance, boundaries, wellness, and peace.

Sanctification enables us to serve God in worship, praise, offerings, sacrifice, spiritual works, and ministry.

Sanctification protects us from:

- ✓ Carnality, ideologies, and behaviors that do not please God
- ✓ Heartbreak and trauma
- ✓ Unnecessary bondages and experiences
- ✓ Soul ties (as sex is spiritual); when we have sexual encounters, our souls are tied to those we sleep with
- ✓ Bondages, transferences, demonization, and spiritual attacks that come from being soul-tied.
- ✓ Addictions, perversions, and sexual propensities that come from being soul tied to others.
- ✓ Memories that draw us back into or cause us to relive sin, heartbreak, and trauma

Anytime we justify not being sanctified, we have not matured with God. This is an indication that we have not pursued God's presence, developed a relationship with His Holy Spirit, and have not consistently studied His word as a lifestyle, so that sanctification of purity, righteousness, and holiness is birthed, cultivated, and evolved in us – formed in us.

Do you want Christ to be formed in you?

Galatians 4:19 *My little children, of whom I travail in birth again until Christ be formed in you.*

In the previous chapter, we learned that holiness requires us to be broken and contrite until we become a living sacrifice. Now we are learning that sanctification requires us to travail. *Travail* means *"toiling, pain, labor, exertion, anguish or suffering resulting from mental or physical hardship, the pain of childbirth."*

As we think about how being ridden of sin can feel like a drag or punishment, we recognize that there is a time of unpleasant work that must be done to produce and sustain us in this sanctification. Sanctification is freely given to us but requires a toiling to manifest its fullness in us as a lifestyle. Many do not want to do the work that leads to their being fashioned in Christ. This is how the warlock and other enticers draw us away from God.

Let me pose it a different way!

When we say we believe in Jesus Christ and His works on the Cross, we are actually declaring that we are dying to sin and are rising in eternal life with Him. When we accept this as our truth, sanctification enters our lives. Sanctification is actually the blood of Jesus and His experience on the Cross. Relinquishing ourselves of sin causes the exchanging of sanctification. Then we must enter a cross experience – fellowship in His suffering – while being resurrected unto God through holiness, sanctification, and righteousness. The work was done over 2000 years ago with Jesus Christ, but we must manifest and live out the work in our own lives.

Until we walk out a consecration season and live it as our truth, we will never love and joy in sanctification. We will always deem it an unattainable burden that steals our fun in life. We will always think that grace is giving us a pass to sin when grace really means power to overcome sin. Such erred doctrine will have us claiming salvation, misrepresenting God, operating through a form of godliness, yet left with open doors that allow manipulation lust, perversion, carnality, worldliness, enticers, demons, and demonic systems. It is important to live this, to disciple people unto true sanctification, and to teach this truth to people as they come for ministry, counseling, deliverance, and healing. Especially when deliverance from sexual acts and sex demons is needed. They cannot be truly delivered without truth and without relinquishing their sins, lusts, needs, and desire to God and allowing him to guide them in restoring what is orderly, proper, and undefiled.

LETS JUST SELAH A MOMENT AND PONDER THAT REVELATION BEFORE SHIFTING FORWARD.

Now back to sexual acts and demonization.

Sexual acts are contrived through the flesh and the mind by way of lustful ideas and appetites.

<u>*Sensual Or Sensuality*</u> - Pertaining to, inclined to, or preoccupied with the gratification of the senses or appetites; carnal; fleshly; lacking in moral restraints; lewd or unchaste. arousing or exciting the senses or appetites; worldly; materialistic; irreligious; of or pertaining to the senses or physical sensation; sensory.

<u>*Sexy*</u> - Concerned predominantly or excessively with sex; risqué: sexually interesting or exciting; radiating sexuality; excitingly appealing; glamorous: Risqué means daringly close to indelicacy or impropriety; off-color; **to be risky.**

<u>Lust</u> - An intense or excessive sexual desire or appetite; uncontrolled or illicit sexual desire or appetite; lecherousness; a passionate or overmastering desire or craving; ardent enthusiasm; zest; relish.

Galatians 5:16-19 *This I say then, Walk in the Spirit, and ye shall not fulfil the lust of the flesh. For the flesh lusteth against the Spirit, and the Spirit against the flesh: and these are contrary the one to the other: so that ye cannot do the things that ye would. But if ye be led of the Spirit, ye are not under the law. Now the works of the flesh are manifest, which are these; Adultery, fornication, uncleanness, lasciviousness.*

<u>Lusteth</u> in this passage is the Greek word *epithymeo*, and means:
1. To set the heart upon, long for
2. Covet (to desire wrongfully, inordinately, or without regard for the rights of others)
3. To turn upon a thing
4. To have a desire for, to lust after
5. To lust for forbidden things

Matthew 5:28 *But I say unto you, That whosoever looketh on a woman to lust after her hath committed adultery with her already in his heart.*

The Greek word for *looketh* is *blepo* and not only means *"to look with the natural eye, but to discern, see, perceive by the senses, to see with the mind's eye to gaze upon."*

Lust will have a person coveting for something that they are not supposed to have or that is not theirs to have. The person will have an ungodly, unhealthy, or demonic appetite for things that are forbidden, things that God deems are wrong, or errored in how they desire a person, place, or thing.

Lust begins in the flesh – generally the eye gates, the spiritual and natural senses, the imagination of a person, the mind's eye. As lust is fed, it opens a third eye where the person begins to desire that which it is looking upon in a wrong way. Inside that third eye, they begin to meditate on that which they are looking at. They commune and entertain thoughts and demons that create an uncontrollable craving and appetite for that which they are gazing upon.

1John 2:16 *For all that is in the world, the lust of the flesh, and the lust of the eyes, and the pride of life, is not of the Father, but is of the world.*

<u>Pride</u> in Greek is *alazoneia* and means:
1. Braggadocio, i.e. (by implication) self-confidence: — boasting, pride, empty, braggart talk
2. An insolent and empty assurance, which trusts in its own power and resources and shamefully despises and violates divine laws and human rights

3. An impious and empty presumption which trusts in the stability of earthy things

Lust is a worldly ambition. It is prideful – haughty. Once the flesh is fed, it increases in pride and fills the person with an empty assurance that they should, can, and need to have what they are lusting for. The person begins to trust in the truth of what lust is feeding them through their adulterous – mind's eye – the third eye. They become driven to want the lusts of the world – the cravings they are having, and become prideful in their pursuit to obtain – covet it.

This is how believers result in believing that certain sexual acts are godly and lawful in and out of marriage when actually they are unholy and impure. Their lust has exalted itself above purity, righteousness, holiness, and the truth that we serve a holy God. He will never agree with perversion.

- ✓ He will never agree with sex outside of marriage.
- ✓ He will never agree with same-sex relationships.
- ✓ He will never agree with sex toys and sex stores.
- ✓ He will never agree with you masturbating to the ungodly region of your imagination.
- ✓ He will never agree with making your spouse dress up and act like porn stars or your favorite secular idol – your entertainment eye candy - just so you can commit adultery with your demonic imagination.
- ✓ He will never agree with swinging and partner swapping.
- ✓ He will never agree with you touching and marrying little children.
- ✓ He will never agree with you raping anyone, not even your spouse.
- ✓ He will never agree with your fetishes and sadistic sex acts.
- ✓ He will never agree with your fetishes or weird proclivities.
- ✓ He will never agree with your down low behavior.

I could go on but I digress. These lusts and thrills are our own imaginations. We can act like God approves, however, that too is our own vain imagination at work. God's love and grace for us is not a sign of approval. Us having no conviction about it is not God's sign of approval. When pride is at work, it makes it hard to receive truth and hear God on what has become a god in our lives. It will be important to consider the sexual acts listed as you and clients seek to explore with God the sexual acts they are engaging in and be open to hearing him for truth and examining his word for divine principles to bring truth. Many people want to heal until they have to give up something they love, crave and that is pleasurable. The stronghold of the flesh and the demons attached to them will have them compromising and striving for a way to keep their pleasures yet still receive some release from the oppressions they bring. Demons and flesh strongholds strengthen when we waver in our deliverance. It will be important to teach people the importance of discipline along with sanctification so they can break free and live in freedom as a lifestyle.

Fornication - Voluntary sexual intercourse between two unmarried persons or two persons not married to each other; the Bible defines fornication as idolatry.

***Ephesians* 5:3-5** *But fornication, and all uncleanness, or covetousness, let it not be once named among you, as becometh saints; Neither filthiness, nor foolish talking, nor jesting, which are not convenient: but rather giving of thanks. For this ye know, that no whoremonger, nor unclean person, nor covetous man, who is an idolater, hath any inheritance in the kingdom of Christ and of God.*

Fornication in Greek is *porneia* and means:
1. Harlotry (including adultery and incest); figuratively, idolatry: — fornication
2. Illicit sexual intercourse, adultery, fornication, homosexuality, lesbianism, intercourse with animals etc.
3. Sexual intercourse with close relatives
4. Lev. 18 sexual intercourse with a divorced man or woman; Mk. 10:11,12
5. Metaph. the worship of idols of the defilement of idolatry, as incurred by eating the sacrifices offered to idols

We discern from this definition that fornication includes a wide variety of sexual activities. Fornication is listed with and compared to idolatry and idol worship. A person may not believe they are worshipping an idol when engaging in various acts of fornication, however, they become their own god when they yield to fornication. They worship their own desires and ideologies, thus sacrificing their bodies in defilement to what they are lusting after. It will be important to cleanse the person from fornication using the blood of Jesus Christ, break covenants of self-idolatry while teaching people how to bring their desires, ideologies, and flesh under the subjection of their spirit man.

***1Corinthians* 9:27** *But I keep under my body, and bring it into subjection: lest that by any means, when I have preached to others, I myself should be a castaway.*

Under is *hypōpiazō* in Greek and means:
1. To hit under the eye (buffet or disable an antagonist as a pugilist)
2. I.e. (figuratively) to tease or annoy (into compliance), subdue (one's passions): — keep under, weary.
3. To beat black and blue, to smite so as to cause bruises and liver spots
4. Like a boxer one buffets his body, handles it roughly, discipline by hardships
5. Metaph. to give one intolerable annoyance, beat one out, wear one out; by entreaties
6. That part of the face that is under the eyes

Subjection is *doulagōgeō* in Greek and means:
1. To be a slave-driver, i.e. To enslave (figuratively, subdue)
2. Bring into subjection, to lead away into slavery,
3. Claim as one's slave, to make a slave, and to treat as a slave
4. I.e. With severity, subject to stern and rigid discipline

Bringing one's desires, ideologies, and body under subjection takes discipline and consistent subjection to God that is comparable to a beating. We do not tell people this truth, they, therefore, think deliverance from such bondage is supposed to be easy, quick, and without challenges. They are expecting a Santa clause God and the work of a magician and God are expecting them to come into a working covenant relationship with him. For we are taught that salvation does this work for us, but the word is clear that this requires our agreement, participation, constant attention, and working of our right to be saved and free from unhealthy, ungodly, and demonic bondage to attain. We will have to cast our flesh down and enslave it to rigid spiritual discipline where we live through the truth, will, and purpose of God.

The Amplified Bible *But [like a boxer] I buffet my body [handle it roughly, discipline it by hardships] and subdue it, for fear that after proclaiming to others the Gospel and things pertaining to it, I myself should become unfit [not stand the test, be unapproved and rejected as a counterfeit].*

Perversion – Any of various means of obtaining sexual gratification that is generally regarded as abnormal. *Pathology* of perversion is defined as a change to what is unnatural or abnormal. The condition of being corrupt. It is a deviation from the original and a twisting of the truth to cause distortion, misalignment, and deviation. It is an ideology and/or a spirit that leads people away from the truth regarding God, his word, his righteousness, his will, and plan for their mind, body, soul, lives, and destiny.

Pervert - To affect with perversion, corruption, twisted ideology; to lead astray morally, to turn away from the right course, to lead into mental error or false judgment, to turn to improper use; misapply, to misconstrue or misinterpret, especially deliberately; distort.

Lustful sexual acts that are improper or operate outside the boundaries of God fall under perversion. So basically this entire chapter is discussing behaviors and demonization that are rooted in perversion.

Philippians 2:15 *That ye may be blameless and harmless, the sons of God, without rebuke, in the midst of a crooked and perverse nation, among whom ye shine as lights in the world.*

Perverse in Greek is *diastrephō* and means:
1. To distort, i.e. (figuratively) misinterpret, or (morally) corrupt: — perverse(-rt)

2. Turn away, to turn aside, to oppose
3. Plot against the saving purposes and plans of god
4. To turn aside from the right path, to pervert, corrupt

Romans 1:21-23 *Because that, when they knew God, they glorified him not as God, neither were thankful; but became vain in their imaginations, and their foolish heart was darkened. Because that, when they knew God, they glorified him not as God, neither were thankful; but became vain in their imaginations, and their foolish heart was darkened.*
It is important to note that though this scripture references homosexuality, it is talking about any sin that exalts itself above God – that becomes a perverse ideology above God.

<u>Wise</u> in Greek is *sophos* and means:
1. (clear); wise (in a most general application): — wise.
2. Wise, skilled, expert: of artificers, wise,
3. Skilled in letters, cultivated, learned
4. Of the Greek philosophers and orators
5. Of Jewish theologians
6. Of Christian teachers
7. Forming the best plans and using the best means for their execution

When operating in perversion, a person becomes wise and learned in what they believe is right and appropriate. They become learned, skilled, and wise in their own ideologies and literally can make a philosophy out of what they believe as if they were a teacher or minister regarding what they believe. They live through – cultivate – execute - their errored wisdom as a lifestyle and even teach others how to live through and take on their wisdom as a lifestyle. This is interesting in this day and age where the government is allowing false educators to come in and teach our children these erred doctrines, while also expecting teachers to instruct children and youth on such ideologies. There is an expectation to become learned in this wisdom and to implement it in the educational system, regardless of how and what the parents of these children and youth believe or desire their children to know and be exposed to.

Verse 24-25 *Wherefore God also gave them up to uncleanness through the lusts of their own hearts, to dishonour their own bodies between themselves: Who changed the truth of God into a lie, and worshipped and served the creature more than the Creator, who is blessed forever. Amen.*

Because the people choose to live through their perverse philosophies, God gives them over to their physical and moral ideologies and behaviors to which he identifies as unclean, impure, lustful, and profligate living. Profligate means utterly and shamelessly immoral or dissipated; thoroughly dissolute, recklessly prodigal, or extravagant. Being turned over causes a SHIFT in them such that they exchange the truth of God for the lie – the perverted wisdom to which they believe – and they become the identity of that erred philosophy - erred doctrine. They begin to worship and service their false doctrine and the idol that it is attached to. God calls their idol a creature.

Creature in Greek is *ktisis* and means:
1. Original formation (properly, the act; by implication, the thing, literally or figuratively) building, creation, creature, ordinance
2. The act of founding, establishing, building etc.
3. The act of creating, creation
4. Creation i.e. thing created, of individual things, beings, a creature
5. A creation, anything created, after a rabbinical usage (by which a man converted from idolatry to Judaism was called)
6. The sum or aggregate of things created, institution, ordinance

Whether that person wants to acknowledge it or not, basically, these perverse ideologies literally and figuratively cause them to create – build an idol. They become idolatrous in their identity, their behavior, and service, as the changes in how they operate in their lifestyle offer worship up to that which they created.

Verse 26-28 *For this cause God gave them up unto vile affections: for even their women did change the natural use into that which is against nature: And likewise also the men, leaving the natural use of the woman, burned in their lust one toward another; men with men working that which is unseemly, and receiving in themselves that recompence of their error which was meet.*

According to the Greek definition vile affection – *atimia* - is an affection that lacks dignity, disgraceful, dishonorable, shameful, contempt, and infamy which is shameful public reproach and condemnation.

It is interesting that being turned over to one's vile affection causes public challenges. The sin itself causes reproach even though in the world's eye, people are accused of being unloving, dishonoring, and disregarding people who choose such lifestyles. The word is letting us know that when God turns us over to our own sin – our perverse ways – our choices SHIFTS us from under his grace, blessings, dignity, honor, favor, to being viewed in a shameful, condemning way. SIGH! This is important to acknowledge because we want to make sure that as we process in deliverance and wholeness with God, we want to be accountable for any hardship, trauma, and challenges, we brought on ourselves. Even as we want others to be held accountable for their actions towards us, we also want to be accountable for how our choices have consequences and judgments. There is reaping regarding the sin we sow.

In this passage of scripture, the women and men exchanged what God deemed natural for that which was unnatural. This is important because God has boundaries and principles regarding what is proper and lawful. Though we think, believe, and feel a certain way, it does not make it right or natural to God. He is not accepting our ideologies, nor is he agreeing with them simply because we choose to think, feel, and behave a certain way.

God turned the people over to what was unseemingly and eventually, they became reprobate – a rejected castaway – left to do as they pleased. Though it appeared that they were benefiting from their sin because they were flourishing and relishing in it, they were really left to reap the natural and spiritual consequences of their sin.

Verse 28-31 And even as they did not like to retain God in their knowledge, God gave them over to a reprobate mind, to do those things which are not convenient; Being filled with all unrighteousness, fornication, wickedness, covetousness, maliciousness; full of envy, murder, debate, deceit, malignity; whisperers, Backbiters, haters of God, despiteful, proud, boasters, inventors of evil things, disobedient to parents, Without understanding, covenant breakers, without natural affection, implacable, unmerciful: Who knowing the judgment of God, that they which commit such things are worthy of death, not only do the same, but have pleasure in them that do them.

The scripture further reveals how living reprobate in vile affections and unseeing behaviors opens the doors to more sin. This is because perversion breeds perversion. The more we expose and engage ourselves to it, the deeper it becomes ingrained in us where we SHIFT deeper into engaging in the vain imagination of our mind and false ideologies.

As you or others are delivered from the perversions that are discussed further in this chapter, this revelation is essential to the deliverance process. Dealing with the roots of lust and perversion and the factors listed below is vital to really purge root issues and process to sanctification where you are able to live in sustaining wellness. Many do not process through in these areas to sanctification. Therefore, they backslid or struggle to maintain healing, because they have been restored and reconciled into complete truth and into the fullness of their God nature and identity.

- ✓ Erred & foolish wisdom
- ✓ Idolatrous thoughts, feelings, & ideologies
- ✓ Self & manmade philosophies
- ✓ Teaching others these idolatrous philosophies
- ✓ Exchanging truth for lies
- ✓ Rejecting God & truth to live in self-idolatry
- ✓ Engaging in vile affections & unseeing behaviors
- ✓ The consequences & accountability factors to one's behaviors

Sexual strongholds and demons can be lodged in the areas below. It may be important to take people through a process and series of deliverance and counseling to cleanse and purge these areas with the blood of Jesus Christ and the fire of God while dealing with any root issues and strongholds that may be lodged there. It may also be necessary to call demonic spirits out of the following areas.

- Mind
- Brain
- Memory Recall
- Mouth
- Tongues
- Hands
- Breast
- Sexual & Reproductive Organs (ovaries, fallopian tubes, testicles, penis, vagina, breast)
- In & around the umbilical cord
- Abdomen
- Rectum
- Rib cage
- Spine
- Pelvic
- Hips & Thighs
- Stimulating nerves
- Blood & Bloodline
- Cells

Also, cleanse with the blood of Jesus and fire of God, break powers and triggers, and bind and cast demons out of the senses.

- Seeing - eyes
- Hearing - ears
- Smelling - nose
- Tasting - mouth
- Touching - feeling, impression, sensation, physical awareness
- Perceiving - sensing, having a conscious awareness, sensation, or recognition of something

Many perverse issues are rooted in unresolved traumas. They can also be generational. It will be important for you and those you minister to, to enter a series of deliverance and counseling sessions to identify personal and generational root issues and traumas. A process of exploration of inner healing may be needed before engaging in deliverance ministry to cast out demonic bondages.

Explore what personal sexual experiences you or the person you have ministered to have engaged in willingly or unwillingly. Deal with the following:

- Root issues
- Break soul ties
- Cleanse & purge specific areas using the list above
- Break the powers of memory recall & triggers

- Break curses & Vows – Break any personal or generational curses and vows off your life, any bewitchment others may have done on or against you or those you are ministering to
- Break Covenants - Cancel any way people or demons have claimed ownership of you & your body
- Break Dedications - Cancel any way you or those you are ministering to may have been offered up or covenanted with idol gods
- Bind & Cast Out Demons

Find out what perversions are in the family lines as that will help with identifying certain lustful cravings, perversions, propensities, and open doors to sexual predators and attacks, and sexual proclivities. There may be underlying roots issues and traumas stemming from what others in your family line have opened the door to that is trying to awaken, track, and draw you or those you minister to, into perversion so it can be further strengthened in the family line.

Knowing, studying, embodying, and living the scriptures are vital to sustaining purity. It is important that you and those you minister know and love truth because it is your greatest weapon against the enemy coming for your deliverance.

- Spend time exploring the scriptures in this chapter with God.
- Journal what he reveals to you.
- Revisit these scriptures often so they can be hidden in your heart.
- Want the purity, righteousness, holiness, sanctification of God as a lifestyle as you seek to be an example of what pleases and represents God.
- Remember sanctification means SHIFTING into a disciplined lifestyle of living through your spirit man. Sanctification requires a beating of the flesh until ungodly thoughts, feelings, ideologies, live under the subjection of the spirit man. Through the process of beating the flesh, one is breaking their will, while exchanging what they want and think is right for what God has ordained for them and for what he has decided is proper through his biblical word. This lifestyle change takes time and a processing of coming into covenant relationship with God as a lifestyle. It will be important to do the work until Christ be formed in you or those you minister to. Commit to entering covenant with God and do not stop beating down your flesh by learning him, learning yourself through him, and living what he regards for your life or the lives of those you disciple.
- Have accountability partners who can empower, support, and uphold you in truth and sanctification.

- Know your purpose and calling and the reason the enemy would want to pervert you and keep you bound and victimized to perversion.
- Ask God for the standard of holiness you need to walk in your calling and live your destiny through those standards.

Colossians 3:5-6 *Mortify therefore your members which are upon the earth; fornication, uncleanness, inordinate affection, evil concupiscence (craving, lust), and covetousness, which is idolatry: For which things' sake the wrath of God cometh on the children of disobedience.*

The Amplified Bible *So kill (deaden, deprive of power) the evil desire lurking in your members [those animal impulses and all that is earthly in you that is employed in sin]: sexual vice, impurity, sensual appetites, unholy desires, and all greed and covetousness, for that is idolatry (the deifying of self and other created things instead of God).*

Galatians 6:7-8 *Be not deceived; God is not mocked: for whatsoever a man soweth, that shall he also reap. For he that soweth to his flesh shall of the flesh reap corruption; but he that soweth to the Spirit shall of the Spirit reap life everlasting.*

The Amplified Bible *Do not be deceived and deluded and misled; God will not allow Himself to be sneered at (scorned, disdained, or mocked by mere pretensions or professions, or by His precepts being set aside.) [He inevitably deludes himself who attempts to delude God.] For whatever a man sows, that and that only is what he will reap. For he who sows to his own flesh (lower nature, sensuality) will from the flesh reap decay and ruin and destruction, but he who sows to the Spirit will from the Spirit reap eternal life.*

New Living Bible *Don't be misled – you cannot mock the justice of God. You will always harvest what you plant. Those who live only to satisfy their own sinful nature will harvest decay and death from that sinful nature. But those who live to please the Spirit will harvest everlasting life from the Spirit.*

Ephesians 5:3-17 God's Word Bible *Don't let sexual sin, perversion of any kind, or greed even be mentioned among you. This is not appropriate behavior for God's holy people. It's not right that dirty stories, foolish talk, or obscene jokes should be mentioned among you either. Instead, give thanks [to God]. You know very well that no person who is involved in sexual sin, perversion, or greed (which means worshiping wealth) can have any inheritance in the kingdom of Christ and of God. Don't let anyone deceive you with meaningless words. It is because of sins like these that God's anger comes to those who refuse to obey him. Don't be partners with them. Once you lived in the dark, but now the Lord has filled you with light. Live as children who have light.*

Light produces everything that is good, that has God's approval, and that is true. Determine which things please the Lord. Have nothing to do with the useless works that darkness produces. Instead, expose them for what they are. It is shameful to talk about what some people do in secret. Light exposes the true character of everything because light makes everything easy to see.

That's why it says: "Wake up, sleeper! Rise from the dead, and Christ will shine on you." So then, be very careful how you live. Don't live like foolish people but like wise people. Make the most of your opportunities because these are evil days. So don't be foolish, but understand what the Lord wants.

Proverbs 17:20 *He who has a crooked mind finds no good, and he who is perverted in his language falls into evil.*

Psalm 101:4 *A perverse heart shall depart from me; I will know no evil.*

Proverbs 6:14 *Who with perversity in his heart continually devises evil, who spreads strife.*

Proverbs 12:8 *A man will be praised according to his insight, but one of perverse mind will be despised.*

Proverbs 15:4 *A soothing tongue is a tree of life, but perversion in it crushes the spirit.*

Ezekiel 9:9 *Then He said to me, "The iniquity of the house of Israel and Judah is very, very great, and the land is filled with blood and the city is full of perversion; for they say, 'The Lord has forsaken the land, and the Lord does not see!'*

Matthew 17:17 *And Jesus answered and said, "You unbelieving and perverted generation, how long shall I be with you? How long shall I put up with you? Bring him here to Me."*

<u>Predators</u> – Predators are any organisms, demonic systems, or people that exist by preying upon other organisms. As I have conducted deliverance ministry, God has highlighted how predator spirits operate in people, against people, and in their generational line. A lot of what God was showing me, I had never heard anyone else speak about before. I begin to do research and found some videos by Apostle Ivory Hopkins on YouTube. He provides clear revelation and understanding of the predator spirit. I encourage you to study his videos. Not just on this topic but all of them. He provides balanced deliverance teachings and shares key weaponry and insights that SHIFTS people to breakthrough and wellness.

- Predator spirits operate or derive through incidents of rape, incest, molestation, prostitution, trafficking, abortion, sex magic, witchcraft practices, idolatry, sexual sacrifices upon altars, and idol gods. They can also operate through physical and verbal abuse, inordinate affections, fornication, adultery, homosexual relationships, and activities.

- Sexual play can open the door to predatory activity, especially if there is a perversion in the family line, or instances of rape, incest, molestation, and the other areas mentioned above. The devil will use children innocently or knowingly engaging in sexual play as a door for predator spirits of oppressing people even children and have them touch other children in and outside of the family, become promiscuous at an early age, masturbating, addicted to porn, drawn to sexual sin and propensities, etc.

- Predator spirits will sexually attack these people sexually throughout the day or in their sleep due to the doors that have been opened up in the areas above. These spirits will harass, torment, rape, molest, beat, mark, weary, people as they constantly attack and drain the life out of them. These spirits operate through astral projection, portals in the dream realm and consciousness, witchcraft (e.i., voodoo, hoodoo, hexes, vexes, potion magic, sex magic, incantations, etc.). They will use pictures, articles that they have taken from the person, blood, fluids, etc., as a point of contact for monitoring and connecting with their prey. They will have high priests and priestesses perform rituals and ceremonies on their behalf as they claim the souls of their prey.

- Predator spirits can operate in the church and ministries where leaders, witches, warlocks, rapists, and molesters, hide behind the Bible and titles while preying spiritually, emotionally, sexually, financially, and ministerially upon members. They usually prey upon children, teenagers, vulnerable people who need to be validated in their identity and calling, those who have already been victimized in their homes and personal lives, those struggling with bondages or sexual sin.

These predators set up systems within the church with non-discerning, religiously loyal members, who do not believe, protect, lie for, contend for, cover-up, the predator's behavior at the expense of the members. We have so many people falling away from the church and God due to predators being allowed to reign in the pulpits by using titles, positions, intellect, religious jargon, scriptures, control, intimidation, manipulation, charm, and seduction, to conceal their predatory operations. Even when victims expose these predators, there is often anything done about their behavior. Some of these predatory systems have been passed down from generation to generation due to the lack of justice being rendered. Sometimes the behaviors of these predators are viewed as "human acts" and they are given a pass. There is nothing human about how they prey on their victims then open them up to continual demonic attacks as they or the demons that work with and through them, astral project, and further rape and torment their victims at night as they sleep and dream. It is important for the body of Christ to begin to come out of their own sinful bondage where they acknowledge the truth of these acts, and put these predatory spirits and systems out of their ministries.

- Predator spirits and systems operate as destiny-killing spirits and even intertwine with the world's system such that they track people even from a young age. They cause attacks upon people in an effort to defile, snare, victimize, and alter their destiny by constantly causing them to be raped, molested, trafficked, prostituted, sacrificed, abused, taken advantage of, etc. These victims live a life of constant hardship, tragedy, trauma, and hopelessness, as they are tracked and dehumanized by these predatory spirits and operations. They will be mad at God and after a while, they will become self-sabotages of their own destiny and opportunity as they live a life striving to hustle, survive, and prey on others before they become the prey. They become ensnared and even offended within the system that created, molded, and shaped them into a predator. It is important to identify these patterns of experiences of behaviors as people come for deliverance. You could be the catalysts for freeing them from this predatory system and helping them to understand God's love, heart, will, and purpose for their lives. To help them to recognize that they are not what they have been through; that God never intended for this to be their lot, and that they still can live a restored life of healing and wellness.

- Sometimes predatory spirits work with other demons as they can operate as a demonic system against a person. Often the person is getting attacked no matter where they are and what they do to stop these attacks. This can be an indication that there is a system of demons working within the generational line, with the predator that is the source of the attacks, or with the demonic realm that has released this attack upon the person.

- Many people associate predatory spirits with the marine kingdom, or the incubus and succubus spirit; sometimes they are correct with this assertion. However, it is important to note that it may not always be the case. It is important to ask God for the source, the root issues and open doors, and the deliverance strategies and weaponry needed to shut the door to these attacks.

Offender - Someone who has violated a criminal, religious, or moral law.

Violate or Violator - To break, infringe, or transgress (a law, rule, agreement, promise, instructions, etc.); to break in upon or disturb rudely; interfere thoughtlessly with; to break through or pass by force or without right; to treat irreverently or disrespectfully; desecrate; profane; to molest sexually, especially to rape.

Sexual Exploitation - Being used for sexual gain or profit.

Sex Addiction - Having an addiction to sexual acts where it has consumed your life and become the god of your life; the sexual act and desire has become your idol.

Sneaky & Risk-Taking Behaviors & Demonic Spirits – These are propensities and/or demonic spirits that have people engaging in sneaky, secret sins and risk-taking behaviors that jeopardize their righteous stance in the Lord. People need to acknowledge and recognize when they are sneaky or risk-takers and address the thrills they get from this behavior. Thrill-seeking is an affect or sudden way of keen emotion or excitement from engaging in a certain type of act or behavior. Thrill-seeking can be pleasurable, awe-striking, intense, fearful yet edgy, exhilarating, and arousing. It awakens sexual endorphins and can be very orgasmic. People love the thrill-seeking factor of doing something that poses a risk or the thought and fun of doing something sneaky and not getting thought. They love reliving the moment over and over after engaging in risky behavior and the continual arousal, rush, and awakening to be more risk-taking and lustily ideas that manifest from mulling over their sneaky behavior. Not dealing with sneaky and risk-taking behavior can cause one to fall and error at significant times in their walk where they are thriving in the things of God. The enemy will come for this propensity and have the person living one life in public and a perverse life in private.

Sneakiness and risk-taking behaviors are rooted in faulty character and flesh issues. The person has an open door in their integrity and to compromise concerning the thing of God. There is a breaking of the will unto true holiness and sanctification that needs to be dealt with so that they won't bend or make excuses for bending to ungodly behaviors.

Promiscuity - Characterized by or involving indiscriminate mingling or association, especially having sexual relations with a number of partners on a casual basis; consisting of parts, elements, or individuals of different kinds brought together without order; indiscriminate; without discrimination; casual; irregular; haphazard.

Seduce - To lead astray, as from duty, rectitude, or the like; corrupt; to persuade or induce to have sexual intercourse; to lead or draw away, as from principles, faith, or allegiance; to win over; attract; entice. Seduction is sneaky. You may not see it coming and even if you do, seduction can have a subtle swag, admiration, beauty, and ambition to it. The seducing person tends to be unique, intriguing, enthralling, charismatic and drawing in some way. They have a way with words and have a way of making what they say appear desiring, needful, and necessary. If you are not discerning, this person will have you entangled in behaviors and activities that unhealthy, ungodly, and deadly to your spiritual walk. When you try to end the relationship, they will have you entangled in drama as they use words and actions that keep you confused, craving, and longing for their seductive nature and character.

Adultery - The voluntary sexual intercourse between a married person and someone other than their lawful spouse. It is important that before you get married, you deal with any personal or generational propensities regarding adultery and any erred mindsets regarding divorce. Many people enter marriage with a mindset that if it does not work out, they can just get a divorce and move on. We should be entering marriage with a mindset to stay married forever, and to marry a mate that we are certain we can and will spend our lives with. We should also be willing to spend time in prayer dealing with anything in use and the generational line that would come for us and our marriage. When we already have a mindset that divorce is a possibility, it opens the door to thoughts and spirits of adultery. Especially in times where the marriage is facing challenges.

Communication is the greatest weapon against adultery. Being able to share your thoughts, feelings, concerns, desires, needs, truths, reproofs, chastisements, corrections, with your spouse is key to setting goals and standards that keep you, your spouse, your marriage, and your household, evolving in a healthy marriage. As a counselor, it amazes me when married people say their spouse does not listen or receive from them. What reasons would you marry someone that you do not regard or communicate effectively with? If I have to pray about everything to get God to intervene on you listening to me or listening in general so that you can regard truth, reproof, etc., then I might as well stay single.

Generally, when there is a lack of communication in the marriage, it was nonexistent during the dating and engagement stage of the relationship. The couple just disregarded making it a priority and not it has become an open door in the marriage. Save yourself some hardship and drama by not marrying anyone you cannot communicate with and who refuses to effectively communicate with you. Adultery love to be a listening ear and void filler for that which you are not getting from your spouse and they are not getting from you. Adultery is unassuming, thrilling, sneaking, seductive, enticing, wooing, and self-serving. Adultery feeds one's cravings, needs, desires, unforgiveness, resentments, and causes a person to enter erred idolatry where they feel justified in their engagement of adultery. It will even have the person making excuses for their adultery or serving it as a punishment to their spouse for them not being fulfilled in some area of the marriage.

Often adultery will have the person believing that their relationship adulterous partner is better than what they have with their spouse. Many times this is false truth and erred philosophy as the adulterous affair is feeding their void so the relationship is exalted in vain imagination and false perception. Counseling is needed along with deliverance to deal with the root issues of adultery. Betrayal has occurred. Many people try to rebuild on what was, however, when betrayal happens, the relationship has been sacrificed and has to be built from the new place it has SHIFTED into. Adultery changes people and the dynamics of the marriage. It also exposes what was not working, lacking, and the open doors that were there in the marriage. For this reason, it will be important to focus on renewing the relationship from where it has SHIFTED to, where the people in the relationship have SHIFTED to, and what is essential in this new place of trust, communication, need for love, belonging, attention, companionship, etc. When focusing on renewing from this new place, the hurt and challenges that occurred because of the adultery are not disregarded. They are factored into the deliverance process and enable the person who committed adultery to be held accountable for their actions, while also both parties being held accountable for what needs to be transformed and instilled into the marriage.

When the focus strives to restore and rekindle what once was, the deliverance and healing are built on a faulty foundation that already self-destructed. When Jesus Christ was betrayed by Judas and denied by Peter, he did not try to restore that relationship that he had with them or the other disciples. Jesus Christ was not the same from the betrayal experience and neither was the disciples. They all were forever changed by the impact of the experiences surrounding the cross and Jesus dying and resurrecting on the cross. It will be important for the couple to focus on resurrecting and learning the power that comes with striving to resurrect in a new place of personal and marriage identity. It is hard to realize that the betrayal experience changed you and your marriage. But resurrection always presents an opportunity to have something better than what once was. That was the entire reason Jesus Christ died and rose again for our sins. You and your spouse or those you are ministering to, can be encouraged in the power of resurrection, and seek to evolve rather than try to be what you once were. Evolve from the lessons you learned from the dreadful experience of adultery, regarding what it identified and exposed in your personality and in the marriage, and what is needed to make sure the reigns are well and closed off in you, your spouse, and your marriage.

Please know that resurrection of marriage takes work. Both parties will have to be willing to do the work. Often people want reconciliation but not a restoration. The restoration requires doing the work to build a solid lasting foundation that can sustain all seasons of one's personal life and marriage. It is being willed to set goals and standards and work on yourself personally and together for the good of the vision of the marriage that God is giving in the resurrected season. When one person is not willing to work on restoration, it keeps the door open to future adultery, drama, division, and divorce. If a spouse just wants forgiveness but does not want to change, then you and those you are ministering to, have to decide if sacrificing the rest of your life with an adulterer is God's will for you or is something you want to subject yourself to. Only you and God can answer this question but is definitely one worth examining.

Amos 3:3 *Can two walk together, except they be agreed?*

We have equated continuous pain inflicted upon us by others be some type of grand identity feet. But truly it is unhealthy and speaks volumes about our own self-care and self-worth. When someone loves you they are willing to do the work to improve and transform themselves and the relationship they have with you for the good of the life and companionship you all are to have together.

When God ordains a relationship, he gives us grace for the people he puts in our lives. We have grace for their sins, their quirkiness, their identity, and who God has called them to be in the earth and in our lives. We have the grace to support them, aid their needs and desires, empower them and SHIFT with them through times and seasons. When there is no grace and you are always overburdened, frustrated, sacrificing your peace and your self-care, bound in drama regarding a relationship, it is an indication that exploration of whether it is God or false obligation and loyalty that is keeping you connecting with that person. Staying stuck in painful - struggle love – type relationships is a generational and ethnic stronghold that has passed down to us within our family line and amongst our ethnic lineage. When God required people to stay in challenging and humiliating relationships, it was for a purpose and revealed prophetic insight and foresight. Otherwise, God made it clear that he desires us to prosper and be in good health even as our souls prosper. God is clear that he desires us to honor, esteem, and regard one another. God is clear that he wants us to separate from anything that causes us harm, pain, heartache, and dishonor.

<u>*Swinging*</u> - This sometimes called wife-swapping, husband-swapping, or partner-swapping, is a sexual activity in which both singles and partners in a committed relationship sexually engage with others for recreational purposes. Swinging is a form of non-monogamy and is an open relationship. Monogamy is marriage with only one person at a time; the practice of having only one mate; the practice of marrying only once during life. Non-monogamy is a marriage of more than one person. Even as this is huge in political, business, and entertainment arenas, swinging has crept in the church. Well, maybe it has not crept in but has always been there and now has become more blatant and glamorized. The believers are partner swapping and even creating connections and secret clubs within the church and body of Christ so they can engage in swinging perversions. When believers have no regard for the covenant of marriage, it weakens the fruit and witness of what it means as believers to be the bride of Christ. It is impossible to minister something you are profaning from. Often these types of behaviors begin in with lust and from past sins of perversion that have not been purged

and sanctified from the heart, mind, and soul, of a person. They then begin to entertain ways to get these needs met inside the marriage bed, while convincing, manipulating, or intimidating, their partners to be a part of their perverse ways. Or they marry a partner who has open doors of perversion, and they use these propensities, to get their spouse to compromise and yield to sneak freaky, lustful perversions.

The spirits behind these types of activities do not play fair. They come to steal, kill, and destroy those involved, their marriages, and the honor of marriage. People come seeking deliverance because their spouse is not in lust – not love – with mates they are swapping with, or who are soul tied to same-sex partners and desires because of swinging. The spirits intertwined in these acts, visit the willing parties upon their beds and have sex with them. Some of these people would rather have sex with the demons that visit them than their marriage partners. They are being gratified through perverse acts, thus normal sexual proper interactions are no longer pleasing to them. I could go on and on but I will digress. The perversions in this chapter are serious and sanctification is key to being delivered from them.

Bigamy – According to law, this is the crime of marrying while one has a spouse still living, from whom no valid divorce has been effected. *Ecclesiastically* bigamy is any violation of canon law concerning marital status that would disqualify a person from receiving holy orders or from retaining or surpassing an ecclesiastical rank.

Polygamy - The practice or condition of having more than one spouse, especially a wife, at one time; *Zoology* defines polygamy as the habit or system of mating with more than one individual, either simultaneously or successively.

Open Marriage - An intimate relationship that is sexually non-monogamous. The term is distinct from polyamory, in that it generally indicates a relationship where there is a primary emotional and intimate relationship between two partners, who agree to at least the possibility of sexual intimacy with other people. Open relationships include any type of romantic relationship (dating, marriage, etc.) that is open. An "open" relationship is where one or more parties have permission to be romantically or sexually involved with people outside of the relationship. This is opposed to the traditionally "closed" relationship, where both parties agree on being with one another exclusively.

Cuffing - This occurs generally in late fall, early winter, is when singles, who were happy dating around in the summer, start looking for a special person to settle down with for the colder months. Some of these relationships last only for the winter while others can lead to longer-term relationships. The focus of cuffing is more to fulfill a void for love and belonging during these seasons, more so than really being focused on finding someone to do life and destiny with. The relationships tend to be birthed out of convenience and opportunity.

Polyamorous - Noting or relating to polyamory, the practice or condition of participating simultaneously in more than one serious romantic or sexual relationship with the knowledge and consent of all partners.

Homosexuality - The sexual desire or behavior directed toward people of one's own sex or gender.

Lesbianism - Female sexual desire or behavior directed toward people of the same sex or gender; gay female sexual orientation.

Bisexual - Noting or relating to a person who is sexually or romantically attracted to people of two or more genders.

Transgender – A person whose sense of personal identity and gender does not correspond with their birth sex.

Queer – An umbrella or slang term used to define a specific community of people, that differ in some way in their sexual orientation from what is usual or normal.

Questioning – A person that is unsure and is questioning their sexual orientation or desires.

Gender Neutral – Not referring to either sex or wanting to be identified self or others by either sex, but only be viewed or to define people in general gender-neutral language or with no gender.

Genesis 5:2 *Male and female created he them; and blessed them, and called their name Adam, in the day when they were created.*

Mark 10:6 But from the beginning of the creation God made them male and female.

Though people have surgeries and strive to change or deny their identity based on how they feel or what they believe about their gender and sexual orientation, genetically, there is no way to change the essence – foundation – of who God created us to be. At our core, we are still the gender God created us to be whether we acknowledge it or not. God distinctly created us male or female for a specific reason that is unique to our disposition, purpose, and destiny. Contrary to what we may feel or think about ourselves, God does not make mistakes regarding how and who he created us to be. When we reject, deny, or alter our gender, we deny the true and unique identity to which God created us.

In order to reject, deny, or alter our gender, we have to give a false or distorted reality of ourselves that is rooted in our own thoughts and feelings. Though our thoughts and feelings are important, God never meant for us to live or operate by our thoughts and feelings. We are spiritual beings and are to live through our spiritual nature. Our thoughts and feelings are gages. They help us to gauge where we are in life and give us insight into what we need to examine with God. We can talk and walk it out with him, receive truth, be restored in the revelation of that truth, so we can gain the insights that deliver, heal, realign us in the divine likeness, order, and spiritual wellness with him.

It is important to be sensitive to how people think and feels and the very real challenges they are having concerning their sexual and gender orientation.

Proverbs 4:7 *Wisdom is the principal thing; therefore get wisdom: and with all thy getting get understanding.*

<u>Wisdom</u> in Hebrew is *ḥakemā* and means:
1. Wisdom (in a good sense): — skillful, wisdom, wisely, wit
2. Wisdom - skill (in war)
3. Wisdom (in administration)
4. Shrewdness, wisdom
5. Wisdom, prudence (in religious affairs)
6. Wisdom (ethical and religious)

It is essential to understand that when dealing with these issues, we are in a war for someone's soul. It takes wisdom to war effectively. We need to use good sense, skill, strategy, ethical and integral tactics, witty ideas, and sound religious doctrines and affairs to win to effectively evangelize, save, and disciple the person. Slinging bible scriptures at people and admonishing them pushes them away from God rather than to him. Every situation and person is different and needs divine intervention based on the strategy and revelation God provides. Often people will need to enter into a counseling process to explore their thoughts and feelings, and root issues regarding homosexuality, lesbianism, queer, questioning, transgender, and gender neutrality. A process of counseling will aid them in identifying where their thoughts and feelings manifested from, resolving any root issues, misperceptions, and ideologies, surrounding how they think or feel, learning how to examine and receive truth from God, and learning how to live the truth of who he has created them to be and what he is saying for their lives. Through this process, any demonic influences or strongholds can be addressed and cast out. Often believers initially try to make this a demonic issue without dealing with the dynamics, circumstances, thoughts, and feelings, surrounding these challenges. Doing this many times cause identity damage, soul wound trauma, and reproach concerning God, his biblical principles, and the body of Christ.

<u>*Downlow*</u> – Though women can be engaged in this sexual practice, downlow defines or pertains to men who secretly or discreetly have sex with other men. Sometimes these men are married with children. They live one life by day and entire life in private. Oftentimes their spouse and family do not know. Their downlow activity is covered up

with lies and leisure activities that are disguised as innocent but are really partners that they are sleeping with. Downlow activity has become common in the Christian community and among fraternities. Many women have been crushed when finding out the secret lives of their husbands. Some women know their spouses are on downlow. They may protect their men and cover their secret lifestyle. Many men tend to waver from being prideful and uncaring in how their actions affect their spouses and families or devastated by their secret being uncovered. Some men contend they are not homosexual or bisexual, and justify their actions as recreational sex. They dread being labeled and shamed and live in a false reality regarding their desires and the stigmas that are attached to their lifestyle. Many downlow men will not wear protection which causes them to infect their spouses with STDs. Many of them believe that wearing protection is an acknowledgment that they are gay and they contend they are not – that their actions are recreational sex.

Women tend to engage in downlow sexual acts with their close friends or other women who show them love, belonging, and companionship. There are also those women who are afraid to admit their same-sex desires so they will have secret relationships with other women.

Meet-up sex apps allow both men and women to engage in downlow behaviors. These people sometimes have fake profiles on these meet-up apps and will meet in parks, alleys, restaurants, hotels, etc. for sex. Such apps can be dangerous as sometimes people are raped, robbed, murdered, and blackmailed by those they meet up with.

Masochism - The condition in which sexual gratification depends on suffering physical pain or humiliation.

Bestiality - The brutish or beastly character or behavior; beastliness; indulgence in beastlike appetites, instincts, impulses, etc.; an instance of bestial character or behavior; sexual relations between a person and an animal; sodomy.

Inordinacy - Not within proper or reasonable limits; immoderate; excessive, unrestrained in conduct, feelings, etc.; disorderly; uncontrolled; not regulated; irregular; to have inordinate affection, lust.

Sexual Voyeurism – Engaging in sexual acts without the consent of the person being observed.

Effeminacy - Means of a man or boy; having traits, tastes, habits, etc., traditionally considered feminine, as softness or delicacy; characterized by excessive softness, delicacy, self-indulgence, etc.

Pornography - sexually explicit videos, photographs, writings, or the like, whose purpose is to elicit sexual arousal. With the rise of social media and internet postings, reels, and branding, pornography has become an issue for all of us. We are inundated with posts, videos, pictures, of half or mostly naked people, couples, children. It has become the norm to show cleavage, imprints of one body shape and private parts; to be gyrating, twerking, bootie shaking, and engaging in sexual dances, movements, impressions, scenarios, and acts, for likes, branding, popularity, money, success, expansion, pleasure, fun, attention, and culture relevance. Personal and business postings and media dialog include sexual insights and jargon for shock value and to draw interest. Even the people of God post sexual content and have sexual dialog and claim it is being human and being real. Married people are sharing pictures, videos, information, and conversations regarding their marriage bed and then telling folks, even the singles that if they do not like it, they can unfriendly them or that they are being too holy as what they are doing is okay because they are married. There is no regard for the fact that singles and struggling people have no idea what will be on their social media pages when they open it, and that a person's post, picture, video, maybe in eye view before that person has a chance to decide if they should unfriend or not. There is no regard for being mindful of the soul and struggle of others or being mindful of how one's actions impact another person.

Mark 9:42 *And whosoever shall offend one of these little ones that believe in me, it is better for him that a millstone were hanged about his neck, and he were cast into the sea.*

Romans 14:13 *Let us not therefore judge one another any more: but judge this rather, that no man put a stumblingblock or an occasion to fall in his brother's way.*

ICorinthians 8:9 *But take heed lest by any means this liberty of yours become a stumblingblock to them that are weak.*

Stumblingblock is *proskomma* in Greek and means:
1. A stub, i.e. (figuratively) occasion of apostasy
2. Offense, stumbling(-block, (-stone)
3. An obstacle in the way which if one strikes his foot against he stumbles or falls that over which a soul stumbles
4. I.e. by which is caused to sin

We would like to believe in our own false ideology that we are not responsible for how our posts, photos, videos, conversations, impact others, but that is an error. We are indeed responsible, not just to those watching or engaged with us, but to God. We are responsible for how to represent God and for how we demonstrate that we are set apart from him.

Pornography is a perverse stronghold that can sometimes take years to be delivered from. There are people who spend hours, days in the back room watching porn. There are wives that cannot get their husbands to come to bed because they are in their man caves masturbating to porn and the demons attached to them. There are grown men and women who were exposed to porn magazines and videos as little children that are now entangled in all types of perverse bondages. There are women, men, children, being exploited right now as you read this so that some addicted person can feed their porn portal. I often tell the women in my ministry to be careful of what pictures they put up online. They are just trying to be sexy and relevant with the times, but some people are taking even the innocent of pictures of them, other women, and children, and using them for perverse purposes.

Some of these people are using pictures and the like in sex magic rituals. This is where they cast spells over your picture to send sexual energy to the person on the picture. As the person becomes aroused by the energy that was sent to them, and starts to yield to masturbation, sexual dreams, and the like, the person astral projects themselves into that person's consciousness and/or dream realm and begins to have sexual encounters with them. Many people will come for deliverance for this. They will contend it is water spirits of incubus and succubus spirits having sex with them. But sometimes it is not these spirits but actual people astral projecting their souls into spiritual realms and laying upon them. These types of acts do have demonic ramifications as that person could be attached to perverse spirits or predator spirits. So that open portal is known as a gateway for demons to visit the person and have sex with them. These demons claim ownership of the person and begin to block their ability to have potential mates in real life; to get married, and even cause affliction to reproductive and sexual organs to cause health and fertility problems.

Proverbs 6:25 Do not desire her beauty in your heart, Nor let her capture you with her eyelids.

Proverbs 23:26 My son, give me your heart and let your eyes delight in my ways.

<u>Masturbation</u> - The stimulation or manipulation of one's own genitals, especially to orgasm; sexual self-gratification; the stimulation, by manual or other means exclusive of sexual intercourse, of another's genitals, especially to orgasm.

1Corinthians 6:18 Flee sexual immorality. Every sin that a man does is outside the body, but he who commits sexual immorality sins against his own body.

Masturbation tends to be a sexual act that opens the door to greater sexual bondage and gratifications of the lust of the flesh. Once the person yield's to masturbation, it becomes their master. It baits the person into being focused on fulfilling the lust of the flesh and feeding one's eye and heart gates excessively as they succumb to its mastery. Some people masturbate when they are stressed, anxious, overwhelmed, and have pint up emotions. What starts out as a desire to have a release, can results in bondage to perversion.

Often people are using imagery of past experiences, present fantasies and desires, magazine and book images and stories, TV and movie shows, songs, and audio recordings; and just fleeting lustful thoughts and impressions that come to them through vain imaginations. As time pass, demonic spirits can enter a person's life and be lodged in the mind, memory recalls, consciousness; in their heart, on their hands and private parts, etc. Many people increase with dreams where they are masturbating or where a demonic spirit is masturbating and having sex with them. This spirit can be lodged in regions of their body and manifest while they are sleeping or it can come upon them at night through open portals of masturbation or via the dream realm.

Some people can become so addicted to masturbation that they engage in this behavior all through the day. Many take to private areas in public settings just to get a release. Some start to engage in pornography to heighten their orgasmic experience. The perversion can even have them masturbating to kid pornography, same-sex pornography, rape scenes, and on and on. Remember perversion just breeds on itself. Perversion has no endpoint. It is a hole that has no bottom. It intends to bury you in its bondage. Some people become so filled with shame, guilt, and condemnation regarding masturbation, that they start to experience sicknesses and illnesses. They begin to let themselves go and have no regard for their appearance. The shame causes them to experience low self-esteem and self-hatred. They may also become isolated and self-rejecting even though others are seeking to draw them into relationships and interaction. This is part of how the spirit of masturbation works. It wants to seclude the person and bind them to more sexual perversion and secret bondage.

<u>Oral Sex</u> - Sexual contact between the mouth and the genitals or anus; fellatio, cunnilingus, or anilingus. Oral sex has become popular among teenagers. They have all types of meet-ups in and around their schools, communities, etc., for the purposes of engaging in oral sex. Young boys pressure females into having oral sex and make them think oral sex is not actual sex. They seduce them into thinking oral sex is popular – everyone is doing it – and engaging in oral sex makes them cool. They are viewed as lame if they do not yield to these requests. Some guys tape the girl performing oral sex on them and then share it with their friends. When they want to shame a girl, they will share the video with everyone in school and even on the internet. So many girls have had their reputations ruined by these acts.

Oral sex is also popular in college and among young and middle-age adults. People drag about giving and receiving oral sex with no regard to health risks or the fact that it is still sex. Even rated PG movies and TV shows have sex scenes that yield inferences to oral sex and present it as an option or foreplay to intercourse. Music reference these acts with such perverse and seduce rhymes and rhythms. Believers engage in oral sex and heavy sexual touching as an alternative to not having sexual intercourse. They do not view this as sex or view it as a lesser sin when truthfully there is no such thing. All sin is a sin to God. Some people – believers and nonbelievers - will have friends and acquaintances whom they engage in casual oral sex with. These partners may be same-sex or opposite sex. In their own learned thinking, this is just for sexual gratification and so the gender or sex act does not matter. Some people have forced oral sex on people and then contend it is not rape. But anytime a person is not in agreement with being touched in a lustful or sexual way, it is a violation and thus is rape.

It is not uncommon to conduct deliverance ministry on people and be led to cast spirits out of the mouth, throat, respiratory system, and stomach.

Anal Sex - The acts of inserting a penis, finger, hand, tongue (or licking which is called rimming), objects in the anis for sexual gratification.

Phone Sex - Sexually explicit telephone conversation engaged in for the purposes of sexual gratification,

Sexting - To engage in the sending of sexually explicit text messages or pictures for the purposes of sexual gratification. Many teenagers and young adults engage in sexting and many forward sex messages to others without the consent of the person they were initially sexting. When starts off as fun, relationship building, and sexual exploration, can quickly become betrayal, scandal, bullying, desecration of character, and in some cases a crime. It is important to teach teens confidence, self-worth, the power of virtue and purity so that they will reject engaging in sexting. Once images are released to others, it is difficult to recover them.

Catfishing – Stealing and using someone else's identity to befriend someone online and start a relationship with them. These relationships result in people engaging in phone sex and sexting, which causes them to develop a soul tie to the person while falling in lust with the person they are being deceived into believing they are talking to. When the truth is exposed, most of the victims are traumatized due to the deception.

Internet, Virtual, & Gaming Sex - Going on websites, apps, groups, social media platforms and engaging in any type of sexual pleasure. This can become very addicting and hard to break free from.

Fetish- An object regarded with awe as being the embodiment or habitation of a potent spirit or as having magical potency; any object, idea, etc., eliciting unquestioning reverence, respect, or devotion; *Psychology*. any object or non-genital part of the body that causes a habitual erotic response or fixation.

People have some wild fetishes. The grown people will be wearing diapers. People will be wanting to lick stranger's toes. People will be peeping in people's windows and even breaking into their homes to steal intimate apparel such as panties, bras, etc. People will carry dolls around and treat them like real babies. People will have an elation to clothing and lifestyles of the opposite sex and will secret or even public lives dressed as the opposite sex even though they do not consider themselves attracted to that gender. People will have fetishes to sadistic sexual practices. I could go on and on but I digress. If the Holy Spirit leads you to ask about fetishes, trust him. People are soul-tied to these items. Therefore they are an open door to them being stronghold by perverse demons. These fetishes are usually the result of an underlying issue so ask about root issues as fetish acts are revealed during deliverance.

<u>*Obsession*</u> – The domination or preoccupation of one's thoughts or feelings, by a persistent idea, image, desire, etc.; beset, trouble, or haunt persistently or abnormally: to think about something unceasingly or persistently; dwell obsessively upon something. Many people with sexual addictions and perversions will have obsessions with certain items, behaviors, and desires. They will be plagued with thoughts and feelings surrounding them and will display anxiety, panic, and addictive-like behaviors as it relates to their obsession. They may need processing of counseling and deliverance before SHIFTING into healing as requiring them to give up an obsession abruptly or without a strategy and dealing with root issues can cause relapse. It can also cause them to increase in pursuing their obsession where the stronghold strengthens in their lives.

<u>*Sex Toys & Sex Stores*</u> - As not to trigger anyone, I will not list various toys and the like. I will state that utilizing sexual toys and going to sex stores comes under inordinacy and perverse acts. I want to share this because having sex toys and lingerie parties have become the norm, even among believers. However, these types of items and acts open the doors to perverse spirits, sexual dreams, demons, and astral projectors laying upon a person at night and having sexual relations with them. It also feeds the flesh and causes it to crave more kinky and even sadistic perversion and even become addicted to perverse acts where they cannot enjoy sex without these items, or they are addicted to sex itself and cannot have a relationship or interaction without desiring or having sex. This can cause many marriages to end in divorce, especially when one spouse is uncomfortable with such acts and the other one is demanding it or decides to fulfill these needs outside of the marriage.

Some people will become so addicted to sex toys that they desire these items over their mates. This is because of the cravings of the flesh and how they have fed it and now it wants what it wants. It is also because demons can attach to these items or oppress the mind, heart, and soul, of a person and cause an addiction to it. The person is drawn to be gratified by the item rather than normal sexual encounters.

Rape - The unlawful sexual intercourse or any other sexual penetration of the vagina, anus, or mouth of another person, with or without force, by a sex organ, other body parts, or foreign object, without the consent of the victim; statutory rape; an act of plunder, violent seizure, or abuse; despoliation; violation.

Incest - Sexual intercourse between closely related persons; the crime of sexual intercourse, cohabitation, or marriage between persons within the degrees of consanguinity or affinity wherein marriage is legally forbidden.

Molestation - An act or instance of interference with or violence against someone; sexual assault or indecent advances.

When a person is raped, molested, or drawn into incest, seeds, traits, and demonic spirits may transfer to their victim. The victim may have a difficult time healing from their experience because of what has been transferred into them and what has become part of their personality. They may not rape or molest anyone, but they may become lustful, promiscuous, addicted, or drawn to perverse acts and sneaking thrill-seeking encounters. They may date or have relationships with several partners at one time, have a difficult time being loyal in relationships, prey on people's hearts with no true desire or ability to commit or govern their hearts. Some of them will brag about how they broke people's hearts or took advantage of them; this is because the traits and possibly even the demonic spirits of the offender have become part of their personality. These traits have to be cleaned out through the blood of Jesus and demonic spirits have to be bound and cast out so that people can be free from these behavior acts and personality traits. And so they can truly heal and be free from the trauma of their experience.

Child's Sexual Play – This is when children are engaging in playful activities that result in them touching one another and mimicking sexual acts that they have to see others do, seen on TV, or picked up through music. Some of these children have been sexually molested and mimic with other children what is occurring to them. They may not necessarily be striving to be an offender, more so than mimicking what has happened to them or what they have been exposed to. I wanted to state this because many people will share these occurrences with leaders, ministers, altar, and deliverance workers. Some of them may have never told anyone before. Some of them may have been willing participants or even the initiators. Many of them are not like an offender who intentionally desires or pursues sexual acts with children or who grows up and becomes an offender of children. Yet, because society has generalized this area, people fear sharing because they do not want to be labeled as a molester or pedophiles. Or they do not want to be shamed and ruined for acts that occurred in their childhood that are not a matter of fact as someone who blatantly molests and preys on children.

There are children that are exposed to child sexual play and as they grow as children and teenagers, intentionally molest other children. Some of these children have been raped and molested and some of them have been exposed to sexual content and behavior that their minds and intellect are not ready for. They become twisted and perverted in their identity and take on the seeds, behaviors, and demonic spirits that have been transferred to them by their predator. People will have their children listening and dancing to pervert music, watching TV shows with sex acts, exposed to same-sex relationships and interactions, sleeping in the bed and room with them while they are having sex, and think the children are not impacted. People will prostitute their children, leave them with perverted family members and friends, put their children in situations where they have to prostitute themselves to survive, etc. Children are impressionable. Also, a lot of these sexual innuendoes have sexual witchcraft spells and idolatry tied to them, and there are always monitoring spirits and familiar spirits lurking, seeking an entryway into children's lives. What may seem funny or necessary as that child encounters it, is not funny or necessary when they are in an unsupervised room with other children. Or when those thoughts, desires, or demonic spirit begins to incite them and they begin to secretly engage unsupervised children in sexual acts. It will be important to create a safe environment for people to share these acts in counseling and deliverance so they and their family line can be free of the traumas, demonic influences, shame, guilt, and condemnation surrounding these experiences.

If you are not a skilled mental health professional (counselor, social worker, psychotherapist, psychiatrist, etc.) that has expertise regarding dealing with rape, incest, and molestation cases, I suggest seeking such professions when the victim desires to pursue charges and/or confront their violator. Such persons will be able to assist the victim with examining their rights and connect them to law enforcement and legal assistance as necessary. It will be important to remain in your zone as a minister and support rather than becoming an investigator, lawyer, judge, counselor, social worker, etc., as doing so without expertise may cause conflict, reproach, scandal, further violation, and trauma, while putting the victim and yourself in challenging and dangerous situations.

Many people have left the church due to being violated by leaders and church members and having saints protect and cover the leader rather than handing the situation over to a professional who can pursue truth in an unbiased manner. Victims are often violated all over again by saints who should be protecting them, supporting them, and aiding them in pursuing justice and wellness regarding what happened to them. This is the reason I suggest involving mental health practitioners who can properly assist, while the delivery worker remains to support an avenue for process, healing, and wellness.

<u>*Spirit Spouse/Spiritual Marriages*</u> - We are the bride of Christ to God and even then this is not a natural marriage, sexual or perverse interaction, but a spiritual marriage where

we have been saved through the works of the cross and have been restored in a covenant marriage with Christ Jesus.

- **Incubus** is a male demon that lies upon sleeping women and attacks them sexually.
- **Succubus** is a female demon that lies upon a sleeping man and attacks them sexually.

Embracing sex with demons is not of God. It is inordinacy, corrupt, unclean, perverse.

Explicit Sex Acts - (According to https://itlaw.fandom.com/wiki/Sexually_explicit) The Federal Trade Commission has defined sexually explicit content in connection with virtual worlds as depictions or descriptions of:

1. Sexual references
2. Full or partial nudity, including depictions of uncovered female breasts, aroused or unaroused male or female genitalia, and unrealistic or overly detailed genitalia
3. Bestiality
4. Sexual acts to or with minors (anyone under the age of 18)
5. Sexual acts include, but are not limited to, penetration/intercourse, and/or oral sex with or without another avatar or any other object, including overt sexual toys and/or sexual aids; or sexual behavior that has a violent context
6. Pictorial depiction of actual or simulated sexual acts including sexual intercourse, oral sex, or masturbation

Prostitution - The act or practice of engaging in sexual intercourse for money.

Brothels - A house of prostitution; whore-house, brothel harlot, a person can be deemed as worthless and used for prostitution; a person may also choose to work in a whorehouse for financial means or gain.

Sexual Trafficking – The action or practice of illegally transporting people from one country or area to another for the purpose of sexual exploitation.

Witchcraft Sex Trafficking - Witches, warlocks, inordinate people, using powerful potions, spells, sex magic, drugs, violence, to control, intimidate, entice, rape, molest, violate a person in a sexual manner. This can be done in actual sex trafficking acts and arenas where they utilize witchcraft practices to subdue, control, and intimidate their victim into being submissive and compliant to being trafficked.

Witchcraft sex trafficking can also be done through astral projection where these persons astral project their souls into spiritual realms, and engage in sexual acts with people as they sleep. They use demon spirits to manipulate the dream realm and use the dream sphere to engage in sexual acts with people or inject sexual desires, enticements, or inferences for the purposes of manipulating people's desires, and ability to live a pure life.

Sex Magic - Spells or rituals used to keep a person under the practitioner's control through sexual relations, incantations, opening portals and gateways, and then attacking through the dream realm and astral projection activity.

Those who experience sex magic will have apparitions that look like the person they had an emotional or sexual relationship with. These apparitions will be actual demons, the soul of that person that has astral projected in their mix, or hypnotic spells sent to draw the person into a sexual encounter with what they believe is the person. As the person submits their body and imagination to the apparition, it gives way for the sex magic to work on them, thus opening a gateway for sexual encounters between them and the person that sent the sex magic spells to occur through the third eye of the victim's consciousness.

In conducting deliverance I have learned via Holy Spirit that there are witchcraft rituals where they send sexual energy to you and when you act on it with thoughts, sex acts and the like it puts the energy inside you and soul tie you to that person and demon that did the ritual on you.

People also sit and meditate on doing sex acts with a person and or actually engage in these acts while thinking about the person and sending energy this way. If the person surrenders to the arousing lust, dream acts, and the like, it can connect the person to the practitioner and the demons they are using and put energy in their body that makes them lust and want to have sex with that person. The practitioner can then open portals through sex magic where they astral Projection into the person's dreams and night season and have sex with them. The person thinks they just have a dream and they having sex with that person's soul through that demon.

SPIRITS THAT ATTACK MINISTERS

From my book entitled, *"Unmasking The Power Of The Scouts, Volume I: Gaining Intel For Victory Over Your Opposition."*

There are times I am ministering and am being attacked to the point where I will stop and pray out loud against the spirit that is attacking me. In other situations, I will call on my armorbearer to pray. My overseer sometimes has her armorbearer walking back and forth behind her interceding as she preaches to help fortify her from attacks.

Many ministers may have experienced these spirits but may not know what they were. That is because many of us expect and accept warfare as we preach or **some of us believe these experiences are our own inadequacies or mishaps rather than demonic interference at work.** I aim to expose these demons so they can be thwarted in the life of ministers. I decree that as you study this list, God will enable you to scout the spirit realm further such that you identify, expose, and cast out these demons that attack ministers.

Zapping Spirit - Strikes or jolts, revelations, and downloads that the minister received from God. One minute they have the information and the next minute it is gone; it's suddenly depleted.

Blocking Spirit - Places a barrier in the spirit realm between the minister and God to block them from receiving fresh revelation and downloads as they minister. Spirit operates like an erected wall upon the brain, skull, imagination, or in the spirit realm to hinder and stifle revelation and communication between the minister and God.

Mind-Binding Spirit - Binds the mind to prevent the minister's brain from regurgitating and releasing the information where it can be understood. May cause confusion, cloudiness, disconcertedness. Sits upon the head and wraps around the head and presses then into the forehead, sides of the head, back of the head, and sometimes the neck; can also sit upon, wrap-around, and press into the brain.

Mind-Blinding Spirit - Spirit blinds - covers - the spiritual and physical eyes, understanding, temples, and imagination of the minister to prevent them from seeing the revelation, seeing the vision, seeing what God is saying. The minister may experience blurred vision or literally blinding. They may have trouble reading their notes, their bible, or the screen as they minister. This is sometimes the reason ministers use readers.

A minister's own anxiety, stress, and pressure they have put upon themselves can bewitch them and causes the mind-binding and mind-blinding spirit to operate and attack them. Those who battle a spirit of perfectionism may experience this as perfectionism causes one to operate in their own strength rather than the strength and excellence of the Lord.

Mind-Controlling Spirit - Minister feels as if they are being controlled, manipulated, discombobulated, or maneuvered; may feel mental pain, pressure, a pressing down upon and around the head, or experience a headache. This spirit may operate like an octopus or squid having tentacles that may press around the head, eyes, ears, temples, neck, and shoulders of the minister. They may have a difficult time focusing, remaining on, or finishing a thought or subject; they may even babble or stutter.

Telepathy - Minister may feel as if they are receiving signals, impressions, or pressure from an unseen force.

Perversion & Lust - The minister may experience perverted and lustful thoughts, images, and feelings, before, during, or after ministry. This can be a demonic attack, witchcraft attack or they can be picking up on the sins of the people, ministry, or region; or the minister has a common sin issue as those he or she is ministering to. Some ministers may become explicit or carnal as they preach, especially if they have a sin issue; they are drawn into making comments that reflect what they are experiencing. Some ministers may be so appalled by what they are experiencing, they may have a difficult time ministering or they may minister a very strong rebuking word.

Twisted Thinking & Error - These spirits cause ministers to twist ideology, misquote God and scripture, use scriptures and concepts out of context; the minister is more focused on building their case and sounding good than being biblically grounded.

Spirit of Pride - The minister may yield to haughtiness and self-righteousness, minister more about self without relevance than about God; minister with high self-importance that comes across as vain, boasting about self rather than glorifying God. Often you can tell this is an attack when it is not the normal character or nature of the minister.

Spirit of Heaviness, Sullenness & Depression - The minister may feel oppressed or depressed with an ungodly weightiness, sadness, may desire to cry for no reason, may be baffled with different emotions, or sense of grief. They May feel bogged down and like something is sitting on them. May have a difficult time praising, worshipping, and exalting Jesus.

Spirit of Fear, Panic, & Anxiety - You probably have watched a preacher experience these spirits and not even know it. You thought they were rambling, sweating, turning red, pulling on their tie, unbuttoning and taking off clothes, was them being hot from that fiery preaching. Sometimes this is the case and other times a preacher may be battling these spirits. They may display uncontrollable profusion, shaking, or panic. They may have moments where they are starring off in space or at their notes while trying to gather themselves. Some ministers may experience internal anxiety, apprehension, panic around the heart, rapid heartbeat, thought racing, nausea, or urge to go to the restroom.

Spirit of Mockery & Insecurity - This spirit taunts the minister before, during, and after they are preaching. It makes them feel inadequate like the people are laughing at them or not listening to them, like what they are ministering is insignificant. It will have them questioning God and themselves. The minister will hear this spirit literally laughing, throwing shade, belittling them. Sometimes the minister will see this spirit working through people in the audience. They will see this sport use people to laugh at them, taunting them, making fun of them as they minister.

Spirit of Religion and Tradition - These spirits operate through suffocation to snuff out the Holy Spirit, glory, and presence of God from operating upon and through the minister. The minister may feel a literal strangulation or suffocation, may feel like his or her throat or respiratory system is shutting down, may start coughing, gagging, having trouble breathing. Religion will erect like a fog, dark blanket type cloud or wall and clog up the heavenliness over a service. It will weigh down heavily on the people, separate them from the preacher and the preached word, and cause them to become mute or dead and dumb. They will stop agreeing with the word as they go into a stupor-type state. It will close the people off from experiencing the full effect of God's plan through that word. It will be as if they are a movie as they are disconnected from what is being released. They may also appear in awe of some of the revelation and signs that manifest through the minister, but nothing will be planted in their spirits as they are disconnected. The ministry will not manifest change or transformation in the lives of the people, the church, and/or the atmosphere because there is a barrier between them and what is going forth.

Tradition will feel like a barricade of resistance which usually presents itself as control, judgment, or refusal to receive. Tradition can be unassuming at first as it tends to be an invisible erected barrier, but the minister will feel it coming to the forefront the minute it challenges a tradition within the people, ministry, or region. Often tradition hits back by trying to bind, shutdown, or suffocate the minister physically and spiritually. It will also release energies of intimidation and control to coward the minister to back off the subject where its high places can remain in tack.

Witchcraft - Hexes, vexes, spells, hoodoo, voodoo, charms, bewitching slander, etc., sent to influence, bind, distract, or stifle the minister in effectively preaching the word of God.

Fiery Darts - Inflamed angry, grievous, lustful, venomous word curses coming from demons, witches, warlocks, wicked people, and ignorant people. May will physically feel like a demonic angry fire or burning sensation. (Quench these word curses).

Friendly Fire - Darts coming from past and present friends and acquaintances who are speaking - releasing ill words against the minister.

Sickness - Afflictions, and infirmities sent to bind and distract the minister with physical ailments. Headaches, stomach aches, nausea, respiratory and sinus issues, heart issues, blood pressure issues, pains in the back, neck, feet, knees, temple, hips, are common attacks ministers experience when preaching the gospel. Some of this is due to witchcraft being sent to afflict certain areas. Demons are also sent to oppress these areas.

Tracking Spirits – These are demonic agents who are assigned to gather intel on a minister and then report it back to their demonic camp. They track ministers by their smell, footprints, voice, fliers, and any other means. They will track the minister from place to place as they move about everyday life, through computer systems and other computerized intel, etc. They will even track you to church and ministry events. They lurk around–eavesdropping on prayers and conversations, to acquire information about the minister then report back so that demonic assignments can be released against them. Sometimes these spirits can be sensed or felt while they follow a person. You know those times it feels like something is following you. It is probably a tracker. They tend to live on the airways, so they rarely will use a body. Although they will oppress people in the minister's inner circle and track them that way. Or they will follow people in the minister's inner circle and track them. Psychics, high priests work with these spirits to track clients and gather intel, so they can have information to share when the person comes for their session. It appears as if the psychic possesses information that only someone in one's private life could have known. They do because the demon tracked the person.

Watcher Spirits - Are spirits that are sent to spy on you after the tracker spirit has shared information on you with his demonic camp. Watchers report on your progress so that further demonic assignments can be released against you. Watcher spirits will even travel to different places as you travel or send messages to other regions that you are coming, share the intel regarding you, so that the demons in that region can be aware of what you will be doing, and can find a way to counterattack your productivity and progress; especially if you are trying to save souls for Jesus. In the past, I use to see these spirits traveling by the airplane when I am going out of town to do ministry. I have learned to pray to cancel their assignments, so they do not track me. Many people share all kinds of personal information on your social media pages. Watcher spirits are sharing that information with the demonic camp. The enemy knew where and how to attack the person because it is on their Facebook page. In the spirit realm, the devil has a demonic library where he keeps files, especially of people who have great callings on their lives. I have seen these libraries and some of these files. Also, the systems of this world, ignorantly help these spirits to collect and maintain information on us. We are constantly being asked for our updated email address, cellphone numbers, etc., when we go in stores or when conducting business transactions.

Scanner Spirits – Use electronics like computers, phones, cameras, to track and gain intel on a minister. They operate as spies that travel throughout areas and regions and transport information to different demonic camps and demonic rankings. They inspect, observe, and survey their enemy or territory for exploitation and military purposes.

Eavesdropping Spirits – Similar to watcher spirits, these demons lurk around eavesdropping on the minister's life, conversations, loved ones, and friends, to gain intel that can be used for demonic attacks. Often these spirits will acquire personal information and then use it to infiltrate a minister's life to gain further personal insight and even to stage a personal attack. It is nothing like being attacked by someone close to a person. Eavesdropping spirits are good for gaining the heart and favor of a minister through personal intel, then causing drama, betrayal, and heartbreak.

Demonic Agents – Are gang or police-type spirits that are sent to intimidate, attack, or seize a minister where they fear or are unable to minister. These spirits love to attack through the dream realm or at night. Sometimes they are in black clothing or maybe dressed similarly like a gang or officers. They tend to surround or corner the person in a dream or within the spirit realm then attack. Sometimes these spirits operate at crosswords on highways or roads. They may operate through police officers or those superior in ministry, community, or business in an effort to intimidate, control, or seize a minister. They like to back ministers in a corner where they will make decisions that usually are outside of the perfect will of God.

SPIRITS THAT ATTACKS VISIONS, TEAMS, & EVENT PLANNING

Some of this information is from my book entitled, *"Spirits That Attack Dancers & Dance Ministries."*

The Lord has revealed these spirits to me over the years while working with team members and preparing for different events in ministry, business, communities, and regions. We experienced a lot of warfare and were able to discern what spirits were attacking us personally, the atmosphere, business endeavors, ministry, and events we were striving to birth forth. After learning how these demonic spirits operate, we were able to be offensive and counterattack to lesson and even thwart warfare before it occurs.

<u>*Deaf and Dumb Spirit*</u> - Inability or challenge to hear or comprehend, instructions regarding the vision, planning, and production of the event. The person will hear God or instructions from leaders, partners, and team members, but there will be a disconnect in their ability to actually comprehend, understand it, and then produce what is being required.

The person being attacked by the deaf and dumb spirit:
- Will at times have a confused and puzzled look on their face. They may also look as though they are not there and are spaced out.
- Will become easily frustrated with themselves because they can hear what is being said or done, but they cannot understand it, and cannot get their mind, emotions, and actions to respond or follow through with what is being required of them.
- Will need things repeated and shown to them over and over, and will be very forgetful.
- When asked questions, they will be confused and unable to answer effectively.
- They may be able to work sufficiently as long as someone is working with them, but when working alone or given an independent task, they will not be able to produce because no true comprehension or understanding took place when being taught or provided instructions.
- They will have insight from God but will not be able to write it down, speak it, understand it, or follow through with it.
- They will have the feeling of "awe man it is right there" but have no ability to grasp it.

   Isaiah 6:9 And he said, Go, and tell this people, Hear ye indeed, but understand not; and see ye indeed, but perceive not.

Mark 4:12 That seeing they may see, and not perceive; and hearing they may hear, and not understand; lest at any time they should be converted, and their sins should be forgiven them.

Zapping Spirit - Steals information by jolting them out of the memory of the brain such that the brain cannot recall what has been downloaded.

<u>Zap in Dictionary.com means:</u>
1. To kill or shoot
2. To attack, defeat, or destroy with sudden speed and force
3. To bombard with electrical current, radiation, laser beams, etc.
4. To strike or jolt suddenly and forcefully
5. To skip over or delete

When a zapping spirit is at work it is literally killing, shooting, and deleting instruction, revelation, and understanding from a person's mind, and it is happening with a sudden speed and force. This is why the person can be executing a task one instance, but in the next moment can no longer remember it or execute it. There is a striking and jolting that is occurring spiritually. The person is bombarded with demonic electrical currents, radiation, and laser beams that are causing death to their ability to retain information.

John 10:10 *The thief cometh not, but for to steal, and to kill, and to destroy: I am come that they might have life, and that they might have it more abundantly.*

Cloaking Spirit – Disguises information where the person cannot spiritually see the vision of what task or endeavor at hand. The insight is masked where it looks like an illusion of its true form. The cloaking spirit will have people improvising their own desires and vision based on what they think it should be or what they thought was required, rather than making sure they implement the true plan and vision.

2Corinthians 11:13-14 *For such are false apostles, deceitful workers, transforming themselves into the apostles of Christ. And no marvel; for Satan himself is transformed (disguised, transfigure) into an angel of light.*

The Deaf and Dumb, Zapping, Cloaking, and Blocking Spirits, can operate through witchcraft spell attacks that are sent against people to steal, distract, and weary those working and planning the event at hand. When they come as spells, there can sometimes be a mist or presence of darkness in the atmosphere or around a person. The person may also experience dizziness, blurriness, or pressure in and around the head. When these spirits operate, bind and cast them out and sever every alliance to any spirits that may be operating in the atmosphere or territory.

- When the death and dumb spirit manifest command spiritual hearing and visualization to come to the ears and eyes and for the eyes of the understanding to be enlightened so that the person can perceive, retain and sustain in receiving and implementing instruction and the vision.
- Cleanse the zapping spirit out of the atmosphere and out of team members and partners. Command insight and revelation that has been zapped out to be restored.
- When the cloaking spirit manifests counterattack it by calling forth God's truth for the vision and illumination of his will to radiate regarding the vision.

Romans 12:2 And be not conformed to this world: but be ye transformed by the renewing of your mind, that ye may prove what [is] that good, and acceptable, and perfect, will of God.

Philippians 4:8 - Finally, brethren, whatsoever things are true, whatsoever things [are] honest, whatsoever things [are] just, whatsoever things [are] pure, whatsoever things [are] lovely, whatsoever things [are] of good report; if [there be] any virtue, and if [there be] any praise, think on these things.

2Corinthians 10:3-5 For though we walk in the flesh, we do not war after the flesh: (For the weapons of our warfare are not carnal, but mighty through God to the pulling down of strong holds;) Casting down imaginations, and every high thing that exalteth itself against the knowledge of God, and bringing into captivity every thought to the obedience of Christ

James 4:7 Submit yourselves therefore to God. Resist the devil, and he will flee from you.

Isaiah 26:3 - Thou wilt keep [him] in perfect peace, [whose] mind [is] stayed [on thee]: because he trusteth in thee.

<u>Blocking Spirits</u> - Blocking spirits use walls, barriers, or troops of demons that have locked themselves together in the spirit realm, where a person or team will have difficulty getting past a particular part of the vision. Team members may keep making mistakes and cannot progress past a particular part of the preparation stage as it relates to tasks for the even.

Psalm 18:29 For by thee I have run through a troop; and by my God have I leaped over a wall.

This scripture lets us know that we must run through these barriers. When encountering them verbally declare that you and team members are blasting through any troops that have set up a siege against you all and the event while using your authority in God to leap over demonic structures that hinder progress in the spiritual realm.

Python Spirits - Wraps around a person's mind or body to squeeze and restrict them where:

- They are limited in their mobility, process, and progress to implement the vision
- There may be an unexplainable tiredness and lethargic oppression where the person finds it difficult to move and press forward in implementing, working on, and completing the vision.
- They feel so weighty, they are physically suffocating, overly exerted in energy, and they are not able to physically keep up with the momentum of producing the vision in the earth.
- It causes confusion, discombobulation, double-mindedness, and thought racing, from the signal faculties in the brain being restricted, weighty, and crushed such that the person becomes stuck and stagnant in progressing and releasing the vision.

Isaiah 61:3 *To appoint unto them that mourn in Zion, to give unto them beauty for ashes, the oil of joy for mourning, the garment of praise for the spirit of heaviness; that they might be called trees of righteousness, the planting of the Lord, that he might be glorified.*

Loose Holy fire to torment python where it releases its grip while commanding this spirit to uncoil and be cast out of your midst.

Spirit Of Pride – The person who operates in pride wants to be in the forefront and center stage of the team and the event. They may overly volunteer for leading roles, reject wanting to do background or mediocre tasks. They will speak against others who they feel have the spotlight, are growing and maturing, or stands out in a unique way amongst the team. This person will seek out accolades and praise then will make comments to further promote personal praise. They tend to be glory stealers and self-idolaters as they will be focused on what they did during vision planning or at the event, versus how God was glorified through the entire team. Many with the spirit of pride will also embellish stories, lie, and even lie on God to make themselves or an experience be greater or more awe-striking than it really is.

Proverbs 16:5 *Every one [that is] proud in heart [is] an abomination to the LORD: [though] hand [join] in hand, he shall not be unpunished.*

James 4:6 *But he giveth more grace. Wherefore he saith, God resisteth the proud, but giveth grace unto the humble.*

Isaiah 42:8 *I am the Lord: that is my name: and my glory will I not give to another, neither my praise to graven images.*

Many prideful people are insecure. Pride is a mask to hide secret feelings and thoughts of inadequacy, low self-esteem, and self-worth. The prideful person tends to be overbearing and self-absorbed in his or her strengths and successes in an effort to prevent these identity issues from being exposed.

1Corinthians 4:18-20 *Now some are puffed up, as though I would not come to you. But I will come to you shortly, if the Lord will, and will know, not the speech of them which are puffed up, but the power. For the kingdom of God is not in word, but in power.*

If not dealt with, pride can cause destruction and even a falling away where restoration is not possible.

Proverbs 16:18 *Pride [goeth] before destruction, and an haughty spirit before a fall.*

Proverbs 29:23 *A man's pride shall bring him low: but honour shall uphold the humble in spirit.*

God requires humility. In order for a person to truly embody the presence of God where lives are transformed through their ministry, he or she must be gracious, meek, and humble. As a team regularly renounce the spirit of pride when praying and preparing for your event. Commit to not giving it any room in the vision, the event, and in your life. The more the team is submitted and humble before God, the greater victory and kingly impact the team and event will have on the earth.

1Peter 5:6 *The Amplified Bible Therefore humble yourselves [demote, lower yourselves in your own estimation] under the mighty hand of God, that in due time He may exalt you.*

<u>**Spirit of Leviathan**</u> - Interrupts and distorts communication between the speaker and the listener. Its' effort is to sow offense, discord, misunderstanding, faultfinding, ungodly judging, mistrust, and suspicion. Someone will say one thing and the person will misinterpret it. A matter that is mediocre can be taken out of proportion where drama and discord arise. This causes people to become offended with one another with no real reason as to why they are offended. Their offense will change the atmosphere of meetings, working on events, and the events themselves as irritation and tempers flare and dominate the area. Job speaks of how Leviathan operates in *Job 41:26-32*. This spirit was at operation between him and his friends who were striving to understand why God allowed the enemy to bring havoc upon his life. This spirit also distorted Job's views where he could not receive wise counsel from God during this time of trial with the Lord.

The quickest way to stifle the workings of this spirit is to repent quickly of any irritation, drama and discord; forgive and reunite in heart and spirit one to another. The unity and love of Christ will dismantle and displace this spirit.

Galatians 6:1-3 The Amplified Bible BRETHREN, IF *any person is overtaken in misconduct or sin of any sort, you who are spiritual [who are responsive to and controlled by the Spirit] should set him right and restore and reinstate him, without any sense of superiority and with all gentleness, keeping an attentive eye on yourself, lest you should be tempted also. Bear (endure, carry) one another's burdens and troublesome moral faults, and in this way fulfill and observe perfectly the law of Christ (the Messiah) and complete what is lacking [in your obedience to it].*

<u>**Mind Binding & Mind Blinding Spirits**</u> – Operate through the stronghold of mind control. These spirits bind and blind the thought life, the mind, and senses to cause affliction, confusion, unexplainable fear of people or of failure, and anxiety. This spirit tends to operate and look like an octopus or a squid. The person may feel pressure or a tormenting headache, feel like something is sticking in their eyes, ears, temples, forehead, or the back of the head. Things may look black as the person strains to see and discern spiritually and naturally. The person may become dull of hearing because the ears will feel clogged or like something is lodged in them. It may also feel like something is sitting on their head or wrapped around their head.

This stronghold of mind control may also plague the person with vile, perverse, unnecessary, or unimportant thoughts. Or may have them panicking and thinking of something over and over to distract them from what is presently important. Sometimes this spirit will swamp the person with constant thoughts of hurts from their past or present life and heart issues that are unresolved. The person may find it difficult to pay attention or to press forward in working on present tasks because of these constant plaguing thoughts and feelings of intense pressure.

Proverbs 15:15 The Amplified Bible *All the days of the desponding and afflicted are made evil [by anxious thoughts and forebodings (prophecy)], but he who has a glad heart has a continual feast [regardless of circumstances].*

Ask the Lord to sever the tentacles of this spirit or use the sword of the spirit to cut them. Break the power of pressure, pain, and torment, and release healing where needed.

<u>**Spirit of Void & Darkness**</u> – This spirit may be at work when there are no blockages, hindrances, blinding, binding, confusion, or discombobulation, yet the atmosphere, eye gates, imagination, and mind is totally black and blank, dark and empty.

We see this spirit in operation in ***Genesis 1:2*** when God was creating the heavens and the earth.

And the earth was without form, and void; and darkness was upon the face of the deep. And the Spirit of God moved upon the face of the waters

This spirit wants a person to think that everything is dead and without form, they cannot see or discern properly, or that there is no potential for creation or manifestation. It operates like a black blanket or cloud, covering everything so the person cannot see behind the scenes. It will smother blackness and void over the plans and seeds of God, and even conceal demonic plans so the person cannot be offensive against the enemy.

This spirit will black out the ability to form and create plans for the vision while covering up revelation, the purpose for the vision, and plots and plans of the enemy. ***Daniel 2:22*** *He reveals the deep and secret things; He knows what is in the darkness, and the light dwells with Him.*

When this spirit attacks begin to release and declare the light, wisdom, and profound, searchable, secretive, mysteries of God to come forth to dispel the darkness.

The Deaf & Dumb, Zapping, Cloaking, Blocking, Python, Leviathan, Mind Binder & Mind Blinder & Void Spirits:

- Prolong the ability to see the assignment of tasks to complete the assignment clearly.
- Prevents and hinders the ability to see how the vision will impact the people, community, region, and/or sphere of influence.
- Prolong the ability to receive insight from the Holy Spirit.
- Prolong and hinder the progress of meetings, planning, completing tasks, which results in the need for additional work and planning.
- Prolong or hinder the ability to learn what is needed to further advance the vision and finalize the event.
- Cause frustration, division, and distractions against and within the vision due to having to constantly teach and review plans and redo tasks.

People on the team are open doors for these spirits when:
- They do not prepare and complete their assignments as it relates to the vision.
- There is no personal cultivation of their personal abilities so they can aid in being an effective team member.
- They are stressed and tired
- They have challenges balancing their home, school, work, business, and ministry life.
- They have a need for attention and use the team and/or the vision as a way to receive attention and get their needs met for love and belonging.
- They are operating in the spirit of inadequacy, insecurity, rejection, the little girl or little boy spirit

It is important to seek God for strategy in order to be proactive and equip ourselves, the team, the vision, and the event against these spirits. It is also important to use the scriptures as weaponry against these spirits. When fortifying in the truth of God's biblical scriptures and strategy, it is difficult for these spirits to gain entrance where they operate to wreak havoc on the visionary, team and the event.

Romans 12:2 And be not conformed to this world: but be ye transformed by the renewing of your mind, that ye may prove what [is] that good, and acceptable, and perfect, will of God.

Philippians 4:8 - Finally, brethren, whatsoever things are true, whatsoever things [are] honest, whatsoever things [are] just, whatsoever things [are] pure, whatsoever things [are] lovely, whatsoever things [are] of good report; if [there be] any virtue, and if [there be] any praise, think on these things.

2Corinthians 10:3-5 For though we walk in the flesh, we do not war after the flesh: (For the weapons of our warfare are not carnal, but mighty through God to the pulling down of strong holds;) Casting down imaginations, and every high thing that exalteth itself against the knowledge of God, and bringing into captivity every thought to the obedience of Christ

James 4:7 Submit yourselves therefore to God. Resist the devil, and he will flee from you.

Isaiah 26:3 - Thou wilt keep [him] in perfect peace, [whose] mind [is] stayed [on thee]: because he trusteth in thee.

Here is a possible strategy to fortify oneself and team against these spirits:
- Praying against these spirits and other areas God reveals before meetings, working on tasks, and releasing the event.
- Cleanse stress, tiredness, weariness, etc. from oneself, team members, and the atmospheres.
- Close gateways within oneself, the team, and the spirit realm that would cause these spirits to operate.
- As these spirits manifest, bind and cast these spirits out and command them not to return again.

Little Girl & Little Boy Spirit - This is a spirit where a person has had a traumatic or painful experience in their childhood and parts of their personality are stuck at that age or are stuck in that stressful, or traumatic event. Because they need deliverance and healing from this experience, they tend to fluctuate between their current age and the age of the traumatic event. A person with a little girl/boy spirit could have experienced a lack of development in an age or stage of life and thus the spirit of the little girl or little boy manifest in them. Psychology calls this arrested development. The trauma has caused them to be imprisoned at a specific age or event in their lives, such that part of their personality is stuck in that age, time, and experience. This person will throw tantrums, sulk, display drama, a sense of entitlement, and victimization. They will be very passive-aggressive and defiant when he or she does not get their way as required to be responsible and accountable for their actions and will do things in an irresponsible or immature way to consistently assist and be cared for. They will constantly ask questions and desire help even though they have the potential to complete the task at hand and will blame others when they do not complete goals and fulfill responsibilities. Due to the need for attention, love, and constant reassurance, they will drain the leader, team members, the vision, and the atmosphere through the manifestation of this demonic spirit operating through them.

Such persons with this spirit will quit the team or event planning over small matters that could be resolved with communication, responsibility, and follow-through. They may also display a pattern of quitting, threatening to quit, stopping and starting, regressing, then returning and claiming they understand their purpose in being apart. The little girl and little boy in them have a challenge committing to the adult responsibilities and finishing what they start. They cycle and never truly progress forward because the little girl and little boy in them dominate their lives and destiny. Until they acknowledge that this spirit is oppressing them, reject being the victim due to past issues, recognize that they are an adult now and have a choice to move forward and be healed, commit to healing underlying issues and maturing as an adult, they will continue to fluctuate between a child and adult, and not achieve destiny.

1Corinthians 24:20 *Brethren, be not children in understanding: howbeit in malice be ye children, but in understanding be men.*

1Corinthians 13:11 *When I was a child, I spake as a child, I understood as a child, I thought as a child: but when I became a man, I put away childish things.*

<u>*1Corinthians 4:14-15*</u> *That we henceforth be no more children, tossed to and fro, and carried about with every wind of doctrine, by the sleight of men, and cunning craftiness, whereby they lie in wait to deceive; But speaking the truth in love, may grow up into him in all things, which is the head, even Christ: From whom the whole body fitly joined together and compacted by that which every joint supplieth, according to the effectual working in the measure of every part, maketh increase of the body unto the edifying of itself in love.*

<u>**Inadequacy, Insecurity, & Low Self-Esteem**</u> - I would define inadequacy as, *"having a feeling of deficiency, feeling incomplete or insufficient regarding life or for a position, task or duty."*

<u>Dictionary.com defines</u> *inadequate* <u>as:</u>
1. Not adequate or sufficient; inept or unsuitable
2. Psychiatry: ineffectual in response to emotional, social, intellectual, and physical demands in the absence of any obvious mental or physical deficiency

In collaboration with Dictionary.com, I would define *insecurity* as, *"a lack of confidence or assurance; self-doubt, instability, inferiority, low self-esteem, fear of what others will think, timidity, shyness, embarrassment, self-consciousness, uncertainty."*

I would define *low self-esteem* as *"having a general negative overall opinion of oneself, judging or evaluating oneself negatively, and placing a general negative value on oneself as a person."*

When inadequacy, insecurity, and/or low self-esteem are in operation, the person will desire to be used by God but will require constant encouragement. This is because these spirits make people feel unworthy, and because they give in to the perceptions of these spirits, they present and act as if they are unworthy. The person will sometimes feel and state that they cannot complete an assignment or task due to some misperceived personality deficiency or misguided physical efficiency. They will want to change the vision over and over, even though they are ready and capable of going forward in the vision and tasks at hand. Such behavior causes the person to be draining to those supporting and encouraging them and causes them to be a hindrance and burden to the vision and team.

A person who is challenged by these unhealthy characteristics of demonic forces is often a risk to relationships and the visions they are a part of. This is due to them being unreliable, uncertain, and unstable in God. Many of them cannot be trusted with the mature things of God as they will lack follow-through, then give unrealistic or poor excuses for their actions. To them, the reasons will appear valid, but to the team and to God, they will be invalid and irresponsible.

Spirit of the Outcast
Dictionary.com defines *outcast* as:
1. A person who is rejected or cast out, as from home or society
2. A homeless wanderer; vagabond
3. Rejected, rejected matter, refused, discarded

My definition: Unwanted, dejected, rejected, belittled, devalued, and at times verbally ridiculed and abused

Ishmael and his maidservant mother were cast out of Abraham's home because Sarah did not want Ishmael to share the throne with Isaac **(Genesis 21:9-13)**.

The lepers in the bible were outcasts. They had to live alone and outside the camp of the Israelites **(Leviticus 13, Numbers 5:2)**.

David was often found outcast due to running from King Saul. King Saul was jealous of David's success. King Saul was often oppressed by a demonic spirit that David's playing of the harp would soothe him from. King Saul was challenged by being subjected to the very man that had the potential, favor, and positive qualities to rule his throne *(1Samuel 18-22)*.

Many people have often felt like an outcast or have been outcast because of their experiences in childhood, as a teenager or an adult, within different group settings, work atmospheres, business endeavors, social and peer interactions, and/or ministries, An outcast persona can also be formed due to a person being peculiar and not really fitting in, or being unable to identify their identity or purpose in life. Sometimes people are outcasts because of their unique identities, giftings, and life visions. People reject them due to being unique or peculiar or because they do not understand who they are and what they possess by way of abilities and talents. This can disrupt a team or event because the outcast person will claim to be for and available to the team but will operate like a long ranger. They will engage in independent and even secretive works and then present them to the team as if it was a team effort or as if they were doing them for the benefit of the team. They will be secretive and guarding of the tasks and duties that are assigned to them or that they are capable of doing and will not want anyone else to know how they did them or what they did to achieve complete their duty. This is because they fear someone taking their place on the team so they engage in this manner to ensure their position within the team. They will have a difficult time connecting with the team, being a team player, and often have to be drawn into team activities, yet when engaging one on one, they do well and shine. They are often jealous of other team members and will at times engage in behaviors to sabotage the unity of the team or to make the person they are jealous of look incompetent. They will seek to operate in ways that uncover and expose the weaknesses of team members and the team while stepping in to do these duties so they can be viewed as the hero and the most important member of the team. They are validating their need for love and belonging through these operations are striving to secure their place within the team even though they are already valued and wanted as a team member.

Sometimes the outcast person will strive to escape and reject religious and traditional doctrines, values, ideologies, and perceptions by becoming very resistant to laws, standards, rules, social, cultural, and norms. This sometimes causes them to be further isolated, rejected, dejected, helpless, hopeless, lawless, imprisoned, and even suicidal. They may end up in jail for breaking the law or cast out of various spheres and arenas for refusing to adhere to laws. They may also imprison themselves by self-sabotaging opportunities because they take on a mindset that everyone is against them and that they have to fight everyone for their right to be unique. They are not able to discern when they are being accepted and being given an opportunity to shine in their peculiar God-likeness. This is because the outcast person has succumbed to operating in a victim mentality.

Wikipedia.com define a victim mentality as *"an acquired (learned) personality trait in which a person tends to regard him or herself as a victim of the negative actions of others, and to think, speak and act as if that were the case — even in the absence of clear evidence. It depends on habitual thought processes and attribution."*

A victim mentality will have a person stuck in outcasting and rejecting what God and others are seeking to make available to them. It is so important to be delivered and heal from the mindset and oppressions of the outcast so the person can SHIFT forth into receiving the people and areas in life that can receive their uniqueness, such that they evolve and achieve all God has for them to do and be.

Keys to Healing From the Spirit of the Outcast
- Spend time in prayer, acknowledge the abuse that occurred. Call it what it was and cancel all the confusion, excuses that others used and even you used to defend, protect, suppress, or remain in false obligation to those that abused you.
- Spend time in prayer forgiving those who ostracized and rejected you and release the situation for God to avenge.
- Cleanse all suppressed hurts and experiences out of your soul, heart, and memories.
- Cast out spirits of the outcast, rejection, fear of rejection, self-rejection, vagabond, wandering, offense, defense, rage and anger, insecurity, inadequacy.
- Spend time soaking in the deliverance and healing power of God.

Controlling Spirits - The spirit of control will attempt to restrain, direct, influence, seduce, and curb the team and the vision to what he or she believes it should be. A person with this spirit is usually combative with the leader of the vision, those in charge, and with team members. They are resistant to being led, taking advice or direction, receiving constructive criticism. Their lives are resistant or closed to the leading of the Holy Spirit. They also resent the leader and anyone who offers guidance to them. They despise them in their heart even though they may present as honoring. However, their lack of honor is displayed in their actions and lack of follow-through. This person may use sarcastic jokes, belittling, negative comments, and subtle remarks to offend others or sway members and the atmosphere to his or her perception so that his or her desires can be implemented. They will become upset and reluctant in being a team player or fulfilling their duties if this is discerned and they are made accountable for these inappropriate actions...

Sometimes this person may be jealous of the leader, and/or want to be the leader. Or they simply just have control issues, and difficulty submitting to anything that is not their idea or that is not under their power or jurisdiction.

Romans 16:17-18 *Now I beseech you, brethren, mark them which cause divisions and offences contrary to the doctrine which ye have learned; and avoid them. For they that are such serve not our Lord Jesus Christ, but their own belly; and by good words and fair speeches deceive the hearts of the simple.*

Control in Dictionary.com means:
1. To exercise restraint or direction over; dominate, command
2. To hold in check; curb
3. To test or verify (a scientific experiment) by a parallel experiment or other standards of comparison
4. To eliminate or prevent the flourishing or spread of

The agenda of a person operating in this spirit is:
- To try to dominate a person, the leader, the group, the vision, and/or the event take command over it, whether that be by constantly drawing attention to themselves or blatantly trying to make adjustments or changes to things.
- To check and curb the team by always being the one to stop the progress and forward motion of the work in an effort to have control over it.
- To diminish and lessen the value and work of the leader, the vision, and team members.
- To test the leader, the team members, the vision, the revelation, and the instructions given and to compare them to their standard or a standard they deem is valuable.
- To eliminate and prevent the flourishing of the gifts, workings, and operations of the entire team, and the opportunities and expansion of the vision and the event.

Confronting this spirit is essential. Silencing their workings is key to extinguishing how they infiltrate and infest the team with erred perceptions and vision that cause confusion, strife, discord, division, and stifling of the vision and the event. If the person is not willing to submit to the vision and to be delivered from this spirit, it will be important to remove them from the team. There is no way to walk together unless there is agreement. Team members need to agree with what God is desiring so they can help build a solid and healthy foundation regarding what is being produced and released on the earth.

Spirits of Intimidation
Intimidation from Dictionary.com means:
1. To make timid; fill with fear
2. To overawe or cow, as through the force of personality or by superior display of wealth, talent, etc.
3. To force into or deter from some action by inducing fear

This spirit causes a person to cower from who they are in God, and what he has granted to their hands. Those operating through this spirit will be focused on instilling fear and inducing (lead, move, persuade, influence, stimulate a synthesis) fear through their blatant passive-aggressive actions. This spirit only has as much power over a person if they succumb to it or rise against it. Some people who operate as passive-aggressive intimidators will act as though they are exempt from any responsibility regarding their behavior. This is because they are not blatantly doing anything against the person, but subtly they are filling them with fear and persuasions that hinder forward movement in God while abusing and bewitching the leader and the team members. That is because this spirit can be equated to mind control.

Sometimes, leaders can operate in intimidation through dictatorship rather than a spirit of encouragement and empowerment. This is a misuse of authority, where they have absolute unrestricted control, and they are the supreme authority. They will leave no room for the members to have a voice, eyes (vision), and ears (hearing) regarding the planning, working and releasing of an event. Thus the team members receive minimal opportunities to grow in who they are as vision carriers and in their own God-identity. When intimidation is at work in a leader, it tends to be the leader's way only or no way. There is no compromise or respect for the members' giftings, callings, or perceptions. Timidity, fear, and control are used to coward the members into submission. The members tend to work and operate from a place of dread while feeling constantly overwhelmed and frustrated. The members will feel a need to be perfect while living under the fear of failing. They strive to live up to the standards that are being required of them rather than evolving in Excellency through God-likeness. There tends to be a lot of bickering behind the scenes as members will voice concerns among themselves and to outsiders rather than to the leader. They do this because they fear being rebuked, chastised, and not having their perceptions validated.

When a person is challenged with a spirit of intimidation, they may be difficult to approach. The intimidator may possess strict rules and regimens about how things should go and will seek to impose those ideas on others. The intimidator may be easily offended and will be good at arguing his or her point. They also may be combative and because they are good at stating their case, others will find it difficult to share an opinion or concern with them. Though this may not be their intent or heart, the person may appear prideful and abusive; their approach tends to be harsh, strict, aggressive, and abrasive. They may have bible scriptures or strong morals and principles to solidify the reasons they think or believe a certain way, yet these measures are used out of context and in error to their true meaning and their biblical or moral intent. Those with issues of insecurities, shyness, etc., will be prey to such leaders and members. They will find it difficult to stand up for themselves and will often be cowardly under the intimidation tactics of these spirits.

Though not always the case, some people operating in the spirit of intimidation may not know it. Speaking with them privately in love about it can be key to helping them be delivered from this ungodly characteristic or demonic spirit. There are also those that know it but do not want deliverance. They may not be willing to be delivered. God may lead you to pray and intercede for their deliverance. If a person finds that the spirit of intimidation is still evident within a leader and change is not their intent, examine if it is healthy to remain a part of the even. God is about empowerment and liberation. God does not require us to be cowered under anyone. When we submit under wrong authority, they become our God, or whatever they are submitted to becomes our God.

Spirits of Rebellion, Stubbornness, & Defiance Against Authority

1Samuel 15:23 For rebellion is as the sin of witchcraft, and stubbornness is as iniquity and idolatry. Because thou hast rejected the word of the LORD, he hath also rejected thee from being king.

In this passage of scripture, one of the Hebrew words for *rebellion* is "*bitterness.*"

Dictionary.com defines *rebellion* as:
1. Open, organized, and armed resistance to one's government or ruler
2. Resistance to or defiance of any authority, control, or tradition

Dictionary.com defines a *rebel* as:
1. A person who refuses allegiance to resists, or rises in arms against the government or ruler of his or her country
2. A person who resists any authority, control, or tradition
3. Rebellious, defiant

When rebellion is present, there may be a bitter root in that person's heart and soul that needs to be healed. This bitterness sometimes stems from past experiences where forgiveness of self and others has not manifested. When a person is bitter regarding an authority figure, they will manifest that bitterness with those in leadership, even when that person has not done anything to offend them. This is because the unhealed breeds a need to avenge and protect oneself from previous trauma. The bitter root of rebellion bewitches the person into thinking their actions are okay and even justifiable. This demonic spirit gives the assumption that the person is entitled to behave rebelliously. It causes them to be stubborn and idolatrous where they only think of themselves, their feelings, needs, and desires while neglecting the good of all parties involved and/or the vision as a whole. The person becomes immovable, uncompromising, and self-absorbed, thus becoming an idol unto themselves. Nothing or no one else is considered in the choices they make, as the aim is to please themselves and fulfill some justifiable need or desire within themselves.

A person who is rebellious – defiant - is generally insubordinate.
Some synonym definitions from dictionary.com as it relates to being *insubordinate* are:
1. Contumacious – stubbornly perverse or rebellious; willfully and obstinately disobedient

2. Refractory - hard or impossible to manage, hard to fuse, resistant to ordinary methods of treatment
3. Recalcitrant - noncompliant
4. Rebellious, insolent; daring, resistant, challenging

People challenged by these demonic spirits will have:
- Difficulty unifying with the vision and team members.
- Resist direction and redirection
- Have challenges following or complying with the rules and regulations of the team and vision.
- Resist following requirements for preparing for the vision and the event.
- Unifies just enough to be apart or on the team, but not enough to be a true team player.
- Can easily fall into backsliding as they do just enough at times to comply but not enough to be truly transformed.
- Will attempt to coast off his or her gifting and will get away with sins because of his or her gift but will be a disruption and open door of bringing warfare and impurity into the vision and the event.

Some of this will show in actions and the work they are required to do. They will constantly do tasks wrong or go the wrong way. They will have to be told constantly that they are going the wrong way – operating contrary to what is required or to the vision. These demonic spirits tend to be lodged in the flesh and will of a person. Therefore, the person may appear very stubborn. When they want to do right, wrong will appear at times - wrong or defiant workings will manifest.

- This person will have to be delivered and healed of past issues that caused them to give in to the bitterness and unforgiveness. Many of these experiences will be related to those in authority taking advantage, neglecting, abusing, or offending them, as some injustice has caused trauma and pain in the person's soul and heart.

- The person will have to practice rooting rebellion out of their flesh and will. A fast may be required to subject their will under the power of their spirit.

- The person will then have to search out the reason God led them to be a part of the event and vision planning, and the reason God led them to submit to that leader. This revelation will help them be accountable for submitting to the rules and regulations of that vision and leader. The person should also be held accountable for what God requires of them when personality traits of rebellion occur in their behavior.

- Because rebellion is rooted in the flesh and will of a person, it will take time to fully process to wholeness. The person and the leader must be willing to work together, as the process of wholeness unfolds. The person who is being delivered must be willing to accept rebuke and correction when necessary to further root this spirit out of their will and personality. Rebuke and correction should be done in love. Sometimes, it is best to take the person aside and speak with them versus handling the situation publicly. The goal is to bring healing and value to the person by building them up in trusting God and trusting those he has given rule over them. Tearing down the person and embarrassing the person could further root rebellion in them and prolong the process to wholeness.

Hebrews 13:17-18 *Obey them that have the rule over you, and submit yourselves: for they watch for your souls, as they that must give account, that they may do it with joy, and not with grief: for that is unprofitable for you. Pray for us: for we trust we have a good conscience, in all things willing to live honestly.*

Philippians 2:3 *Let nothing be done through strife or vainglory; but in lowliness of mind let each esteem other better than themselves.*

1Peter 3:8-9 *Finally, be ye all of one mind, having compassion one of another, love as brethren, be pitiful, be courteous: Not rendering evil for evil, or railing for railing: but contrariwise blessing; knowing that ye are thereunto called, that ye should inherit a blessing.*

Spirits of Murmuring and Complaining - Spirits of murmuring and complaining can oppress a person when they are angry, frustrated, agitated, tired, stressed, weary about life, or about challenges concerning what God has granted to their hands. When spirits of murmuring and complaining set in, a person can become rebellious and resistant to the rules and regulations, expectations, and requirements that God is requiring. They may begin complaining and murmuring about how matters are conducted, speak against the leader, find fault and voice complaints against team members, speak against God and the vision. Such actions can draw other team members into complaining and murmuring while speaking against the vision, leader, and team members.

Murmuring and complaining tend to be rooted in ill will or resentment. This can cause emotional sickness, displeasure, bitterness, offense, insult, and feelings of injustice in their souls and heart. When not dealt with, this person's emotional sickness spreads and contaminates the souls and hearts of people. This spirit is contagious and loves company, and essentially needs company and attention in order to thrive. Murmuring and complaining opens the door to sin and idolatry as people's souls and hearts begin to deny, resist, reject, or become dull to the truth, and they begin to walk in their own plans and perceptions. These plans and perceptions are often in the effort to immediately satisfy the flesh and the soul and are often against the will and plans of God for their life, destiny, and the vision they are part of. When this occurs, you may have members leave the team before the vision goes forth, while encouraging others to leave. They will start operating by their own rules and standards and rally people to uphold their point of view.

Ephesians 4:29 *Let no corrupt communication proceed out of your mouth, but that which is good to the use of edifying, that it may minister grace unto the hearers.*

Corrupt in Greek is *sapros* and means:
1. Rotten, i.e. Worthless (literally or morally): — bad, corrupt
2. Putrefied corrupted by one and no longer fit for use
3. Worn out, of poor quality, unfit for use

Philippians 2:4 *Do all things without grumbling and faultfinding and complaining [against God] and questioning and doubting [among yourselves], That you may show yourselves to be blameless and guileless, innocent and uncontaminated, children of God without blemish (faultless, unrebukable) in the midst of a crooked and wicked generation [spiritually perverted and perverse], among whom you are seen as bright lights (stars or beacons shining out clearly) in the [dark] world.*

Spirits of Competition & Comparison - The spirit of competition can operate consciously or unconsciously within a person or among team members. This spirit can also be very overt or subtle, depending on who it is manifesting through. It can operate through the most prideful person or the shyest, insecure person.

The spirit of competition will have a person competing with the leader or with team members. This demonic spirit will have a person competing in their mind as they are plagued with thoughts of needing to be seen, perfect, or better than everyone else. This person may strive to change the vision to what they believe it should be. Their reason will be more in the effort to outdo others than truly having the revelation that benefits the vision or the event.

The spirit of competition manifested among the disciples. In ***Matthew 18:1-6, Luke 9:46-48, and Luke 22:24-27***, we find the disciples asking Jesus who is the greatest in the kingdom of heaven. Jesus pulled a child close to him and expressed that unless we come unto him as children, we will not inherit the kingdom of heaven no matter how great we are. Jesus went on to express that if we offend or cause one another to sin or stumble in our conduct or thought we will be judged harshly. He then stated that the humble is the greatest among us all.

Jesus encourages us to be cautious with entertaining such thoughts and actions. Whether intentional or unintentional, conscious or unconscious, when the spirit of competition is at work, it breeds sin and stumbling in the conduct and thoughts of others. The spirit of competition draws others into competing, comparing, challenging, becoming jealous and envious, while causing discord and strife on to another. Even those who may not be participating are now having thoughts of whether they are adequate and living up to par. It is important for leaders to be discerning of when this spirit is surfacing and it is important for dance members to cast down thoughts of competition, and deal with underlying issues of inadequacies and insecurity that cause these spirits to have an open door in their lives.

It is important for people to know their gifts and callings and how they impact the team and the vision. This will also aid in dismantling competition and comparison spirits as the focus will be on using one's purpose to glorify God and fulfill his will rather than rather than validating one's own insecurities, while glorifying self.

Galatians 5:23-26 The Amplified Bible *Gentleness (meekness, humility), self-control (self-restraint, continence). Against such things there is no law [that can bring a charge]. And those who belong to Christ Jesus (the Messiah) have crucified the flesh (the godless human nature) with its passions and appetites and desires. If we live by the [Holy] Spirit, let us also walk by the Spirit. [If by the Holy Spirit we have our life in God, let us go forward walking in line, our conduct controlled by the Spirit.] Let us not become vainglorious and self-conceited, competitive and challenging and provoking and irritating to one another, envying and being jealous of one another.*

<u>Mocking Spirits</u>
Proverbs 3:34 *Surely he scorneth (mocks) the scorners (mockers): but he giveth grace unto the lowly.*

<u>Scorneth and Scorners in this scripture is the Hebrew word *lus* and means:</u>
1. Properly, to make mouths at, i.e. To scoff
2. Hence (from the effort to pronounce a foreign language) to interpret, or (generally) intercede
3. Ambassador, have in derision, interpreter, make a mock, mocker, scorn(-er, -ful), teacher
4. To be inflated, act as a scorner, show oneself as a mocker

Essentially when a person mocks others, they are servicing as an intercessor, ambassador, teacher that is thus training others how to disrespect someone or something. It is okay to laugh and have fun. It is however important to be careful in not making comments that belittle, ridicule, abuse, and devalue team members. It is especially important to not become so familiar where blatant hurtful comments are made that can be offensive rather than funny.
It is important, to be honest in recognizing that some jokes are really disguised abuse. They are heart issues manifesting the truth of what a person feels, thinks, or believes.

Mocking Spirits are a hang out in the atmosphere and among relationship interactions, so they can take advantage of opportunities to operate through familiarity and a lack of regard. They tend to strike when it is least expected while using mimicking, quick wit, judgmental comments, harsh or blatant jokes to cause offense, strife, and division.

The mocking spirit actually births division as one of the definitions of mock is to attack. When someone is under attack it is them against whatever is attacking. They are not on the same side. The person is hiding behind jokes and laughs that throw darts at the person they are mocking. Mockery operates as a disguise to speak and hurt someone with words that a person really wants to say but passively aggressively mock to get their point across. They reject handling their challenges and issues in a healthy manner where they sit down and converse with the person in a healthy dialog. Do not allow mocking spirit to hang out and operate. Be committed to stopping these spirits in their tracks. Teach the team healthy communication and conflict resolution skills so they can handle concerns and challenges in a healthy manner, mature conversations that produce wellness and fruitfulness.

One of the synonyms of scorn is contempt. When a person is treating someone with the contempt, they are being mean, vial (repulsive, disgusting, filthy, foul), and worthless. It is an act of showing disrespect, and dishonor. A person may not think of this or be mindful of this when they are having fun, joking, and playing games. The person is actually disrespecting, dishonoring, taunting, treating someone as if they are worthless, and putting them down. This is unacceptable as team members should be esteeming one another higher than they esteem themselves.

Another word for mock is mimic. When we are mimicking others, we are copying and imitating another person's actions, the things that they say, how they behave, etc. and essentially, we are making fun of and ridiculing who a person is. We are also making fun of their personality, their attributes, and how they may express themselves and interact. This can cause much harm to a person, by making them feel rejected, isolated, bullied, inferior, and inadequate. They may begin to self-reject and self-isolate to avoid ridicule. They may become offended, withdrawn, and wounded. They may feel abused amongst those who should be loving them, encouraging, edifying, comforting, and building them up rather than tearing them down. We cannot give the enemy any room to infiltrate by allowing the mocking spirit to hide behind jokes, fun, games, and laughs that really abuse, harm, and wound others.

We must be sensitive to the Holy Spirit so he can bring correction when we have crossed a line with people or just in general. Be humble enough to repent quickly when there is an unction in your spirit that something you said or did may have offended, been misinterpreted, or could have become an open door to strife or division. When you feel convicted, even if that person or team does not hold you accountable, hold yourself accountable, by repenting to the person and even the team if necessary.

Leaders must also hold themselves and team members to this standard as when mocking spirits invade the ministry, it breaches safety and trust. Members then start to feel unsafe and as if they cannot trust the members and the ministry with their insecurities, weaknesses, fears, shortcomings. The ministry should be a safe place to grow, but the operating of this spirit makes it battling ground rather than safe ground, and as people step onto the ground to come forth in who they are, learn, and grow, they are getting shot down and killed in a place where they should be coming alive and awakening; where they should feel safe to not have to guard themselves and be free to be who they are as they learn and grow more in God and who God is in them. This spirit actually sabotages a person's growth because it makes them feel uncomfortable to be themselves and to take strides out of fear of being mocked and ridiculed, so instead, they stop stretching out to learn and grow because they are guarding and shielding themselves from this spirit. It also sabotages relationships in this same manner because the person becomes guarded and no longer comfortable to just be themselves, and they become abused and wounded in the relationship and eventually the relationship perishes and we see people disconnecting from the ministry that should have been helping them to grow and connect to God. I also believe that this spirit causes church hurt, and it sends people away from the church and away from God when truly this spirit and these actions are not a representation or true depiction of the church and who God is.

We must make sure that our ministries are cultivated with the nature and character of who God is and a spirit of love, honor, and respect where people feel they can be empowered and grow. Therefore, address mocking spirits quickly by repenting and forgiving one another. The more you practice this, the more it will become a part of your ministry culture. God will also honor the humility of team members and the ministry, and there will be an increase of power and anointing that will flow through the deep unity that radiates within the team.

Matthew 18:15 *Moreover if thy brother shall trespass against thee, go and tell him his fault between thee and him alone: if he shall hear thee, thou hast gained thy brother.*

Luke 17:3 *Take heed to yourselves: If thy brother trespass against thee, rebuke him; and if he repent, forgive him.*

1Peter 3:8-9 The Amplified Bible *Finally, all [of you] should be of one and the same mind (united in spirit), sympathizing [with one another], loving [each other] as brethren [of one household], compassionate and courteous (tenderhearted and humble). Never return evil for evil or insult for insult (scolding, tongue-lashing, berating), but on the contrary blessing [praying for their welfare, happiness, and protection, and truly pitying and loving them]. For know that to this you have been called, that you may yourselves inherit a blessing [from God – that you may obtain a blessing as heirs, bringing welfare and happiness and protection].*

Spirit of Betrayal - Sometimes there will be a person that may be planted by the enemy to betray the leader or the team. Spirits of betrayal are not uncommon and should not shock us, for **Matthew 24:10** says, *And then shall many be offended, and shall betray one another, and shall hate one another.* If you are successful then you will experience betrayal at different levels of your ministry. There is really no way to avoid spirits of betrayal. We can try to prepare for them but doing so causes us to be guarded in our interactions, and accusatory towards those who mean well towards us. We are not able to relax in our interactions because we fear being hurt, berated, and assaulted by the very ones we are to love and esteem. We should be conscious that betrayal may occur through the most unlikely of persons. And though you can never prepare for betrayal, here are some keys that can be utilized when exploring the spirit of betrayal. I would also encourage you to study the story of Judas and Jesus (*Luke 22*) for further assistance in identifying and dealing with spirits of betrayal.

- The betrayer is often self-serving and seeking to prosper in finances or position. The challenge is the betrayer is willing to sell you out to get his or her needs or desires met.
- Whether conscious or unconscious, the betrayer wants to be you and will seek to replace you. I say unconscious because some insecure or inadequate people tend to be subject to the spirit of betrayal and not even realize it until they have betrayed you. Their desire to replace you will be by way of selling you out or eliminating you in some way where they can defile or diminish your reputation and take your place.
- The betrayer is usually operating in carefully crafted words where they appear as if they are for you and are invested in what God is doing in your life and in the ministry. Or maybe they are but their insecurities cause them to be an open door to steal your heart then stab you in it.
- The betrayer operates in a projected loyalty or even in a pure loyalty. They can walk with you and the vision for seasons and even be your personal confidant. They may give you beneficial wise counsel; flatter you with kind and encouraging words, and even prophecy into your life. It will appear or be as if they are very supportive and that they see what God desires to do in your life and in the visions, he has granted to your hands.
- The challenge with this is during the times where you or the visions are in a vulnerable state or a season of transitioning or elevation, you do not realize that the betrayer is not for you.
- Something may shift in them or nothing shifts, but the truth of who they are will begin to reveal itself. One major key is the relationship with you and/or the vision shifts, which is where the betrayal begins.
- Again please know that you cannot escape betrayal so even as it is unfolding, it must continue in order for the fullness of your transition and/or the vision's transition to taking place. All of the actions of the betrayer are calculated and covered by false loyalty, and often go unnoticed until the moment of the blatant

act of betrayal. Therefore it is no way to stop the betrayal because it has intertwined itself with the process of the transition. This is the reason I contend that some experiences people call betrayal are not betrayal. When betrayal really occurs, the consequences cannot be changed. Betrayal unleashes a series of events that cannot be stopped, and that goes for all parties involved.
- The betrayer may not even realize their actions until they see the consequences, and even then, the betrayer may not care or take responsibility for how their actions impact you and the vision.

The main challenge with dealing with those who operate in a spirit of betrayal is that it causes a breach in a covenant. There can be reconciliation where forgiveness and healing of hurts occur, however, the covenant cannot be restored to its original state. The issue of trust will always be a factor; therefore, a new covenant has to be made to bring security to the betrayal never occurring again. And even then, it takes an abundance of work on both parties to restore the relationship. Sometimes, there is one person that is not willing to do what it takes to build a new covenant so even if these relationships are reconciled, the relationships are never restored. There also has to be the realization in that the person or ministry being betrayed enters a new place, so in order for the betrayer to unify with that person or ministry again, it has to be on the new level, as that person or ministry is not who they were and where they used to be once the betrayal unfolds and the transition is complete.

Regardless to whether you know who is going to betray you like Jesus did, or you are caught off guard, I liken the pain of betrayal to someone who was a friend or loyal foe, coming up and stabbing you in the heart. You now feel tricked, led astray, confused, and exposed to everyone. You do not know who to trust and so all kinds of thoughts and feelings flood your heart and soul as shock and trauma overtake you. It is important however not to get caught up in vindicating or defending yourself and or the vision while being so focused on the experience of betrayal that you and/or the vision do not continue forward in transitioning to where God is taking you. Even in the midst of the pain, it is essential to press onward as God unveils victory on your behalf.

Romans 12:19 Dearly beloved, avenge not yourselves, but rather give place unto wrath: for it is written, Vengeance is mine; I will repay, saith the Lord.

Overcoming Betrayal
- Spend time acknowledging and releasing all anger, rage, pain, hurt, shock and awe, slander, trickery, dishonor, false loyalty, manipulation, lies, deceitful control, need to vindicate and defend self, offense to God, and cleanse these attributes out of your heart and soul by applying the blood of Jesus.
- Forgive the betrayer and all parties involved; release the situation itself to God.
- Cast out the spirit of betrayal, murder, shock and awe, trauma, pain, mistrust, confusion, untruths that are lodged in your soul and heart.

- Cast out all demonic spirits of division and disunion operating between you and other people or you and the vision. These spirits tend to be lodged in the spirit realm and intertwined in the atmosphere of those parties involved, and where the betrayal occurred.
- Break the power of bewitchment and memory recall, and cleanse out the power of triggers that cause you to relive the situation over and over in your mind.
- Cleanse out all daggers and stabbing sensations and impressions.
- Ask God to heal your heart and soul such that the feelings of vulnerability and exposure are fused.
- Fill your soul and heart with God's love, acceptance, truth, and confidence.
- Spend time decreeing out who God says you are and the truth of who he says you are, and who and what he has called you to be.

You may have to complete these prayer steps multiple times to really heal your heart and soul from the effects of betrayal.

Spirits of Performance and Entertainment – People who operate in performance and entertainment spirits tend to be validated by their gifts and callings, and what they do rather than who they are. They take credit for the planning, the work, vision, and/or the success of the event without regarding the team or the glory God is to receive. It is okay to be proud of yourself and the work that you do. It is okay to receive accolades, rewards, and praise, for your investment and work. But when it is the identity of you it is an idol. Especially when it steals glory from God and disregards the work of others. Be mindful to esteem the good in everyone that was part of the vision or event. And create a team culture where the members accolade and empower one another so that there can be regard and honor for who each member is and what they do within the vision and event.

Proverbs 2:3 *Let nothing be done through strife or vainglory; but in lowliness of mind let each esteem other better than themselves.*

Spirit of Perfection - A person operating in this spirit will be very hard on themselves because they will always be striving to reach an unrealistic standard and level of perfection. In God we operate in his spirit of excellence where he is perfecting us; but through a spirit of perfection, we strive through our own strength, and through our own standards to perfect ourselves. We cannot be perfect within ourselves because it is God who perfects us.

A person manifesting this spirit will become easily frustrated, sensitive, and hard on themselves if they cannot get things right the first time, and if you correct and give them instructions. If they cannot get the movements right immediately, this is viewed as imperfection. If you give them a correction, they hear this as you telling them that they are not perfect. They will feel as though they have failed and are displeasing you when truly their need for unrealistic perfection has caused them to forget the reality that a learning process is natural.

The leader and team members may be hesitant to talk to this person, and very cautious as they try to find the best way to speak to them such that they can receive in a healthy manner. The leader and team members will not want them to be so hard on themselves, and will not want them to feel bad. This will become a burden to the leader and team members because it is an extra task in having to take the time to figure out how to talk to this person where they can receive, yet not succumbing to the spirit of perfection that they operate in. It will also become a burden to the person manifesting the spirit because they will be operating out of their own strength, and always striving and working extremely hard to reach their unrealistic standard of perfection. It will become extremely tiresome, weighty, unnecessary pressure on them, and it can cause anxiety. However, you do want and need to speak truth to them so that they recognize that they are operating in their strength and not God's ability to perfect that which concerns them.

The spirit of perfection is a threefold cord that consists of perfection, shame, and guilt. When the person sees the imperfection or it is revealed to them by another person, they become ashamed about it and then begin to feel guilty about not being able to be perfect. And then in a means to do away with the shame and guilt of not being perfect, the person will then focus on striving to perfect themselves, so that they no longer feel ashamed and guilty. Where there is a spirit of perfection there is always shame and guilt making the person feel bad, discouraged, and low about themselves. Shame and guilt also reinforce the person to cycle in perfecting themselves. It causes the person to go around and around in a circle striving for perfection. As soon as they see the imperfection, they want to fix it. They will never be perfect which is the reason they need God. If we were perfect, there would be no point in having a relationship with God.

Communication, love, and processing of deliverance and healing are needed to root out the spirit of perfection. The person needs to be cleansed of false realities and standards of perfection and the words of others that embedded this spirit where they felt as though they had to be perfect because others expected them to be. They need to be cleansed of fearing failure, being displeasing, and from feeling ashamed and guilty about not being able to perfect themselves. The threefold cord of perfection, shame, and guilt need to be broken. And they need to receive the truth that they cannot be perfect within themselves, but only God can be their perfecter.

Psalm 18:30-35 As for God, his way is perfect: the word of the Lord is tried: he is a buckler to all those that trust in him. For who is God save the Lord? or who is a rock save our God? It is God that girdeth me with strength, and maketh my way perfect. He maketh my feet like hinds 'feet, and setteth me upon my high places. He teacheth my hands to war, so that a bow of steel is broken by mine arms. Thou hast also given me the shield of thy salvation: and thy right hand hath holden me up, and thy gentleness hath made me great.

Psalm 138:8 *The Lord will perfect that which concerneth me: thy mercy, O Lord, endureth for ever: forsake not the works of thine own hands.*

Hebrews 13:20-21 *Now the God of peace, that brought again from the dead our Lord Jesus, that great shepherd of the sheep, through the blood of the everlasting covenant, Make you perfect in every good work to do his will, working in you that which is wellpleasing in his sight, through Jesus Christ; to whom be glory for ever and ever. Amen.*

<u>**Spirit of Offense**</u> - This spirit can work amongst a team through members taking offense to correction, constructive criticisms, pure jokes (not meant for harm), conversations, etc. when their intention was not to be offensive but to have healthy communication and interaction with the person. This spirit can operate between leader and member, and member and member. It is difficult to communicate with a person operating in this spirit because you never know what will trigger the offense. This person typically becomes offended without warning. The leader will try to give this person correction, and constructive criticism, but the person will immediately feel as though they are being wronged, attacked, and that an injustice is being done to them. Also if the team is sharing laughs, jokes, and conversations that include the person, and they perceive that these things are geared to harm them, they will become offended and feel like the team is ganging upon them, and bullying them. This causes division within the team, because the offended person always feels as though it is the leader and the team members against them. Yet the team accepts them and wants to embrace them, but the walls created by offense keep them at a distance.

The leader and members interacting with this person will feel as though they are being accused, as they are generally made out to be the suspect, while the person manifesting the spirit is always the victim. But truly in this instance, the offended person has become the offender. The leaders and members may shut down and not want to interact and have a relationship with this person, or they may continuously go on an unnecessary search within themselves trying to figure out what they are doing wrong when really it is not their issue. It is the person's issue or rather, the spirit of offense at work.

There are instances where a person manifesting this spirit will not know they are offended. They will contend they are being wronged and attacked. But often they are reliving or filtering through past hurtful experiences as they are interacting with others. They truly are being offended and hurt all over again by the past that they have not let go of and are still bound in. They are not being offended by the team, and the team should not take responsibility for their past experiences. Be sensitive to discerning this spirit because it will drain you, have you confused, wondering what is wrong, and searching for yourself unnecessarily. When yielding to this pattern of behavior, you will become just as bound as the person with the offensive spirit.

This spirit operates through:
- Miscommunication & misperception - Where the person continually misunderstands what is being said and communicated with them.
- Unhealed issues of the past where they have been abused, ridiculed, bullied, and truly offended, but they are harboring this offense and reflecting it upon you when you say something that reminds them and takes them back to this offense.
- Triggers - Words and actions that remind them of things that happened in the past that take them back to reliving the past offenses.
- Insecurities, inadequacies, and low self-esteem that has come in through past offenses, experiences, abuse.
- Victim spirit – Where the person thinks everyone is against them and hurts them.

Teaching and demonstrating how to express ones' feelings, concerns, and how to resolve conflict is key to bringing healing to someone with the spirit of offense. They may be surprised at what is being discussed because of their justifications, but speak truth to them in love, because they need to be free. This will also provide an avenue for them and the entire team to engage in healthy communication and conflict resolution skills.

This person also needs to go through a deliverance process, where they are cleansed from all past offense, bitterness, unforgiveness, anger, abuse, ridicule, bullying, and triggers that cause them to revisit the past. In addition, the person may need deliverance from unhealthy perception, poor or confused hearing, and judging situations through a negative well. This will be a process, as this spirit can be deeply rooted and enmeshed in a person's personality, character, and behaviors. They will need much love, patience, and encouragement while they process through to wholeness. They will also need someone to help them walk this out. Having a mentor or counselor will aid in the deliverance because this will break the mindset it is them against everyone else. They will see that they have people that are with them, they will not feel alone, and the walls of offense can begin to be broken down.

Proverbs 18:19 *A brother offended is harder to be won than a strong city: and their contentions are like the bars of a castle.*

Leviticus 19:18 *Thou shalt not avenge, nor bear any grudge against the children of thy people, but thou shalt love thy neighbour as thyself:I am the Lord.*

1Thessalonians 5:11-13 New Living Translation *Wherefore comfort yourselves together, and edify one another, even as also ye do. And we beseech you, brethren, to know them which labour among you, and are over you in the Lord, and admonish you; And to esteem them very highly in love for their work's sake. And be at peace among yourselves.*

1Thessalonians 5:15 New Living Translation *See that none render evil for evil unto any man; but ever follow that which is good, both among yourselves, and to all men.*

Spirit of Defense
Defense in Dictionary.com means:
1. Resistance against attack; protection
2. Something that defends as a fortification, physical or mental quality, or medication
3. The defending of a cause or the like by speech, argument, etc.
4. The denial or pleading of the defendant

This spirit operates through self-protection. If a person is manifesting this spirit they will feel as though what is being spoken has the potential to cause them harm, so they will immediately become defensive in order to protect and shield themselves. This spirit can manifest when the leader is giving correction, instruction, and constructive criticism. But it will also manifest in general conversation, and when the leader and team members are interacting and communicating with this person. This spirit operates frequently through fear, insecurity, and pride. But it is all in means to self-protect.

Different ways the spirit of defense manifests:
- Fear - as they fear being hurt. They protect themselves because things remind them of past hurts that they have received through harsh, hurtful experiences with past leaders, their peers, or those who have had some type of authority over their lives.
- Insecurity - Due to them not being secured in who they are, they will become defensive in times where they feel like they have to assert and prove to you, the team members, and even themselves who they are.
- Pride & haughtiness - As they will be in denial if they do not agree with whatever you are sharing with them. They will feel as though they are always doing everything correctly and that they don't need any correction. This will make it difficult for the leader to interact and communicate with this person because they will become defensive when the leader gives them corrections and instruction on how to improve and better themselves. And if the team is trying to help them with their assigned tasks, they will also respond to them in this same manner. The team will find it hard to unify and work as a team with this person because they can become defensive no matter what is said.

A person dealing with this spirit will have a hard time receiving from people, therefore, pride, insecurity, and/or fear will need to be cleansed. Due to a lack of reception, this person has difficulty growing personally in their gifting, and this also challenges their growth with the team. The person may not recognize that they operate in this spirit.

This spirit can be embedded in a person's personality, behaviors, and identity. They need to submit to mentoring and the process of deliverance and healing. They require truth throughout the process to keep them accountable and honest. They need to be cleansed from fear and the past where they were abused, criticized harshly, and mistreated by leaders, parents, peers, or any authority figure where they felt defenseless. All word curses and pacts they made in saying that they would never be defenseless again and that they would protect and defend themselves need to be broken. All revenge-seeking, and wanting to avenge themselves from their hurtful experiences, harboring the past through unforgiveness and bitterness needs to be cleansed. They need to be cleansed from any insecurity, and healed to a place of wholeness within themselves where they understand that who they are will speak for itself, and who they are is great in the Lord. They need to be cleansed from strongholds that cause wrong thinking and feeling that the corrections and help of others diminish who they are because it actually enhances it. Moreover, they need to completely relinquish all rights to protect and shield themselves and receive healing in trusting, and relying on God as their protector and shield.

Psalm 5:11-12 But let all those that put their trust in thee rejoice: let them ever shout for joy, because thou defendest them: let them also that love thy name be joyful in thee. For thou, Lord, wilt bless the righteous; with favour wilt thou compass him as with a shield.

Psalm 36:7 How excellent is thy lovingkindness, O God!
therefore the children of men put their trust under the shadow of thy wings.

2Samuel 22:2-3 And he said, The Lord is my rock, and my fortress, and my deliverer; The God of my rock; in him will I trust: he is my shield, and the horn of my salvation, my high tower, and my refuge, my saviour; thou savest me from violence.

Spirit of the Enabler
Dictionary.com defines *enabler* as:
2. To make able; give power, means, yield competence, or ability to; authorize
3. To make possible or easy
4. To make ready; equip (often used in combination)

Ephesians 5:11 - And have no fellowship with the unfruitful works of darkness, but rather reprove them.

When we enable people, we are actually authorizing them to mistreat, mishandle, and take advantage of us. There is usually a false or erred loyalty or obligation associated with being an enabler. The enabler is not really wanting to aid a person and operates through self-inflicted pressure or pressure and manipulation imposed by the person seeking assistance. Generally, this person presents as the victim, entitled, privileged, and as if the enabler is required to aide them. They will make statements to make the enabler feel bad about themselves as if they have to help them. It will be an attack against the enabler's morals, standards, and character, where they are made to believe that they are not the good person they present as if they do not give the person what they want. The enabler often volunteers from tasks and roles they really do not have the heart to do but feel obligated to do. They will then be angry and passive-aggressive for having to do them. They will sometimes take their indirectly take their anger and aggression out on the person they helped, or on others that they really should be helping but assert their right not to help in the effort to gain some control over their right to make their own decisions.

The enabler is challenging to have on a team or part of an event because of these behaviors. They are subject to quit and refuse to complete tasks abruptly and it can be detrimental to the excellence and advancement of the vision planning and the release of the event. It will be important to discern a person who is an enabler and making sure people are being part of the team because they have a heart and clarity about who they are to the vision and the event and how their gifts and callings are essential to what God is releasing in the earth. Often such persons SHIFT back and forth between an enabler and a fixer.

Spirit of the Fixer - Please note that this is a broad revelation of the fixer spirit. Some may not possess all these qualities but may still be bound by the fixer spirit.

Dictionary.com defines *fixer* as:
1. A person or thing that fixes
2. Informal. A person who arranges matters in advance through bribery or influence

Dictionary.com defines *fix* as:
1. To repair; mend
2. To put in order or in good condition; adjust or arrange
3. To make fast, firm, or stable
4. To place definitely and more or less permanently
5. To settle definitely; determine
6. To direct (the eyes, the attention, etc.) Steadily
7. To attract and hold (the eye, the attention, etc.).
8. To make set or rigid
9. To put into permanent form
10. to put or place (responsibility, blame, etc.) on a person

A fixer has a driven need to repair, rescue, or help someone while attempting to fit the person into their personal perception of how they believe someone should be, what they feel would perfect the person or the person's life. The fixer tends to bombard the person with their own ideas and perceptions of what the fixer believes it will take to make the person perfect. The fixer also tends to only accept the person if the person conforms to the fixer's perceptions, eventually yielding to what the fixer believes it will take to perfect the person's life.

A fixer can also be someone who has the best interest of others at heart. The fixer sees a person's potential but cares more about the person changing than the person cares about it themselves. Such a person (fixer) ends up playing roles in the person's life that they should not. The fixer resorts to being more to the person than they should be. The fixer is striving to be the rescuer and although some of their perceptions can be useful and beneficial, the well through which these ideas are filtered, is usually by way of negativity, a critical mess, a need to control, a need to be needed and a need to fix others. Most fixers have unresolved hurts, painful pasts, or challenging experiences and as a result, they use their fixer mindset in an effort to rescue others from hardship.

Some fixers fear being hurt due to unresolved issues from their past. This leads to their striving to perfect those who desire a relationship with them. The challenge to this (for the fixer) is that they now try to make the person consistently fix things about themselves in order to please the fixer so the person can remain a part of the fixer's life. By the time the person fixes one thing about themselves, the fixer has already presented another thing to fix. The person finds themselves constantly jumping through hoops to try and please the fixer. However, the fixer cannot be pleased because their issue is actually not that person, but the fixer's own need to be healed. They engage in their relationships through their past unhealed pains and fears of being hurt again.

Some fixers have the heart and compassion of God, the gift of discernment and help, and the gift of administration. They are called to lead, shepherd, train and equip people, yet they use their gifts in an unhealthy or unbalanced manner. They end up becoming God and/or an enabler in peoples' lives. Their need or drive to be the savior of the person causes them to be more to the person than God has said, or it causes them to take on more than God is requiring. This type of fixer possesses great positive qualities and giftings but needs balance in making sure they are allowing God to be God. If they allow God to be God, they will not end up hating their lives and callings and resenting those whom they are called to help as a result of becoming and bearing more than God has intended.

Fixers tend to build a lifestyle of false peace and false perfection. They do this by holding on to people through superficial and surface relationships. If you penetrate their walls, you will find some mental instability and inabilities to truly trust, relax, and rest in the love and security of the relationship.

Anytime you are imperfect, the fixer takes this as a personal attack against themselves. They view your downfalls as your hurting them, betraying them, and dishonoring them, especially if they gave you advice on a matter but you did not implement it or were not consistent in utilizing it. "*How dare you not take their advice and run with it.*" The fixer tends to punish the person by ending the relationship or threatening to end it if the person does not correct this betrayal immediately.

The fixer will also use silence and abusive threats to control and manipulate a person into feeling guilty and ashamed of not following through with their advice.   The person will often feel beat down, condemned, confused, and double-minded by the negative words and negative perceptions that the fixer speaks towards them. The person will feel confused and double-minded because what the fixer says or is suggesting may have a point of truth, but the method is all wrong. Therefore, the person wavers between wanting to submit and rebelling against what the fixer is suggesting.   Also, unless the person does everything the fixer says, the fixer negates any progress the person makes. It is usually all or nothing for a fixer, so the person tends to be abusively corrected and chastened despite any progress they have made.

There are instances where the fixer will obtain information about the person's past failures, and then when the fixer is correcting and chastising the person, the fixer will belittle the person reminding them of these failures. Fixers use these failures to cause the person to feel as if they will never change and will never have success if they do not adhere to what is being demanded of them.

Sometimes the fixer's perceptions of the person are rooted in their own past hurtful experiences with other people. The fixer, however, casts these perceptions onto the person and assumes that the person is also that way, even if the person is in no way similar to the person that hurt the fixer.

A fixer checks upon the person to ensure that the person is doing what is demanded of them. The fixer will also ask certain questions in an effort to get the person to admit that they have not changed or have not followed through with what was requested. The fixer tends to attack the person's character placing the person in a position of having to defend themselves. Fear causes the person to lie in order to avoid being rebuked or shut down altogether if they have not done what was required of them. Any of these positions causes the fixer to become angry and feel betrayed. What follow is usually verbally abusive or controlling manipulative acts for the purpose of forcing the person into subjection to the fixer's demands.

Though the fixer appears to celebrate you when you achieve success from doing what you were told to do, the fixer's motive of celebration is not due to your being transformed but it is because you implemented the fixer's ideas. You will recognize this when the fixer takes credit for your achievement even though you did the work. The fixer will contend that you only acquired victory because of them, and without them, you are a failure waiting to happen.

Because fixers view themselves as the helper, it is very difficult to get them to pursue deliverance and healing from their fixer mindset. If they do acknowledge their issues, it is generally with the mindset that the only reason they are broken is because of the person they are fixing; they feel that if they fix you, that fixes them.

The fixer relationship tends to resemble Jezebel and Ahab from the bible. To Jezebel, Ahab was inadequate. She was always using control, fear, manipulation, threats, murder, and negative methods to fix situations that King Ahab had reign over (*1Kings 18-19*).

Because of the emotional soul ties and bewitchment that occur between the fixer and the fixee, it can take years before the fixee realizes they are being abused and needs to end the relationship. The fixee has close calls of ending it but tends to talk themselves out of it when rewarded with the fixer's attention and seductive accolades The fixer makes the fixee believe that these accolades are due to the fixee's good behavior in submitting to what was required of them. However, the fixer's behaviors soon return and the fixees are entangled again and striving to comprehend whether the confusion and chastising they are receiving is actually abuse and unhealthy to their overall wellbeing.

The fixer can also possess many good qualities that make the fixee want to work on the relationship, to please the fixer, and even prove themselves to the fixer. The fixer tends to have the person so bewitched that the person feels as though they will be losing out by ending the relationship. The fixee ends up feeling that they are hopeless and cannot live without the fixer. These very misconceptions are what keep the cycle of the relationship going. Eventually, the fixer tends to leave the relationship with regret, feeling that years of their life have been wasted on something that never could have been healthy; they feel that they have lost themselves in a relationship that bred only unhealthiness and identity theft.

Some of us have become fixers or have been groomed as fixers through our family roles and traditions. We have been the smart ones, the successful ones, the responsible ones, or the reliable ones in the family. We have been the oldest kid, the family curse breaker, or have had to step up due to insufficient parental roles in the family. Some have had to rely on themselves and take care of others, particularly siblings. Thus, we have been molded and shaped into the fixers.

Some of us have become successful and have felt obligated to go back and fix or take care of capable family members. We feel obligated because they are family and now there is the unrealistic pressure to take care of them or enable them. This fixer mentality has been groomed within us due to the wounds of a difficult childhood, false or unhealthy cultural obligations, guilt and shame of being successful while other family members remain in poverty or role reversals where the child has had to be the parent or has had to fulfill parental duties as a child or teenager. This is not your burden to bear. Let God lead you as to when you are to assist and help your family. Do not engage in savior roles that only God can fulfill.   God is the only fixer and He has promised that if we walk with Him, He will perfect (make sound) the things that concern us.

Psalm 138:8 *The Lord will perfect (make sound) that which concerneth me: thy mercy, O LORD, endureth for ever: forsake not the works of thine own hands.*

DEMONIC BINDINGS TO OLD PARADIGMS & SEASONS

From my manual, "*Fivefold Operations Volume II: Shifting Into Vision Casting.*"

As you strive to SHIFT from the old paradigm into a fivefold paradigm, certain spirits, cycles, and psychological attacks will come for you. They want to SHIFT you back and keep you tied to the old.

Psychological Warfare (Study the story of Nehemiah) - Derives from territorial spirits, powers, spells and word curses, and witchcraft sent from witches, warlocks, and demonic chatter from demons, ungodly, foolish, or ignorant people. Words live on airways and demons pick them up, especially the negative ones. Then they speak them back to you to distract, weary, and kill your progress or stance in God. This warfare causes anxiety, insecurity, wrestling, and questioning God's word.

Break the powers of wrestling and questioning. Boldly muzzle and silence demonic voices by telling them to SHUT UP! Break the powers of spells, soothsaying, psychic powers, and telepathy being sent against you. Use the blood of Jesus to cleanse airways and frequencies of ungodly, negative, and demonic words that have been spoken about you.

Mental Warfare - can come from the insecurities of your soul - your inner man, or from the principalities and powers and frequencies and airways within your midst. It entails a continuous flood of vile thoughts, misperceptions, mental oppression, fear and doubt, confusion, forgetfulness, migraines, demonic suggestions, and impressions. The voices of your soul, or of the enemy are strong and speaking continually to weaken your mind, your stance, and your ability to journey in the truths, purposes, strategies, visions, and momentum of the Lord. You may feel crazy and like you are losing your mind, focus, faith, and stability.

It is important to deal with the wounded and insecure issues of your soul as this will help silence mental warfare. Also, muzzle the mouths and airways of demonic forces around you while cleansing mental instability and pressuring words that have been released concerning you within the frequencies and airways of your region.

Emotional Warfare - Attacks your emotions and senses while causing double-mindedness, confusion, frustration, pressure, depression, and oppression. Makes you feel dramatic and out of control like you are on an emotional rollercoaster. Can cause you to appear manic, bipolar, or schizophrenic. Can operate through condemnation and uses shame and guilt of being unstable to further draw you away and isolate you from your supports and accountability partners. Causes weeping, uncontrollable crying for no apparent reason, or regarding things that would not warrant crying. Evokes thoughts of suicide, death, and failure thoughts. Attacks your body's hormonal system to further confound emotional instability and affliction (e.g., PMS, thyroid issues, digestive issues, blood pressure issues, migraines, anxiety, panic, nervousness, body aches, and pains).

Insecurity, immaturity, unworthiness, and/or comparison, fear of the unknown, fear of failing, life stressors, burnout, can open the doors to this attack. Bewitchment from people, witches, and demons can also cause this attack.

You must be discerning that this attack will occur or you will give fully into it. You will spend days distracted, losing time, focus, and momentum due to succumbing to it. It will in turn, take time to SHIFT out of it due to its impact. It will feel like you are SHIFTING up out of a pit or dark place.

Receiving prayer and encouragement immediately is key to nullifying this attack. Come up out of this attack by reconnecting with supports, receiving prayer, fellowship, and truth. Spend time soaking in the love of God; spend time rehearsing and decreeing out promises, and prophecies of God.

Financial Warfare - Will come as the spirit of Python to squeeze out the vision finances and cause financial hardship. Come to make you believe you cannot fund the vision; it is too big and cannot be financed. Will cause psychological warfare of worry regarding money. Apostle Jackie Green, founder of The Enternational Prayerlife Institute, says this spirit will *"cause attacks in areas of job security, bank accounts, old bills arise from the past, garnishment of wages, stress on the church finances and unexpected expenses eat away at monies. Enemy will attack your faithful tithers and givers to cause them to leave the church or be attacked in their income so they cannot give."*

Consistently contend against the spirit of Python. Continuously release the vision to God and declare miracles and prosperity blessings to manifest on your behalf. Take on the mindset that the vision is God's so he will find it and expect him to do just that. Share your concerns and fears with God concerning finances and allow him to build and encourage your faith as needed. Ask God for witty ideas for creating multiple streams of income. Command prophetic words and promises concerning finances and prosperity to manifest in your life. Decree out wealth transfers from the wicked and for favor with people to sow consistently into your life and vision. Decree into the glory and SHIFT heaven to earth on your behalf. Deal with any brass heavens, poverty spirits, and personal and generational strongholds that may be hindering the flow of favor, mercy, grace, and prosperity.

Proverbs 8:12 *I wisdom dwell with prudence, and find out knowledge of witty inventions.*

Psalm 104:24 *O LORD, how manifold are thy works! in wisdom hast thou made them all: the earth is full of thy riches.*

Philippians 4:19 *But my God shall supply all your need according to his riches in glory by Christ Jesus.*

Proverbs 13:22 *A good man leaveth an inheritance to his children's children: and the wealth of the sinner is laid up for the just.*

<u>Python Spirits</u> - Spirits that come to slowly squeeze the life out of the vision carriers, members, and the vision. This spirit comes as depression, heaviness, financial hardship, subtle drainage of an area/s of your life and vision. It will wrap around a person, family, situation, and ministry, or region, vision, while using its body to squeeze and restrict them where:

- They are limited in mobility and progress
- There may also be unexplainable tiredness and lethargic oppression where energy, movement, and progress is slow or thwarted
- There will be a weightiness, physical suffocation, overexertion in energy, and sluggardness to being in step with the momentum of God
- It causes confusion, discombobulation, double-mindedness, and thought racing, from the signal faculties in the brain being restricted, weighty and crushed

Python comes to squeeze the life out of people, families, churches, ministries, relationships, and the region spiritually, physically, financially, economically, mentally, and emotionally, etc. Comes against new ministries and businesses with a vengeance to thwart and abort the vision and hinder them from planting and developing. Seeks to kill them early by causing constriction and suffocation. This is done through suffocation and constriction. Death is generally slow and painful. The snake:

- Sits on the person's shoulders and makes them sluggish and lethargic
- Will wrap around a person, ministry, or region to attempt to constrict to squeeze out the life, production, zeal, fruit, and success of that person, ministry, or region
- Will wrap around the head revelation and vision and cause headaches and pressure

Also works through:

- Divination/Soothsaying (Gothic, astrology, and Baal)
- Pharmakia (hallucinate drugs, street drugs, prescribed pain pills, psychiatric drugs)
- Apathy – makes a person, atmosphere, or region lethargic, sluggish, indifferent, passive, cold, lacking a drive for life

- Depression – especially strong in the fall leading to the winter months. Winters tend to be very long, the cold weather is bitter and hard, which makes life secluded and difficult
- Heaviness (constant feeling of a weighing down)
- Word curses, witchcraft
- Fear – sluggardness and indifferent feelings sensations causing anxiety, fear, fear of dying, fear of failing
- Discouragement - the hopelessness that tends to hit a person or atmosphere when there are not any challenging situations going on or heightens when situations may be occurring
- Infirmity – will cause sicknesses that come in the form of feeling pressured or weighed down. Can also cause respiratory illnesses or sensations like inability to breathe or choking

Isaiah 61:3 *To appoint unto them that mourn in Zion, to give unto them beauty for ashes, the oil of joy for mourning, the garment of praise for the spirit of heaviness; that they might be called trees of righteousness, the planting of the Lord, that he might be glorified.*

Break the head and tail of the python. Loose Holy fire to torment it where it releases its grip while commanding this spirit to uncoil and be cast out of your midst. Continuously decree, promote, and release life and that more abundantly as death cannot flourish where God's light and resurrection life dwells.

Spirits of Fear - These spirits will come in the form of spiritual warfare. They will constantly try to make you feel insecure, inept, and inferior of the SHIFT you are embarking upon. They will be attempting to break you down - weary you - until you give up altogether or return to what is comfortable and familiar.

- Fear of failing
- Fear of looking ill-equipped
- Fear of engaging in false and erred doctrine
- Fear of making the wrong decisions and moves
- Fear of leading people wrong
- Fear of losing control and order of people and the ministry
- Fear of losing what has already been built
- Fear of losing members
- Fear of being alone - losing friends, loved ones, ministry partners who do not understand or believe in fivefold
- Fear of losing destiny and ministry momentum

- Fear of being ridiculed and judged
- Fear of the warfare of SHIFTING into a new paradigm or that accompanies fivefold ministry
- Fear of not having avenues to be trained and equipped
- Fear of not being ready for fivefold ministry and all it entails

Stand on the word against these spirits:

2Timothy 1:7 *For God hath not given us the spirit of fear; but of power, and of love, and of a sound mind. SHIFT!*

1John 4:4 *You are of God, little children, and have overcome them, because He who is in you is greater than he who is in the world.*

Philippians 4:13 *I can do all things through Christ who strengthens me.*

John 10:27 *My sheep hear my voice, and I know them, and they follow me:*

Isaiah 11:2 *The Spirit of the LORD will rest on Him--the Spirit of wisdom and understanding, the Spirit of counsel and strength, the Spirit of knowledge and the fear of the LORD.*

John 14:27 *Peace I leave with you; My peace I give to you. I do not give to you as the world gives. Do not let your hearts be troubled; do not be afraid.*

Romans 8:15 *For you did not receive a spirit of slavery that returns you to fear, but you received the Spirit of sonship, by whom we cry, "Abba! Father!"*

Romans 8:31 *What then shall we say to these things? If God is for us, who can be against us?*

Isaiah 54:15-17 *Indeed they shall surely assemble, but not because of Me. Whoever assembles against you shall fall for your sake. "Behold, I have created the blacksmith Who blows the coals in the fire, Who brings forth an instrument for his work; And I have created the spoiler to destroy. No weapon formed against you shall prosper, And every tongue which rises against you in judgment You shall condemn. This is the heritage of the servants of the Lord, And their righteousness is from Me," Says the Lord.*

2Corinthians 2:14 *Now thanks be to God who always leads us in triumph in Christ, and through us diffuses the fragrance of His knowledge in every place.*

<u>**Destiny Killing Spirit**</u> - Attacks personally and generationally. It wants to kill your destiny, and any way God's plan for your life impacts your success, advancement, lineage, and present and future generations.

John 10:10 The thief cometh not, but for to steal, and to kill, and to destroy: I am come that they might have life, and that they might have it more abundantly.

This spirit usually begins its attack at a young age, even at birth, and then attempts to kill the person's identity, purpose, and hope at a young age. This is the reason so many believers, especially leaders, experience challenging childhoods. The enemy is striving to kill the person before they realize there is a plan for their lives. This spirit knows that if you align with true fivefold, destiny is inevitable.

It will do everything possible to murder or get you to murder, altar or stifle the vision and plan God is providing for your life. It will blatantly try to kill you, send people to try to kill you spiritually and naturally through words, enticements, seductions; come through sickness and affliction, try to steal and kill the seeds you plant, release constant warfare to get you to quit, present favorable or easier altering paths so you compromise. You have to want what God has for you more than what the devil or man can offer. You have to get to a place of being souled out and wanting to please God at all cost.

Identify personal and generational destiny-killing spirits, how they come for you, when they come for you, and how they manifest in people and in situations around you. Break their powers over your life and generational line. Cancel their assignments against your life and generations. Close up doors in and around you that allows them to enter your sphere of influence. Break and resist cycles and behavioral patterns of sabotage, disobedience, rebellion, and anti-submissiveness as this opens the door to the operation of destiny-killing spirits.

<u>*Backsliding Spirit*</u> - This spirit will cause you to relapse into old familiar habits, religious and traditional behavior, and activities. This spirit will make you believe that what you had was better than where God is taking you. It will have all types of excuses as to the reason you should stay or return to the old. It will point out all your flaws, the challenges of moving forward, make you feel obligated to the old, and be responsible for others not being able to fill your position. It will cause you to endure psychological and mental warfare that makes you feel insecure and the unknown and the future. It will present the old as productive, fruitful, beneficial, and prosperous. And even if these attributes hold truth, if it is not where God wants you then you are in sin due to disobedience and are reaping from an illegal place of familiarity. Such harvest often comes with consequences where you eventually ensure drama and calamity from the place or people to which you are reaping or receive the judgment of the Lord due to being disobedient.

Spend time repenting for backsliding ways, cycles, sin issues, and disobedience towards the purposes of God. Break the powers of rebellion and anti-submissiveness and break all soul ties with the old (e.g. the people, ministry, positions, duties, etc.). Spend time closing doors to the old and decreeing out new doors, visions, and purposes. Spend time seeking God for clarity, vision, and love for the new SHIFTED vision he is bringing you into. Seek accountability partners that can help you remain grounded in the new vision. Be obedient to what God is saying while fasting weekly to kill your flesh and subject your soul to your spirit where you can walk confidently in the will and purposes of God.

Spirit Of The Crab - This spirit moves sideways and never forward, and attempts to get you to do this as well. It will try to sidetrack you, delay, and sideline you from the purposes of God. It will try to get you to feel that you are not ready and will present all types of excuses as the reason you should wait, should not go forward, and the reasons you are not equipped to do what God has already told and trained you to do. When natural crabs are clumped together, they will pull one another down in order to get ahead or out of a sticky spot. This spirit operates in the same manner. It tries to pull you down or off the correct path with God especially when you are gaining some progress and momentum in God. It attempts to pull you to a place of sidetracking, backsliding, and regression. It will attempt to stifle your success and advancement where you are working on the same thing over and over again, while never progressing or moving past a certain point in your life.

This spirit will also try to keep your soul tied to the old by providing opportunities that appear to be favorable, profitable, and for the betterment of all parties when really it is just to keep you attached to the old and distracted in advancing where God is taking you. Break this spirits legs as it uses its claws of words, belittlement, error, obligation, false loyalty, plan B, seduction, manipulation, intimidation, pride, sin, poverty, and low-level mindsets and behaviors, etc., to snatch you back down to its downgraded level or a level beneath God's will for your life. This spirit will be seeking to own and use you but you will not be aware of it because of the flattery and seduction to which it presents.

Spirits of Religion & Tradition aka Ungodly Vision Dictators - People will come and want you to be and implement a traditional paradigm when God has given you a unique fivefold blueprint. They are going to want Sunday services, bible studies, Sunday school, men's ministries, women's ministries, and so on. They will not have vision for your blueprint but will see the potential of the old inside the physical space God has given you. They will speak against your vision, question it, and tell you how unrealistic and far-fetched it is. They will sow seeds of fear as it relates to your ability to succeed, fund the vision, or draw people to the vision. They will tell you how great and safe the religious and traditional paradigm is and make you feel it is best for you and those God has called you to.

Do not allow people to dictate, implement their familiarity on you, or place a vision on you that God did not give you. If they cannot align with the vision God sets, then they are not your remnant and that is okay. There is a ministry, business, etc., for them. Encourage them to connect to them, while remaining true to the blueprint God has called you to. You will know your remnant. Your remnant will value the vision and want to align with it. They will want who you are and what God has called you to do on the earth. If they want an altered vision implemented then they need to run with it by planting it themselves - not you.

Do not allow it to sow seeds of negativity, discord, fear, and witchcraft curses into you or your ministry. Have a clear understanding of your identity, purpose, and vision so you can immediately shut down this spirit when it manifests. Be okay with silencing this spirit with the truth of the vision and rebuke and correct it and anyone else that agrees with it. Do not give these people major roles in your ministry until they show clear signs of being delivered from this spirit. Otherwise, they will sow tares and wreak havoc in your ministry and the unity of your team. They will seek to get people on their side as they release subtle word curses to discredit you and the vision and to draw people back into familiar paradigms that appear more logical and easier to implement. Value quality over quantity and know that few is better than having people on the team that do not have your heart for the vision.

<u>**Legalism**</u> - Is the act of putting ungodly laws or the laws of the land above the gospel of Jesus Christ, above the laws and standards of God, or above what God is purposing concerning your life or situation. These laws can be laws of your community, state, nation; laws on your job, laws of an organization, policies, and procedures, legal requirements; school rules or requirements, culture trends, traditions of man, your family; laws and doctrines of ministries and businesses, that are used by the enemy to stifle what God has purposed, is planting, building, etc. Or that wants you to disobey the laws and standards of God's word.

You have to trust God to prevail for you. It will initially appear as you will not win. Do not waver or fear. But stand decreeing and contending for the judgment, justice, and purpose of God to manifest, as he will prevail for you.

<u>**False or Immature Place Holders**</u> - Be okay with people gleaning but not being your remnant. There will be seasonal people, inconsistent followers, church hoppers, and sojourners. Per Apostle Oscar Guobadia, Founder of the Brook Place Ministries in United Kingdom London, sojourners are those you instruct and impart into but are not your remnant). You will always have people like this show up at your ministry and that is okay. They can be a blessing to you in certain ways as they glean and connect with you and your ministry and you and your ministry can be a blessing to them. Accept what they can give, do not take it personal when they do not support and invest sufficiently; and do not see it as dishonor when they are not committed to your vision. They are not supposed to be committed because they are not your remnant. Yet, they may be just as important to awakening revival reformation in the region as you are as

they may be connected to someone else's ministry or sent to be a temporary assistant. Or they may be sent to give what they can but nothing more. Receive them for where they are and do not give them complete access to the vision. Do not give them positions that they are not capable of filling. If they want more access to the vision then give them goals where they can mature into vision carriers. They will either mature where you can effectively utilize them or they will leave. Either way you are operating responsibly with protecting yourself and the vision.

THWARTING DEMONIC WITCHCRAFT ATTACKS

It is important in being offensive to know that demons and witchcraft will attack you and to have some awareness of how this may operate. This is just a cheat sheet list of some of the demons and witchcraft experiences you and others may encounter as you release your purpose in the earth. Remember you are **VICTORIOUS! SHIFT!**

Zapping Spirit – Bombards, jolts, snatches, strikes, deletes, steals, kills, revelation, thoughts, and understanding from the mind, such that the brain cannot release the correct information to the people or maintain the information God downloads to them.

John 10:10 *The thief cometh not, but for to steal, and to kill, and to destroy: I am come that they might have life, and that they might have it more abundantly.*

Blocking Spirits - Use walls, barriers, or troops of demons that have locked themselves together in the spirit realm, where you will have difficulty getting past a particular barrier. This will feel like a wall, gate, ceiling, door, object hindering breakthrough or a pathway from opening. You may also feel this in your mind and heart where you cannot seem to SHIFT pass a certain thought, issue, or barrier that has lodged itself in these areas.

Psalm 18:29 *For by thee I have run through a troop; and by my God have I leaped over a wall.*

This scripture lets us know that we must run through these barriers. When encountering them, verbally declare out blasting through any troops that have set up a siege against you and then use your authority in God to leap over demonic structures.

Tracking Spirits, Demonic Watchers, Squatters & Hitchhiker Spirits

- *Tracking Spirits* are demonic agents who are assigned to gather intel on you and then report it back to their demonic camp. They track you by whatever means necessary. They will track you from place to place as you move about everyday life, through computer systems and other computerized intel, etc. They will even track you to church and ministry events. They lurk around – ease dropping on your prayers and conversations, to acquire information about you then report back so that demonic assignments can be released against you. Sometimes you can feel these spirits following you. You know those times it feels like something is following you. It is probably a tracker. They tend to live on the airways, so they rarely will use a body. Although they will oppress people in your inner circle and track you that way. Or they will follow people in your inner circle and track you. Psychics, high priests work with these spirits to track clients and gather intel, so they can have information to share when the person comes for their session. It appears as if the psychic possess information that only someone in your private life could have known. They do because the demon tracked you.

- *Demonic Watchers* are spirits that are sent to spy on you after the tracker spirit has shared information on you with his demonic camp. Watchers report on your progress so that further demonic assignments can be released against you. Watcher spirits will even travel to different places as you travel or send messages to other regions that you are coming, share the intel regarding you, so that the demons in that region can be aware of what you will be doing, and can find a way to counterattack your productivity and progress. Especially if you are trying to save souls for Jesus. In the past, I use to see these spirits traveling by the airplane when I am going out of town to do ministry. I have learned to pray to cancel their assignments, so they do not track me. Many people share all kinds of personal information on your social media pages. Watcher spirits are sharing that information with the demonic camp. The enemy knew where and how to attack the person at because it is on their Facebook page.

  In the spirit realm, the devil has a demonic library where he keeps files, especially of people who have great callings on their lives. I have seen these libraries and some of these files. Also, the systems of this world, ignorantly help these spirits to collect and maintain information on us. We are constantly being asked for our updated email address, cellphone numbers, etc., when we go in stores or when conducting business transactions.

  It is good to pray against tracker and watcher spirits consistently, as your purpose will alarm to demons wage war against you. Blind these spirits and declare amnesia of any intel they have collected on you. Send them wandering in dessert land until Jesus return or send them back to their camps confused and discombobulated. Declare their kingdom will attack them for not having any information to report. Use the fire of God to zap and burn out any information the enemy has stored on you in his demonic library and computer systems. Cancel their assignments in the spirit realm and annihilate anyway they are working with principalities and powers in my region and other regions to track and attack you. Ask God to place a hedge around you and to give you a stealth bomber anointing, so you can go about undetected to the enemy.

- *Stealth Bomber Anointing - Psalms 18:28-29* For thou wilt light my candle: the Lord my God will enlighten my darkness. For by thee I have run through a troop; and by my God have I leaped over a wall.

- *Enemies Destroying One another – 2Chronicles 20:21-22* When he had consulted with the people, he appointed those who sang to the LORD and those who praised Him in holy attire, as they went out before the army and said, "Give thanks to the LORD, for His lovingkindness is everlasting." When they began singing and praising, the LORD set ambushes against the sons of Ammon, Moab and Mount Seir, who had come against Judah; so they were routed. For the sons of Ammon and Moab rose up against the inhabitants of Mount Seir destroying them completely; and when they had finished with the inhabitants of Seir, they helped to destroy one another.

- *Squatter Spirits* are short plump looking demons that squat on your property or land to keep the gateways open for tracking and watcher spirits to track you and for other spirits to attack you. Squatter spirits are usually unlawful. They may not have any legal right to be on your land or property. They usually take advantage of you not paying spiritual attention, or if God has promised you a land or building and you do not lay claim to it, they take up residence to and occupy it. Their presence becomes a blockage to you acquiring it. They can sit on land and hinder you from acquiring property and buildings that God has promised to you. They will also sit on your land and manifest spirits of gloom, doom, and depression. That is the reason sometimes you may pull up at events, and there is a dark presence on the parking lot or even in the building. Squatter spirits have laid claim to the land. They are there to make people apathetic, sullen, dull, and dead to the move and presence of God.

    When there is a blockage in you acquiring land, a building, or things appear dark and gloomy around your land and property, examine if you have squatters. Put these illegal demons off your property and close any portals and gateways that have opened to give access to other demons.

- *Hitchhiker Spirits* are opportunists. They hang out at gas stations, stores, in appliances and different items within stores, etc., and then get in the car with people and go home with them. These spirits also like to hang out at churches and Christian events and then go home with people. Therefore, we cast the devil out of folks, and these hitchhikers look for vulnerable culprits to go home with and oppress.

    Some demonic spirits that are cast out in meetings hang outside the church until services are over and go home with folks they oppressed or find other spiritual homes to demonize. This especially occurs at events with mass deliverance and breakthrough. It is beneficial to have intercessors praying during or after the service to further displace these spirits.

Python Spirits - Wrap around a person, family, situation, ministry, or region, while using its body to squeeze and restrict them where:

- They are limited in mobility and progress.
- There may also be unexplainable tiredness and lethargic oppression where energy, movement, and progress are slow or thwarted.
- There will be a weightiness, physical suffocation, overexerted energy, and sluggardness to being in step with the momentum of God.
- It causes confusion, discombobulation, double-mindedness, and thought racing, from the signal faculties in the brain being restricted, weighty, and crushed.

Isaiah 61:3 *To appoint unto them that mourn in Zion, to give unto them beauty for ashes, the oil of joy for mourning, the garment of praise for the spirit of heaviness; that they might be called trees of righteousness, the planting of the Lord, that he might be glorified.*

Break the head and tail of the python. Loose holy fire to torment python where it releases its grip while commanding this spirit to uncoil and be cast out of your midst.

Spirit Of Leviathan The King Of Pride – Leviathan is the king of pride. Leviathan Interrupts and distorts communication between the speaker and the listener, between God and the person/ministry, and within atmospheres. Its' effort is to sow offense, discord, irritation, anger, misunderstanding, faultfinding, ungodly judging, mistrust, and suspicion. Job speaks of how Leviathan operates in ***Job 41:26-32***. This spirit was in operation between him and his friends who were striving to understand why God allowed the enemy to bring havoc upon his life. This spirit also distorted Job's views where he could not receive wise counsel from God during this time of trial with the Lord. This spirit will enter in when the ministry is under heavy warfare, is in the middle of intense ministry or transition, or is on a time schedule. Quick repentance and forgiveness is the easiest way to combat leviathan. The unity and love of Christ will dismantle and displace this spirit.

Galatians 6:1-3 The Amplified Bible BRETHREN, IF any person is overtaken in misconduct or sin of any sort, you who are spiritual [who are responsive to and controlled by the Spirit] should set him right and restore and reinstate him, without any sense of superiority and with all gentleness, keeping an attentive eye on yourself, lest you should be tempted also. Bear (endure, carry) one another's burdens and troublesome moral faults, and in this way fulfill and observe perfectly the law of Christ (the Messiah) and complete what is lacking [in your obedience to it].

Cut the head and the tail off of this spirit, and release fire to burn its fruits and roots, while casting it out of your sphere.

Mind Binding & Mind Blinding Spirits – Witches love to operate through the stronghold of mind control. These spirits bind and blind the thought life, the mind, and senses to cause affliction, confusion, unexplainable fear of people or of failure, and anxiety; have trouble paying attention, experience mind wandering and racing thoughts. This spirit tends to operate and look like an octopus or a squid. You may feel pressure or a tormenting headache, feel like something is sticking you in the eyes, ears, temples, forehead, or the back of the head. Things may look black as you strain to see and discern spiritually and naturally. You may become dull of hearing because the ears will feel clogged or like something is lodged in them. It may also feel like something is sitting on your head or wrapped around your head.

This stronghold of mind control may also plague you with vile, perverse, unnecessary, or unimportant thoughts. Or may have you panicking and thinking of something over and over to distract you from what is presently important. Sometimes this spirit will swamp you with constant thoughts of hurts from your past or present life and heart issues that are unresolved. You may find it difficult to pay attention or to press forward in working on present tasks because of these constant plaguing thoughts and feelings of intense pressure.

Proverbs 15:15 The Amplified Bible *All the days of the desponding and afflicted are made evil [by anxious thoughts and forebodings (prophecy)], but he who has a glad heart has a continual feast [regardless of circumstances].*

Ask the Lord to sever the tentacles of this spirit or use the sword of the spirit to cut them. Break the power of pressure, pain, and torment, and release healing where needed.

Spirit Of Void & Darkness – This spirit could be at work when there are no blockages, hindrances, blinding, binding, confusion, or discombobulation, yet the atmosphere, eye gates, imagination, and mind are totally black and blank, dark and empty. We see this spirit in operation in *Genesis 1:2* when God was creating the heavens and the earth.

And the earth was without form and void; and darkness was upon the face of the deep. And the Spirit of God moved upon the face of the waters.

This spirit wants you to think that everything is dead and without form, you cannot see or discern properly, or that there is no potential for creation or manifestation. It operates as a black blanket or cloud, covering everything so you cannot see behind the scenes. It will smother blackness and void over the plans and seeds of God, and even conceal demonic plans so you cannot be offensive against the enemy. It will block out the ability to see the vision, receive revelation, understand the purpose for ministry engagements and events, and discern the plots and plans of the enemy.

Daniel 2:22 *He reveals the deep and secret things; He knows what is in the darkness, and the light dwells with Him.*
When this spirit attacks, release and declare the light, wisdom, profound, searchable, secretive, mysteries of God to come forth to dispel the darkness.

Spirits Of Fear – Different types of fear can be sent through witchcraft and territorial attacks. Fear is a distressing emotion, concern, or anxiety aroused by impending danger, evil, pain, sweating, rejection, etc., whether the threat is real or imagined. It is the feeling or condition of being afraid, frightened, panicked, anxious disheveled, frenzied, overwhelmed, gripped, shocked, or traumatized with terror. Fear can be sent as a spell or assignment through the atmosphere, imparted into the mind or imagination through mind manipulation, bewitchment, or telepathy; imparted via dreams, or through demonic creativity or stirring via witchcraft of a traumatic or startling event to incite fear. Fear tends to attack unaware; it can have no real basis for manifesting, but its presence is very real, intentional, and demonic.

2Timothy 1:7 *For God hath not given us the spirit of fear; but of power, and of love, and of a sound mind.*

When we yield to fear, we SHIFT from under the authority, love, and stability of God. We believe the lies, misperceptions, misconceptions of the enemy, while, relenting to instability, weakness, and helplessness. We also resort to believing we are worthless, under-appreciated, devalued, and that our life is not worth living. The more you meditate and yield to the thoughts, the greater the fear and the oppression of its assignment. Fear is an attack and assignment against the truth of your identity and against your salvation and refuge in God.

Bind and cast out the spirit of fear. Break the powers of how it is manifesting, fall out of agreement with any ways you agreed with fear, close portals to it operating again, use scriptures to build your identity, and fortify yourself in the love and worth of God.

Spirit Of Confusion – Causes chaos, disorder, upheaval, forgetfulness, cloudiness, frustration, blankness, and discombobulation. May be unable to distinguish right from wrong, truth from lies, clearness from distinctiveness. Such attacks cause uncertainty of self and others, the uncertainty of one's calling, confusion of one's destiny vision will cause you to question your identity, your team, supports, and God. You will begin to airways as the chaos causes a tossing to and fro between reality and delusion. The enemy wants you to fear failing, fear doing the Lord's work, fear walking in faith, fear man, fear the devil, fear being obedient, and on and on. Anytime you feel fearful, if it is not a reverenced fear from the Lord or God warning you about something, then deal with it as a demonic attack.

1Corinthians 14:33 For God is not the author of confusion, but of peace, as in all churches of the saints.

Break the powers and spells of confusion and bewitchment. Cleanse out all effects of how the spirit is operating in your life, atmosphere, and ministry.

Spirit Of Sluggardness – The spirit of the sluggardness is sent to cause inactivity, idleness, laziness, relaxation, dullness, and disinterest. There may be exhaustion where you are sleeping for long periods of time or no apparent reason, not wanting to be bothered, or wanting to hide from people and responsibilities. You can be indolent, slow-moving, sluggish, averse, or disinclined to work, be active, or exert energy. This spirit will cause you to lack wisdom, vision, and energy in knowing when to plant, work, and invest. It feels like a weight laying upon you. It can sometimes feel cold clammy, wet, moist, or slimy where you feel uncomfortable or unclean. You have intent and heart to work, but no drive.

Matthew 26:41 Watch and pray, that ye enter not into temptation: the spirit indeed is willing, but the flesh is weak.

Proverbs 6:6-9 Go to the ant, thou sluggard; consider her ways, and be wise: Which having no guide, overseer, or ruler, Provideth her meat in the summer, and gathereth her food in the harvest. How long wilt thou sleep, O sluggard? when wilt thou arise out of thy sleep?

Bind and cast out the spirit of the sluggard. Break its power off your physical body, health, mind, and heart. You may also have to break its power off the body, health, mind, and heart of your ministry, region, and people you oversee. Cleanse your foundation, life, and ministry of any patterns of sluggardness, laziness, making excuses, and inconsistency.

Spirit Of Slander & Accusation – This spirit releases fiery darts, word curses, accusations, gossip, ungodly reports, malice, and defamation against one's character, ministry, or work. The slander is generally false or the true being used in a slanderous way to incite shame, shunning condemnation, and destruction.

Sometimes you cannot resolve slander in the natural; it often has to be dismantled in the spirit realm. When slander cannot be resolved, know that God judges the slanderous.

Matthew 12:36 But I tell you that every careless word that people speak, they shall give an accounting for it in the day of judgment.

Other times slander can be resolved through healthy conflict resolution skills and healthy communication. But the spirit of slander and accusation is still at work in your soul and in the spirit. It will need to be rebuked, and its assignment will need to be canceled. The true report of the Lord will need to be declared into your life and the spirit realm.

Proverbs 11:9 The Amplified Bible *With his mouth the godless man destroys his neighbor, but through knowledge and superior discernment shall the righteous be delivered.*

Proverbs 26:20-22 *Where no wood is, there the fire goeth out: so where there is no talebearer, the strife ceaseth. As coals are to burning coals, and wood to fire; so is a contentious man to kindle strife. The words of a talebearer are as wounds, and they go down into the innermost parts of the belly.*

<u>**Spirits Of Affliction & Infirmities**</u> – Sometimes your purpose will endure constant or seasonal attacks in this area. Some attacks may be related to soul issues or a part of the generation lineage. God may send an affliction as a form of buffeting to keep you or others humble and submitted to him. Other times afflictions and infirmities are sent by witches and territorial spirits to bind, distract, hinder, and attack your purpose. When words curses are released, they may come in the form of affliction. It is important to really pray over your food because the enemy and witches will inflict by casting spells upon meals and drinks.

Many times, we may go to the doctor, and they are not able to cure or relieve us of ailments. When there are no open doors for affliction and infirmities, then it is most likely due to territorial warfare or witchcraft. It is also possible to carry the afflictions of the people, ministry, land, and region you are governing. Often when I pray deliverance and healing prayers for myself, I pray for these areas as well for when they are delivered and healed, I at times am relieved of afflictions and infirmities.

There are also instances where I will manifest the ailments of the region or the witches and territorial spirits of the region are attacking me because of the calling and mantle upon my life. If the region is afflicted with sickness and disease, you may incur different afflictions as it relates to what is in the region. The Holy Spirit can reveal to you how to counterattack this to judge and break whatever is binding you such that deliverance is your portion.

Psalm 34:17-20 *The righteous cry, and the Lord heareth and delivereth them out of all their troubles. The Lord is nigh unto them that are of a broken heart; and saveth such as be of a contrite spirit. Many are the afflictions of the righteous: but the Lord delivereth him out of them all. He keepeth all his bones: not one of them is broken.*

God has promised to deliver the righteous from every affliction. This is so key to remaining in a posture of peace and confidence that he will deliver, especially when the affliction and infirmity release feelings and reports of helplessness, no cure or death. But you know God will deliver you. Trust him and not your feelings or reports of man.

<u>*Spirit Of Jezebel*</u> – Jezebel tends to manifest everywhere (e.g., on the job, in your ministry, on your team, in the service, in the boardroom, at the grocery store, at the family gathering, online, in your email). I believe this spirit tracks people, especially apostles and prophets. It also shapeshifts from person to person, where it manifests in different situations. Or it sets up a Jezebelic system and this demonic system works against the person to track them. Though some people you encounter will have the Jezebel spirit, this spirit also oppresses insecure people or people who have a need to be validated. It uses them to frustrate, control, intimidate and challenge the mantle and work of those it is tracking.

Jezebel will seduce, manipulate people and situations to stir up strife against the person and the work their purpose. Jezebel will gain personal knowledge and entail on the person, particularly about their past, then use it to launch witchcraft drama and conflict against them and the vision of the ministry. This spirit is so manipulative and webbing, that it will have you questioning yourself even though your motives of pure for the people and work at hand, you are delivered from that sin, and you have not done another wrong.

Jezebel must be confronted naturally and spiritually. Its' actions must be exposed in both realms such that the influences and works are totally annihilated off the people, ministry, region; and in regards to any seeds and fruits, it may have planted within the word of people, ministries, and the region. When confronted Jezebel will be defensive, prideful, and will seek to gain the approval and strength of the naysayers to prove that her actions are Godly and for the good of the people and the ministry. Jezebel is intelligent, skilled, and knows how to articulate where its' plot sounds like the true will of the Lord. The situation will most likely get messy and very confrontational, even unto death (spiritually and or naturally), before it gets better. Jezebel, however, will not submit to leadership or the vision of the ministry, as it usurps authority. As this is exposed, people will discern its true intent, such that its plans are revealed and thwarted.

Jezebel will come very abrupt, matter of fact, and strong. This is because of the demons operating behind the scenes to strengthen her assignment and the witchcraft that has been sent to fortify its work against them and the work of the ministry. Jezebel is not stronger than the Lord and is not stronger than his chosen vessels. Do not allow Jezebel to cower you. Stand up to this spirit, deal with it naturally and in prayer, then watch God get glory through every situation.

2Kings 9:9-11 The Amplified Bible *I will make the house of Ahab like the house of Jeroboam son of Nebat and like the house of Baasha son of Ahijah. And the dogs shall eat Jezebel in the* *portion of Jezreel, and none shall bury her. And he opened the door and fled.* **[Fulfilled in II Kings 9:33–37.]**

Micah 5:12 *And I will cut off witchcrafts out of thine hand; and thou shalt have no [more] soothsayers.*

Revelation 2:20 *Notwithstanding I have a few things against thee, because thou sufferest that woman Jezebel, which calleth herself a prophetess, to teach and to seduce my servants to commit fornication, and to eat things sacrificed unto idols.*

<u>Spirit Of Goliath</u> – Goliath seeks to defy the name, plans, and work of the Lord. Goliath will challenge a person and use intimidating tactics to get them to back down from fulfilling the vision at hand. Witches and territorial spirits will send constant intimidating thoughts to the person through the well of Goliath. The thoughts are so intense, piercing, and continuous that the person will start to feel overwhelmed, burdened, inadequate, angry, and want to give up, hide, or separate themselves from people and the vision. The person will not want to war against Goliath for fear that they will be defeated. There will also be natural confrontations within the person's life that will strengthen and confirm the attacks being sent in the spirit realm. These attacks may come through family members, bosses, etc. It is usually through people who have a level of authority and influence and is being used to cower, isolate, and cause a withdrawing of the person from walking in their mantle and from the vision.

Sometimes the witchcraft attacks coming through Goliath can cause pain, such as migraines, stomach aches, panic attacks, or chest pains. An unwarranted fear or intimidating presence may be accompanied by these attacks. Goliath is big in stature and boastful in puffed-up chatter, but the person is greater, and so is the authority of God in the person's life. Do not go back and forth in mindless and puffed-up words with Goliath. Persons know who they are, so they have nothing to prove to Goliath or anyone else. Use your weapons and authorities to smite him in the forehead. Explore the heart of situations concerning Goliath, then use the word of God to stab him in the heart with the sword of God's word and plans for your life and the vision at hand, then cut off his head to totally solidify his defeat against you and God's vision.

1Samuel 17:48-51 The Amplified Bible *When the Philistine came forward to meet David, David ran quickly toward the battle line to meet the Philistine. David put his hand into his bag and took out a stone and slung it, and it struck the Philistine, sinking into his forehead, and he fell on his face to the earth.*

So David prevailed over the Philistine with a sling and with a stone, and struck down the Philistine and slew him. But no sword was in David's hand. So he ran and stood over the Philistine, took his sword and drew it out of its sheath, and killed him, and cut off his head with it. When the Philistines saw that their mighty champion was dead, they fled.

__The Spirit of Saul__ – This spirit is a rebellious, disobedient, witchcraft spirit that does not have the maturity to adequately govern their lives, the people's lives, or the region he has been placed over. In the chapter regarding the identity of a person, I spoke about the importance of only submitting to the voice of the wise-hearted, as they have a clear vision for destiny and calling on your life as a person. Saul is the people's choice, so this type of coverage is allowed by God but is not ordained by God. It is essential to have the correct coverage and affiliate partners, as otherwise, you can subject yourself and your life's vision to a Saul Spirit. This spirit recognizes the destiny and calling on your life but is jealous, envious, and in competition with it. People who operate as Sauls tend to be very insecure, battle inadequacy, are mentally unstable and waver between loving who you are and hating you were ever born. Their instability will hinder their ability to adequately lead and support you. As much as they will use you or encourage you to go forth in your gifts and calling, they will also seek to kill you and the vision God has given you. You will want to be loyal to Saul, but Saul does not know or honor loyalty. You will not receive the same honor and dedication that you seek to give. And you will be constantly fighting and maneuvering around Saul, such that you respect who they are in God, yet not allowing their position in your life to take you out. Pursue God-ordained covering and partnership. And break ties with anyone who begins to operate in a Saul Spirit in your midst (***1Samuel 18-24***).

__The Spirit of Amnon__ – Ammon spirits uses familiarity, deception, manipulation, seduction, and a false or erred sense of love to strip the purity and innocence of the leader, the people, and the vision. This spirit is perverted because it appears to have the heart of God and the best interest of people and the vision but is internally anguished by twisted thoughts of lust and ungodliness. Not expecting this spirit to be among us, creates the perfect environment for it to attack and defile us, the innocent, the weak, the vulnerable, and the areas where our ministry, members, and vision are not adequately covered or watched. This spirit will only get worse as perversion is normalized and legalized in society. We must create an environment that sounds the alarm on rape, molestation, sexual sin, perversion, and inordinacy, such that this spirit does not have its way in our sphere (***2Samuel 13)***.

__Spirit of Absalom__ – This spirit usurps godly authority by acting on decisions and strategies that were not discussed with the leader or leadership team. Whether there was an injustice, a situation they believe should be rectified or addressed, they will take matters into their own hands, with no regard to how their actions impact the leader, the people, or the vision. When Absaloms have decided in their eyes that the leader is weak, passive, or ill equipped, they will continue to engage in behaviors to usurp the leader's authority and will become enraged with bringing reproach upon the leader's name, destiny, and life's vision. Absalom may have the best resolution, appropriate response or strategy at the time, but Absalom is a heart matter.

Proverbs 21:2 *Every way of a man is right in his own eyes: but the LORD pondereth the hearts.*

Luke 16:15 *And he said unto them, Ye are they which justify yourselves before men; but God knoweth your hearts: for that which is highly esteemed among men is abomination in the sight of God.*

We can have the right answer, correct response, the greatest of wisdom, but where is the posture of our heart regarding how to present and utilize that information where it edifies God, his people, and his kingdom? Absaloms operate out of emotions, retaliation, and revenge. They are self-absorbed, immature, temperamental, and brash in their actions even though it appears as if what they are doing is benefiting or seeking justice for God or for others. Absaloms will use underhanded schemes and tactics to draw the people and the vision from under the leaders' shepherding, and into the kingdom they are building for themselves. They deem their leadership grand over all others and will use the needs, desires, weaknesses, and emotions of the people to seduce and manipulate them to come under their control.

Absaloms can come in the form of family members, team members, friends, mentees, and spiritual children, as this spirit has some type of inheritance or covenant to the leader and the vision but does not value relationship or covenant. They only value what they deem right in their own eyes and will sacrifice the leader to prove that their way of leading is righteous and justified. David was passive and wanted to spare Absalom because he was his son. When Absalom is not dealt with, this spirit causes generational consequences upon the life of the leader, the vision, and that leader's sphere of influence. You must confront Absalom and teach vision carriers of your mantle and ministry how to identify Absalom. As once Absaloms plans unfold, everyone can be affected, and so can the generational inheritance (*2Samuel 13-19*)

<u>*Spirit of Judas*</u> – This spirit operates as a demonic scout or infiltrator for the purposes of identifying you to your enemies or the enemy, so they can kill you and the work God has granted to your hands. God may allow Judas to be a part of your ministry for the specific purpose of further unfolding your destiny and revival authority in him. Remember Judas was used to fulfill the prophecy of Jesus being crucified and annihilating the powers of death by raising from the grave with all power – resurrection power in his hand. Experiencing the spirit of Judas is heartbreaking but understanding its greater purpose is essential to processing through the painful experience and allowing God to exalt you to the next dimensional SHIFT of revival glory and authority that is due to your life. Often, we are blinded by the Judases in our midst. But Jesus

knew exactly who Judas was and what role he would play in his life. Jesus did not be less to Judas because he would betray him. Jesus imparted, loved, and cultivated Judas' destiny just as he did the other disciples and apostles. We too must be discerning of everyone's role in our inner circle. We must be clear about their strengths, weaknesses, and propensities to sin and abilities to hurt us, while still being who God has called us to be in their lives, despite what they may or may not do to us. Study the story of Jesus and Judas and ask God to identify the keys to how to handle Judas' experiences. If you discern that someone is a Judas, seek God as to whether the Judas was allowed by him for a greater purpose or is a demonic assignment completely orchestrated by the enemy. If God allowed it, seek wisdom on how to lay down your life and process through the experience, such that you do not abort the salvation that others will receive from your experience. And so that you will not abort the resurrection SHIFT in power and authority that God has ordained for you as he defies death and hell on your behalf. If it is completely a demonic attack, then displace Judas from your life and realm of influence; and seek God on how to nullify any impact his presence caused you and your ministry. *(Matthew 26-27, Mark 14:18-21, Luke 22-23, John 6:64, John 10:17-18, John 12:21, John 13:21-30)*

<u>*Spirit Of Death, Hell & The Grave*</u> – There are a host of spirits that operate in this category. They can attack the person, families, ministries, businesses, visions, and regions. Often there will be a dark presence and experience of doom and gloom, extreme heaviness upon the atmosphere, over your life, in your heart, and chest. There can be flooding thoughts of dying and killing yourself, suffocating, wanting to die and be with Jesus even though it is not time to leave the earth. There can be constant near-death experiences, impending death, fears of tragedies, feeling something bad will happen, demonic dreams to instill fear of dying; attacks spiritually and physically through the spirit of murder, sabotage, and self- sabotage.

<u>*Spirits of Death, Hell, & The Grave*</u> – These spirits operate as a demonic threefold cord against you. It is a prideful spirit as the bible says hell enlarges itself and is pomp.

Isaiah 5:14 *Therefore hell hath enlarged herself, and opened her mouth without measure: and their glory, and their multitude, and their pomp, and he that rejoiceth, shall descend into it.*

When this spirit attacks, it tries to exalt itself against the plans and destiny that God has ordained for your life. It is arrogant and swells itself as if it has governmental rule and authority over your life. *Pomp* is *saon* in the Hebrew and means "*uproar, as a rushing, destruction, horrible, noise, tumultuous, crash.*" This threefold cord crashes down on your life and creates all kinds of havoc. It causes a major disturbance, disruption, commotion, and uproar in your life and/or vision. Matters are so turbulent that death feels inevitable. But you must understand that as long as you remain:

- ✓ Clear and confident in your identity
- ✓ Clear in who God is to you
- ✓ In alignment with Jesus
- ✓ In his purpose for your life
- ✓ Grounded in Jesus being the cornerstone of your life and vision

The gates of hell shall NEVER prevail against you.

Matthew 16:15-19 He saith unto them, But whom say ye that I am? And Simon Peter answered and said, Thou art the Christ, the Son of the living God. And Jesus answered and said unto him, Blessed art thou, Simon Barjona: for flesh and blood hath not revealed it unto thee, but my Father which is in heaven. And I say also unto thee, That thou art Peter, and upon this rock I will build my church; and the gates of hell shall not prevail against it. And I will give unto thee the keys of the kingdom of heaven: and whatsoever thou shalt bind on earth shall be bound in heaven: and whatsoever thou shalt loose on earth shall be loosed in heaven.

Much of the turbulence and the noise are to get you to fear, become confused about your identity, and God's word and works in your life so that it can have an open door to unleash the plan that is at the gates of hell. It will roar loud, constantly, and like a riot coming from every which way to attack you. You will have to consistently contend to overthrow it, but you are already victorious against death and hell. Jesus saw to that your own stance solidifies that truth in your life and vision. Command the enlargement of hell to attack and turn in on itself and silence every storm and assignment from hell sent against you.

<u>*Coffin Spirits*</u> – The coffin spirit work with the demons of death, hell, and the grave. Coffin spirits want to bury you alive or before your time. They want to bury your destiny and vision, so you cannot walk in their purpose. You will literally feel as though you have died, been put in a coffin, buried six feet underground, and covered with dirt. The grave spirit locks you down where you cannot get out of the coffin. Life will appear dark, gloomy, hopeless as if there is no escape, and you will feel like you are suffocating and trapped in a buried coffin. But you have the keys to heaven and earth, to bind and to loose. Rebuke and judge the threefold cord of death, hell, and the grave, break the locks and seal of the coffin spirit and bury every spirit in the coffin that tried to bury you.

<u>*Premature Death*</u> – This spirit is in operation when a person, vision, business, ministry, etc., dies before its God-appointed time. Many believe premature deaths are preventable. There could be some truth to that in some cases. One of the ways the Lord has had me combat premature death in my life is to examine the family illnesses, health challenges, sin, and behavioral patterns, and make changes so that these issues will not be a factor in my life. I have also examined this with the Lord concerning my destiny

and life's vision. As I have considered the demonic and unhealthy family patterns and how to thwart them, my destiny has prevailed against premature death spirits that do not want me to succeed in life. Regionally, I have examined with the Lord how this spirit operates against ministries, businesses, and those chosen to do a great work for the Lord. I have received some valuable keys from the Lord for pressing, contending, and sustaining against this spirit where I will not succumb to regional death spirits, and how to help others in this area.

Spirits of Abortion – There are instances when the enemy wants to abort what God has breathed life on. The enemy will always try to get you to quit, give up, throw in the towel, and sabotage your own progress. He will always be sending plans to abort your revival fire, your vision, and to stop the work of the Lord that you are doing. Especially at the beginning of launching your revival vision, this spirit will be on a mission to kill, still, and destroy you and your work. There will be a constant contending you will have to do to fortify yourself against this spirit. As you begin to sustain in your revival vision, the attacks from this spirit will lesson but remain alert and vigilant as it will always be looking for an entryway into your life and vision.

Stillborn Spirits is when you give birth to a baby, vision, business, ministry, etc., but it is born dead. It is lifeless without fruit, substance, or the breath of life. Generally stillborn occurs because what you were birthing stopped developing, failed to fully develop, failed to advance in its process or success while in the womb, was hindered in tapping into its actualized potential, or did not realize or was cultivated in its own value or worth, the womb had some complications or infractions, therefore it did not progress and birth forth properly. Sometimes we can become aware of a stillborn in the womb, but often we are not aware of a stillborn until it is born. Either way, the experience is heart-wrenching, and whether we have an open door or not, the experience appears as happenstance, it is a demonic attack on what God has granted to your hands, so deal with it accordingly.

Spirits Of Suicide floods you with thoughts of hopelessness, worthlessness, rejection, lack of purpose for living or going forward, doom, and gloom. Makes you feel like killing yourself is the only option for coping with whatever you are experiencing in life. This is a demonic coping skill as God would never want you to kill yourself and even to consider it as an option for handling life matters is demonic in nature. This spirit wants you to be responsible for killing your own destiny and life's success. Sometimes there is nothing challenging occurring, and this spirit will attack. Especially if you have entertained this spirit at some point in your life, then it will visit you at times in an effort to get you to agree with taking your own life. This spirit has increased its assault on the world as even children are considering suicide as an option for handling life experiences. We must be aware of the wiles of this spirit and seek to thwart it in our lives, families, and regions.

Many people will encounter these spirits but will not pray against them. It is important to be offensive against these attacks and not take them lightly. Cancel witchcraft spells and assignments, rebuke spirits of death – send them back to hell if necessary. Cleanse out dream impartations of fear, death, and tragedy and cancel assignments sent through dreams. Continually agree and decree out life and that more abundantly over yourself, vision, and ministry partners. Remember as a person, you have resurrection power. Use it to overthrow the enemy.

John 10:10 The thief cometh not, but for to steal, and to kill, and to destroy: I am come that they might have life, and that they might have it more abundantly.

James 5:16 Confess your faults one to another, and pray one for another, that ye may be healed. The effectual fervent prayer of a righteous man availeth much.

I decree that you would always have a desire to pray, a love to pray, a fervency to pray, and that perseverance in prayer and warfare is infused into your mantle and calling. I decree that you are fearless and fierce against demons and demonic attacks. I decree that every demon that combats you will be quickly exposed, that you take joy in knowing that you prevail over every demon and that the end result is that you are victorious. May you SHIFT with increasing in your identity and authority even now. May you SHIFT in towering all the more in wearing the truth of your mantle, experiencing God, and him receiving limitless glory out of your life and revival vision. **SHIFT!**

OVERTHROWING PRINCIPALITIES & STRONGHOLDS

From my manual, *"The Great Awakening: Igniting Regional Revival."*

In this chapter, I will share some principalities that I have encountered during regional work to activate your mantle all the more in identifying, discerning, and mapping the operations of demonic forces. As you study this chapter, ask Holy Spirit to identify the principalities, territorial spirits, powers, etc., in your region so you can journal them and use it to BEAT DEVILS DOWN!

<u>*Leviathan*</u> - Operates through a curse (curse can be generational or otherwise). It is the king demon of pride that seeks to steal the kingly anointing. Pride operates greatly among traditional, personal, spiritual, political, and family beliefs. Regionally there can be a haughty disposition among the people and even in the atmosphere of the region. This is a controlling spirit that desires self-glory; the desire to be served, glorified, be known among people. Attacks wealthy ministries and businesses and releases a climate and aroma where they present themselves as better than everyone else. Jezebel gives this demon power through false gifts, healings, miracles, etc., to seduce people from their rightful place in life and the kingdom. Seeks to stop growth in a person or region by having them glorify self rather than God or above God. Also works with schizophrenia and its attachment spirits. This principality attacks in another way in that it can cause learning disabilities, and will work with the deaf and dumb spirit to disable the learning, or hearing of a person or region. Can be the reason a person cannot speak in tongues. Causes miscommunication where this spirit gets in the middle of conversations and hearing and distorts or mutters what is said so that there is a miscommunication and/or misunderstanding and twisting of words to cause confusion and disorder). Will dig its tail into the person or region and wraps itself around its victim or region suffocating it (Snatch out his tail, crush his head, and severe the body). Other spirits that work with this principality are as followed:

- ❖ Serpent Spirit – Sly, craftiness, and conning spirit; can also be a python that constricts, cobra which is a highly venomous (poisonous) spirit, or leviathan spirit. Can wraps itself around neighborhoods, communities, or the region as a whole or slithers over and about the region to release venom, crafty schemes, etc.
- ❖ Religious Spirit, False Doctrine, False Prophecy, and Legalism.
- ❖ Spirit of Traditionalism - Change is not easily initiated or embraced.
- ❖ Sabotage & Self Sabotage - This spirit works with the destiny-killing spirit to sabotage progress, destinies, marriages, ministries, businesses. It comes through psychological and mental warfare where it plagues people and regions with demonic and vile voices, so they will quit and want to move out of the region.

- ❖ Racism – Can work within the church, in communities, in the politics and climate of the community, and the region.
- ❖ Lying Tongue, Tale bearing, Gossip, Exaggeration – Demonic operations are due to personal unfulfillment, slandering others, need to feel adequate at the expense of others; stretches the truth, steal God's glory by fantasized and exaggerated stories that have minimal truth to them yet gives and distorted or false impression of a person, community, or region.
- ❖ Quarreling – Can operate in families, schools, and neighborhood kids and families; combative spirit sows discord, faultfinding, slander, and is an accuser of the brethren.
- ❖ Stubbornness – Resistant to change, resistant to the things of God; there can be a physical stiffness in the neck, neck pain, etc., that can be a sign of leviathan as work.
- ❖ Apostasy - Renouncing or abandonment of loyalty or duty; lack of loyalty and honor within the region and people.
- ❖ Intolerance or Condensation - Has challenges progressing in the things of God or taking in a lot of God.
- ❖ Unteachableness – Resistant to being taught; rather remain ignorant than to be taught or admit an unknowing of something. Make excuses for not needing to be taught or wanting to invest in being taught. Causes people and the region to be stifled of growth due to a lack of knowledge, willingness to learn, and progress past the current state.
- ❖ Critical and Condoning Spirits, Negative Attitudes and Mindsets - operate with leviathan to belittle people and the region so hopeless to override the vision for change.
- ❖ Spirit of the Antichrist – Anti-Christ, anti-teaching, preaching, and establishing Jesus and his kingdom within people and the region.

<u>Jezebel & Ahab</u> - Comes against the apostolic and prophetic voice, the vision of persons, those carrying the voice and vision of God, and those seeking to bring change in a people, land, or regions; is rooted of witchcraft and rebellion. These principalities rebels against God's word and authority and the things of God. Counterfeits God's authority.

Works through the lust of the flesh, the lust of the eyes, and the pride of life. Focus on self-glory and self-gratification, while drawing people to serve them and idol gods. Intelligent, hardworking, success driving, power-driven, power-hungry, perfectionistic, and domineering. Uses control, manipulation, lust, and seduction to draw in the hearts of people for personal gain. Tends to have unrealistic expectations of others and uses self-pity and manipulative witchcraft words and tactics to win the compassion of others. Can be aggressive, deceitful, overbearing, extremely or underhandedly calculous and evil. Tends to be unrepentant in how their actions affect others but demand repentance of others who may knowingly or unknowingly hurt or challenge them. Very vengeful. Vengeance is sometimes passive-aggressive, underhanded, and callous, but dominated by a strong rage to destroy at any cost and with no regard to the consequences of their actions. Can appear submissive and supportive, but usually overtly despises authority, and will overthrow authority to control the people, land, and region. Other spirits that work with these principalities are as followed:

- ❖ Bullying, Intimidation, Combating Spirits, Goliath, Spirit of Saul - Prevalent in the school systems and traditional regional businesses, and ministries. Love to attack fivefold ministries and revival movements to kill the glory of God.
- ❖ Overbearing Spirit, Sharp Tempered - Intolerance for anyone who resists its demands.
- ❖ False Confidence, False Authority, Counterfeit Spirits, Pride, False Pride, Insecurity – Works among those who have been abused, those who have made lots of mistakes, and among those who are confused about or have no vision for their lives. Provides vision that appears to be God's will or a way to personal fame and glory. Will have people idolatrously sacrificing themselves unto the death for personal growth and success.
- ❖ Whoredom, Sexual Perversion, Seduction, Fornication work with these principalities. These acts are really sacrifices to idols for ritualistic purposes, fame, power, and destruction of purpose and destiny. People do not know that what they are doing is a sacrifice to idols but because these spirits plaque the region, land, or people, the workings of these behaviors automatically become a sacrifice to idol gods.
- ❖ Adultery, Divorce – Operates through curses to destroy God's order of family and to destroy covenant with God.
- ❖ Flattery, Sympathetic Witchcraft, Sensuality, False Enthusiasm works with these principalities to seduce and draw the people to themselves.
- ❖ False Doctrine, False Prophecy, Spirits of Error, Compromise, works with these principalities to distort and usurp the truth of God.
- ❖ Angry, Retaliation, Murder, Rebellion works alongside these principalities to control, incite fear, and chastise people who do not yield to their rule.
- ❖ Female Dominance, Male Passiveness, Doubting Manhood, Passive Quitter - Pouting when it does not get its way operates with these principalities to usurp God's will for man to be the head of families and the kingdom rule God has set in a place where men are the leaders. Feministic movements are on the rise to soften and dismantle the strength and Godly stature, authority, and position of the male role in families, communities, and regions.

- Call evil good – Narcissists, restless and has no peace; never satisfied -speaks contrary to the order of God; is adamant, relentless, bloodsucking, and unfearing in its stance.
- Idolatry, Idol Worship, Witchcraft - self-harming, sacrificing of women and children are prevalent among these principalities.
- Greed, Lying, Manipulation - uses position and false power to manipulate others.
- Lust for material things, worship of enterprise, success, profit, promotion, wealth will be the mindset of the people and the region when these principalities are working.
- Confusion, No Unity, Disobedience, and Resentfulness work alongside to keep people and communities at odds. Strong in gang communities and among ethnic-driven communities and ministries.
- Sullenness, Depression, can be evident in a people, land, or region while displaying the domination, effects, and characteristics of these principalities.
- Workaholics - Gets needs met through work ethic and through the strengths of others.
- Considering God's things trivial; no godly order is in operation, but manmade and demonic control is evident.
- We must also consider the children of Jezebel and Ahab and Sibling Rivalry - will work with the contrary and/or spirit of competition; will work in families and groups of people. The children of Jezebel and Ahab have their spirit, characteristics, and nature.
- Ahabs have an inability to designate and delegate authority, leaving things of GOD to wife.
- Spirit of Abandonment works with these principalities as they will have people abandoning children, jobs, homes, responsibilities with no regard to how their actions impact others; this is usually done as punishment, retaliation, or to avoid consequences for their actions.
- Denial - spirit causes people to deny even what is in front of them; usually, live in a false or self-absorbed reality.
- Spirit of Competition, Covetousness, Envy, Jealousy, Self-Seeking, Self-Serving are all workings among these principalities.
- Browbeating Spirits work with these principalities - Even in an attempt to build up people, people are verbally torn down first then built up. This is also a stronghold in the churches, school systems, social service agencies, and households. Rather than instilling compassion, this spirit instills fear, shame, and/or guilt in an attempt to change behavior.

Athaliah - Mother of Jezebel. Comes to steal the priestly anointing which is the royal seed; the royal seed does not just include the children of leaders but encompasses all those under the kingly anointing. They are present and future leaders in the kingdom. This principality works with the destiny-killing spirit to dethrone those children and youth that God wants to use from birth to be leaders of their generation. This principality desires to rule and lead in place of God's chosen youth. This principality will even use family members to kill and thwart the destiny of these youth. They will abuse, literally kill, spiritually, and mentally kill the child until they cannot be who God has called them to be.

Babylon - The spirit of the world, of this age. This is a Canaanite goddess idol of fortune and happiness, the supposed consort of Baal and her images. Historically, Nimrod the son of Cush, a descendant of Noah's son Ham, founded the Kingdom of Babel. According to Strong's Concordance, Babel means "confusion, by mixing." There were a group of people in the bible who desired to build a tower from earth to heaven. God confounded, confused them, and scattered them to deter this operation. The city was named Babel (*Genesis 10-11*). Babylon derived from this place as being the city of rebellion against God. In *Revelation 17:5* Babylon is called the great, mother of prostitutes and the earth's abominations. Babylon is its own kingdom set up directly against and in rebellion to the Kingdom of God. In scripture not only did they have their own demonic altars and treasures, but they often defiled God's altars, temples, and treasures, and used them for their own idolatry practices. Babylon wants to rule and reign its own kingdom of the world, as well as defile and overtake God's kingdom. It desires to overtake the people who are of God's kingdom and defile their temple which belongs to God and persuades Godly people to come under its customs and idolatry. The world serves Babylon. It is a kingdom contrary to God's kingdom and seeks to govern the people, land, and region with its own self-focused systems and principles.

Babylon is rooted in pride, idolatry, self-idolatry, sin, murder-ungodly bloodshed, demonic sacrifices, greed, anti-Christ, evil world system, rebellion, drunkenness, sexual sin & immorality, mixture, polytheism, blasphemy, perversion, inordinacy, lust, magic, witchcraft, sorcery, mediums, psychics, false authority, violence, the harlot, fornication-indulge in unlawful lust, practice idolatry, prostituting of the body to the lust of another, and the giving over to unlawful intercourse, due to being given over to idolatry and serving these principalities. It is strongly rooted in the mindset of people, in the land and regions. Even those who serve God, have some Babylon ways and tendencies that need to be rooted out of their mindsets and behaviors. They tend to desire to fame, success, fortune, and lusts of Babylon while claiming to serve and be sold out to God.

<u>*Belial*</u> – Is a very wicked, vile, undermining spirit of destruction. One of its Hebrew translations means "*Ungodless*" and one of its Greek translations is the word "*Satan.*" This lying, deceiving demon cause people to draw away from serving God and his kingdom. It may come to people appearing as a dreamer or a prophet of God with signs that appear to be Godly. Then when the people are enthralled, it will implement idolatrous practices as its intention is for people to worship other gods, not the true and living God. It usually misguides people who are not really sold out to God, or who have open doors and propensities to waver in the commandments and standards of God.

Deuteronomy 13:1-3 *If there arise among you a prophet, or a dreamer of dreams, and giveth thee a sign or a wonder, And the sign or the wonder come to pass, whereof he spake unto thee, saying, Let us go after other gods, which thou hast not known, and let us serve them; Thou shalt not hearken unto the words of that prophet, or that dreamer of dreams: for the Lord your God proveth you, to know whether ye love the Lord your God with all your heart and with all your soul.*

God demands no compromise with Belial. This is a challenge because many people will compromise the commandments standards of the Lord for family members, friends, jobs, personal gain, etc. They will put aside their biblical principles and succumb to pagan, cultural, and ethnic traditions, with no regard to this being idolatry and witchcraft. This has become such a norm until many are lukewarm and unable to discern witchcraft and idolatrous practices. God says we should be putting these people, even loved ones and anything connected to Belial to death. Meaning we should be despising them and turning away from them, and even turning the people who do them, over to their own demise, such that they receive the consequences of their actions.

Verse 6-10 *If thy brother, the son of thy mother, or thy son, or thy daughter, or the wife of thy bosom, or thy friend, which is as thine own soul, entice thee secretly, saying, Let us go and serve other gods, which thou hast not known, thou, nor thy fathers; Namely, of the gods of the people which are round about you, nigh unto thee, or far off from thee, from the one end of the earth even unto the other end of the earth; Thou shalt not consent unto him, nor hearken unto him; neither shall thine eye pity him, neither shalt thou spare, neither shalt thou conceal him: But thou shalt surely kill him; thine hand shall be first upon him to put him to death, and afterwards the hand of all the people. And thou shalt stone him with stones, that he die; because he hath sought to thrust thee away from the Lord thy God, which brought thee out of the land of Egypt, from the house of bondage.*

Regions should reject Belial, and persons and revival ministries should judge and destroy the works of Belial.

Verse 11-17 *And all Israel shall hear, and fear, and shall do no more any such wickedness as this is among you. If thou shalt hear say in one of thy cities, which the Lord thy God hath given thee* *to dwell there, saying, Certain men, the children of Belial, are gone out from among you, and have withdrawn the inhabitants of their city, saying, Let us go and serve other gods, which ye have not known; Then shalt thou enquire, and make search, and ask diligently; and, behold, if it be truth, and the thing certain, that such abomination is wrought among you; Thou shalt surely smite the inhabitants of that city with the edge of the sword, destroying it utterly, and all that is therein, and the cattle thereof, with the edge of the sword. And thou shalt gather all the spoil of it into the midst of the street thereof, and shalt burn with fire the city, and all the spoil thereof every whit, for the Lord thy God: and it shall be an heap for ever; it shall not be built again. And there shall cleave nought of the cursed thing to thine hand: that the Lord may turn from the fierceness of his anger, and shew thee mercy, and have compassion upon thee, and multiply thee, as he hath sworn unto thy fathers;*

Belial causes younger generations who were raised in the church or those who know the way of the church, to turn to perverse ways and bring reproach upon the church.

1Samuel 2:12 *Now the sons of Eli were sons of Belial; they knew not the Lord.*

Eli was a high priest in Israel, yet his sons did not have a relationship with the Lord or have no regard for the ways of the Lord.

Verse 22-25 *Now Eli was very old, and heard all that his sons did unto all Israel; and how they lay with the women that assembled at the door of the tabernacle of the congregation. And he said unto them, Why do ye such things? for I hear of your evil dealings by all this people. Nay, my sons; for it is no good report that I hear: ye make the Lord's people to transgress. If one man sin against another, the judge shall judge him: but if a man sin against the Lord, who shall intreat for him? Notwithstanding they hearkened not unto the voice of their father, because the Lord would slay them.*

Eli's sons not only sinned, but they also sinned on the church steps. They defiled the temple and gave the impression to onlookers that this behavior was okay. Despite knowing the laws of God, they had no regard for their life or the consequences of their actions. And even though Eli verbally confronted them, he did not stop them from bringing reproach upon the Lord and the Lord's house.

This is how the spirit of Belial operates. It will have reputable saints resorting to respect of person when it comes to the ways of the Lord. This is the reason some people in the church can sleep around and sin and still be allowed to preach and minister, while others are sat down and chastised for their actions. This is one of the reasons the world does not want to come to church and why many who have been hurt within the church do not want to return. There is a blatant sin done against God in the open among the saints, by leaders and sheep, but everyone keeps having church like nothing is wrong with these behaviors. When onlookers say something about the reproach, no consequences are ensued. And the leaders who operate in Belial behaviors will play the *"I am human"* card, or will make the saints feel like they have no right to confront their sin. The scripture *"touch not my anointed,"* has been inappropriately used to avoid accountability of treacherous behaviors among leaders (***Psalms 105:15***). Leaders are held to a higher standard, and there is no way around that (***Provers 16:12, Matthew 18:6, Acts 20:18, James 3:1, Hebrews 13:17***). This was one of the reasons Eli was judged. He was held accountable for not implementing the same consequences for his sons that he would have for anyone else who had done such file things on the doorsteps of the Lord.

2Chronicles 6:16-18 *Now therefore, O LORD God of Israel, keep with thy servant David my father that which thou hast promised him, saying, There shall not fail thee a man in my sight to sit upon the throne of Israel; yet so that thy children take heed to their way to walk in my law, as thou hast walked before me. Now then, O LORD God of Israel, let thy word be verified, which thou hast spoken unto thy servant David. But will God in very deed dwell with men on the earth? behold, heaven and the heaven of heavens cannot contain thee; how much less this house which I have built.*

I believe the Spirit of Belial uses the offenses of church hurt and the falls of Christian leaders to cause saints to rebel against coming to church and to be suspicious of being connected to, sowing into, and fellowshipping with the church. The other challenge is that this spirit has caused the body of Christ to be a church divided against itself. I say this because even though leaders and ministries recognize that church hurt has occurred, many of them have not made changes within themselves, their ministry teams, the relationship dynamics, and the ministry climates of the ministries, where people will feel safe to be restored to the church. We, therefore, have one side bashing the church and the other side demanding that rebels return to the church. Those that are bound to church hurt and have rejected the church are now experiencing some misalignment with their destiny and calling, which is the plan of the spirit of Belial. He wants to destroy God-ordained destinies. These people attempt to reorder their destiny by serving God at home, doing ministry on social media sites, etc., while their church hurt spills onto others that they minister to. The leaders and ministries that are demanding the hurt to return tend to operate in pride, entitlement, a lack of compassion, and regard for the trauma they have endured at the hands of leaders and saints within the church. They do not realize that if they do not transform their hearts towards those hurt by the church, it impacts them and the body of Christ, as there is no salvation or ministry if people do not want to be a part of it. People need to be aware of how this spirit is operating because it is wreaking havoc in the body of Christ.

<u>**Baal**</u> – Baal means Lord. Historically, Baal is an ancient idolatrous Canaanite god worshipped within regions. He was the supreme god worshiped in Canaan and Phoenicia. He is known as a fertility god who enables the earth to produce crops and helps people to produce children. Those who worship him believe that Baal he is in absolute control over nature and over people. They believe he has charge over the rain and the weather, and man's survival was dependent upon this god's provision.

Different regions worshipped Baal in different ways, and special denominations of Baalism are at work on the earth. Regions that rely heavily on agriculture and the weather to produce wealth are strongly rooted in Baal worship. Baal worship also consists of sensuality, and involves ritualistic prostitution in the temples; some of the reasons for human trafficking, prostitution houses, brothels, and strip clubs is due to the oppression of these principalities. Sexual worship, prostitution, human sacrifice of children, ungodly bloodshed, fertility, good fortune, wealth, god of thunder, lightning, winter storms, vegetation, magic, self-mutilation, sexual immorality, incest, god of the sun are a few of its origins. It is important to consider Baal worship where there is a lot of senseless murder in regions. Witches and warlocks are releasing curses and spells to incite killings, so the blood goes into the land and is offered up as a sacrifice to Baal. We just think people have no regard for life and are killing one another. But they are under the domination of principalities and powers that use their godless lifestyle and life hardships as open doors to demonic operations.

Human sacrifice is also a practice of Baal worship, especially the sacrificing of a firstborn child. The priests of Baal also appeal to their god in wild abandon worship that includes loud, ecstatic cries and self-inflicted injury, cutting another person or the sacrificing of an animal. In *1Kings 17*, you will find the prophet causing drought to stifle the workings of Baal. In *1Kings 18*, you can study the prophet showdown between Elijah and the prophets of Baal. Baal prophets love to attend ministry events and challenge the ministers in the spiritual realm. This is the reason you will hear a minister say, "I know a witch is in here." These Baal prophets will be contending and attempting to inflict the minister as they proclaim the gospel. The minister is discerning this behavior and exposing the witch. I saw do more than expose it by acknowledging its presence among you, judge it and kill its workings by speaking God's judgment over it and canceling what it is seeking to do to you and the people.

1Kings 18:40-41 *And Elijah said unto them, Take the prophets of Baal; let not one of them escape. And they took them: and Elijah brought them down to the brook Kishon, and slew them there. And Elijah said unto Ahab, Get thee up, eat and drink; for there is a sound of abundance of rain.*

Judges 2:12-13 *And they forsook the Lord God of their fathers, which brought them out of the land of Egypt, and followed other gods, of the gods of the people that were round about them, and bowed themselves unto them, and provoked the Lord to anger. And they forsook the Lord, and served Baal and Ashtaroth.*

<u>Asherah</u> – Works with the principality of Babylon as it provides high places and groves that yield sexual acts to demons. The *Asherah Pole* as defined on Wikipedia is a "*sacred tree or pole that stood near Canaanite religious locations to honor the goddess Asherah.*" This Asherah Pole is a demonic altar, shrine, and figurine. I know you are wondering the

reason I am telling you this. But as a regional person, it is essential to understand your mandate to deal with idolatry. You have to know what the people, land, and region is bound to, so you can use the revival fire to break it off their lives, the land, and the region. I am just awakening your spirit man to greater enlightenment, so you can discern the idols in your region. Some of these idols are ancient and have governed regions for centuries. They are not going to just give the land to you. And they surely will contend with you whether you acknowledge the war or not. You must know that it is yours, break its powers, and gut out its workings.

Exodus 34:13-17 New International Bible *Break down their altars, smash their sacred stones and cut down their Asherah poles. Do not worship any other god, for the Lord, whose name is Jealous, is a jealous God. "Be careful not to make a treaty with those who live in the land; for when they prostitute themselves to their gods and sacrifice to them, they will invite you and you will eat their sacrifices. And when you choose some of their daughters as wives for your sons and those daughters prostitute themselves to their gods, they will lead your sons to do the same. "Do not make any idols.*

You may know the goddess Asherah as the Queen of heaven. It is the goddess of motherhood and fertility. Asherah operates through perversion, pornography, sexual immorality, and idolatry. These acts are used to offer up sexual sacrifices to the demonic altar of Asherah. These sexual altars are often found in occult practices, covens, and shrines. We think altars tend to be built in a specific location and you have to actually go to that location to offer up a sacrifice. However, it is important to realize that altars are platforms. Dictionary.com defines altar as, *"an elevated place or structure, as a mound or platform, at which religious rites are performed or on which sacrifices are offered to gods, ancestors, etc."* TV, social media, the internet, ad displays at stores, your job, etc., are all platforms. They are all altars designed to get our attention and get us to buy into and trade our time, money, morals, beliefs, destiny, life, heritage, etc. for their product. Sadly, because these platforms are altars, they have crept into normal society through pornography and perversion released through media via TV shows, music, commercials, social media, ads, and clothing. In relation to the principality of Asherah, these platforms are all shrines and trading floors for offering up sexual sacrifices to the devil – to idolatry. Sexual games are also ways to which the altars of Asherah creep into the lives of youth, adults, and even marriages.

Kissing games, sex games, partner swapping, etc., are all trading altars of Asherah. Due to media, it is very difficult to escape pornography and perversion. Even if you are not pursuing it, it is subject to manifest in a TV show, commercial, social media page or while you are searching the web. This has made children more curious, exposed, and vulnerable to engaging in sexual acts at an early age while desensitizing the world to perversion and pornography. This principality is strong in the world at large. This spirit works with incubus and succubus (spirits that sexually assault people in their dreams and sleep, rape and molestation, and astral projectors (people who use their soul to travel in the spirit realm illegally). Asherah often uses these platforms as open doors to enter the dream realm to sexually molest people in their sleep. When you watch shows with sexual content or explicit, implied sexual content, you are saying you agree with these acts. Since you are taking in these acts into your life, the spirit feels it has a right to act on that trade. Thus, expecting payment of entering your dream realm and sleep realm and sexually assaulting you. Even if we did not intend to watch something that was sexual, if we are subjected to it, it is important to cleanse any seeds that were sown in the eye gates, imagination, mind, and emotions, repent if necessary, so you can close portals that will allow the altars of Asherah to feel like it can trade with you.

At different times of the year, sexual sacrifices are intensely offered on these altars. As these altars are worshipped by cults, witches, and warlocks, an increase of mental and psychological sexual warfare floods the thoughts and minds of people due to the release of these practices into the atmosphere of the region. Such an increase in thoughts causes people to give in to sexual acts of masturbation, pornography, fornication, infidelity, perverse acts, and inordinate affections and behaviors. Sometimes, it is not the person wanting to sin but being driven to sin by what is in the airways, land, and region. We must be aware of these altars, and how they operate so, we will know how to break people, lands, and regions free.

Deuteronomy 16:21 New International Bible *Do not set up any Asherah pole beside the altar you build to the Lord your God.*

2Kings 18:4 *[Hezekiah] removed the high places, smashed the sacred stones and cut down the Asherah poles. He broke into pieces the bronze snake Moses had made, for up to that time the Israelites had been burning incense to it.*

Also, study *Ezekiel 8*

<u>**Python**</u> - Comes to squeeze the life out of people, families, churches, ministries, relationships, and the region, spiritually, physically, financially, economically, mentally and emotionally, etc. Comes against new ministries, businesses, and visions with a vengeance to thwart and abort the vision and hinder them from planting and developing. Seeks to kill them early by causing constriction and suffocation. This is done through suffocation and constriction. Death is generally slow and painful. The snake:
- Sits on the person's shoulders and makes them sluggish and lethargic
- Will wrap around a person, ministry, or region in an effort to constrict and squeeze out the life, production, zeal, fruit, and success of that person, ministry, or region

- Will wrap around the head, revelation, and vision, and cause headaches, pressure, slow spiritual and natural death.

This principality also works through:
- Divination/Soothsaying (Gothic, astrology, and Baal).
- Pharmakia (hallucinate drugs; street drugs, prescribed pain pills, psychiatric drugs).
- Apathy – makes a person, atmosphere, or region lethargic, sluggish, indifferent, passive, cold, lack of drive for life.
- Depression – especially strong in the fall leading to the winter months. Winters tend to be very long, the cold weather is bitter and hard, which makes life secluded and difficult. Uses the winter season to steals the momentum of people and vision carriers.
- Heaviness (constant feeling of a weighing down).
- Word curses and witchcraft spells are released to bring depression and mental instability.
- Fear – sluggardness and indifferent feelings and sensations causes anxiety, fear, fear of dying, fear of failing.
- Discouragement - the hopelessness that tends to hit a person or atmosphere when there are not any challenging situations going on or heightens when challenging situations are present.
- Infirmity – will cause sicknesses that come in the form of feeling pressured or weighed down. Can also cause respiratory illnesses or sensations like the inability to breathe or choking.

Schizophrenia – This principality is strong in ministry circles and regions. It makes the people double-minded, insane, and weary about life and the things of God. There can even be a weariness in the atmosphere where things are generally chaotic, draining, and stressful, even for those who appear to be living the "good life" or a region that appears to be advancing. When things get stressful, often people feel out of their minds. People often use phrases like "*I am losing my mind,*" "*I'm going crazy.*" Schizophrenia also works in the atmosphere, especially in churches and businesses. It will make things confused and scattered. Things will not flow, and there will be weariness, confusion, emptiness, and pressure in the atmosphere; even in an atmosphere that appears to be productive, but the seeds will be blown away rather than sowing and flourishing into that environment. A prime giveaway is when there is uneasiness, instability, or uncertainty in the atmosphere and people cannot figure out what is going on even in what should be routine situations. Also working in this area is the spirit of strong delusion. If given over to Schizophrenia, one can acquire a split personality or the perception of a split personality of rebellion & rejection.

Mental Illnesses, labels placed on kids, and the distribution of psychotic medication are huge regional and even national strongholds. Physicians are quick to label diagnoses and prescribe medication for mental and emotional issues. This is witchcraft and pharmakia at its strongest. Saints are being diagnosed with depression, bipolar disorder, Manic Depression, Schizophrenia and are taking psychiatric medication, and the body of Christ has minimal to no strategy for helping people deal with mental oppression, so they can be set free. Many psychiatric medications can be bought on the street and are easily accessible, even to children. People are taking these medications for recreational use, to further experience Pharmakia altered realities, where they escape the stress, mental oppression, and the challenges of life. Many children are labeled special education and/or with learning disabilities, hyperactive, attention deficit, and are being prescribed medications for behaviors that may be demonic spirits at work.

Abortion - The Spirit of Molech & The Spirit of Ammon – These are principalities and curses that operate to spiritually and/or physically abort, cause miscarriages, murder, and premature death to the purpose and destiny of people. There are a lot of projects that have started in some regions but are not complete and have been left unfinished for years. A lot of churches began projects, but they fall through or start yet end after a few months or years due to this spirit at work. They will be after your revival fire. They want you to sacrifice your revival vision to their altar of death. I decree consuming resurrection power to beat this principality down.

Barrenness & The Spirit Of Miscarriage – These principalities can operate as a generational curse. Afflicts the spiritual and natural womb, making it difficult for women, ministries, lands, and regions to get pregnant with children and with the things of God. Causes impotence in men where they cannot conceive children or the purpose and plans of God. Works with the spirit of Eve to cause torment during menstrual cycles and cause female problems such as tumors, fibroids, cancer that block the womb and make pregnancy difficult. Makes it difficult for people to conceive, carry, and birth God's vision or sustain in God's vision. Makes the region hard, barren, and infertile where it has difficulty producing the will, purpose, and plan of God. Rages against the finisher anointing as people will start off in the plans, will, and destiny of God, but never complete goals or fulfill destiny. The vision miscarried or becomes stagnant and halted. People will carry around visions but never give birth. They remain in the incubation stage of destiny and their life's vision.

Isaiah 54:2-3 Enlarge the place of your tent, and let the curtains of your habitations be stretched out; spare not; lengthen your cords and strengthen your stakes, for you will spread abroad to the right hand and to the left; and your offspring will possess the nations and make the desolate cities to be inhabited.

The Message Version 1-5 "Sing, barren woman, who has never had a baby. Fill the air with song, you who've never experienced childbirth! You're ending up with far more children than all those childbearing women." God says so! "Clear lots of ground for your tents! Make your tents large. Spread out! Think big! Use plenty of rope, drive the tent pegs deep. You're going to need lots of elbow room for your growing family. You're going to take over whole nations; you're going to resettle abandoned cities. Don't be afraid--you're not going to be embarrassed. Don't hold back--you're not going to come up short. You'll forget all about the humiliations of your youth, and the indignities of being a widow will fade from memory. For your Maker is your bridegroom, his name, God –of–the–Angel–Armies! Your Redeemer is The Holy of Israel, known as God of the whole earth.

<u>Poverty</u> – This principality is not just about money but poverty mindset, poor self-perception, poor presentation of self, poor housekeeping, poor hygiene, poor execution of destiny, and the calling that is on a person's life. People also tend to be tightwads, stingy, and make excuses for not sowing and investing, while spending money on materialistic and frivolous things and endeavors. People are constantly seeking to swindle, hustle or acquire a free or cheaper way to pay or obtain things. When encouraged to sow into their lives, invest in destiny and their future, or to sow into the lives of others they are gleaning from; defensive walls erected in the spirit around and within them. Many people will hold back the little bit they are willing to give with minimal to no discernment that the investment is for the good of their growth and advancement. This principality assaults churches in an effort to close them down and /or keep them from advancing and impacting the region. As a result, many hustling dealings occur within the administration of churches to keep them afloat. This causes unrepented sin to linger in the churches, which hinders the financial blessings and promises that are due to people and ministries.

Many regions have an area that is severely oppressed with poverty. Crime is very high, and the regard for life is low. This principality works with the spirit of Cain, causing people to kill their brothers and sisters as a result of greed, jealousy, and stinginess. The focus is survival at the expense of neighbors, generations, communities, and the region. Most do not feel safe and feel helpless in breaking the strongholds of poverty and escaping the generational and poverty-stricken cycles of the community. This principality targets intelligent, driven youth and people in the community, often causing catastrophes of hardship, murder, and violence to further incite hopelessness upon families and the community. Destiny killing spirits, spirits of tragedy, and death and hell run rampant in these communities snuffing out royal seeds that have been chosen by God to break the powers of poverty and idolatry while restoring the name and blessings of God back into the generational lineage.

<u>Sexual Perversion</u> – We seem to be driven in a sex-driven age. The desire for purity and the protection of innocence and holiness is a rarity. The need to contour and alter one's

looks, body parts, etc., has stolen the identity and divine beauty of many as we strive to appear more sexually and sensually appealing to one another rather than to God. Sex is everywhere, and the crossing of boundary lines and standards has made it difficult not to be violated by the perversions and twisted mindsets and behaviors of others.

- Homosexuality – Huge stronghold among males, females, teenagers, and college students; teens are becoming comfortable with homosexuality due to abuse, videos, inordinate friendships, experimentation, playing sex games, and rap music. This spirit is targeting children, using open doors in their identity or challenging experiences, to cause them to want to change their gender. There is an agenda released in the world to normalize homosexuality to distort God's will and standard for marriage and family and stifle the purity of children being born through Godly marriage covenants and family covenants. This agenda is also being used to silence saints and ministries from speaking against sin, proclaiming the gospel of Jesus Christ while releasing reproach and judgmental disdain upon the body of Christ so cannot save souls and advance the kingdom of God on the earth.

- Sexual Abuse, Physical Abuse, Incest, Wounded Spirit, Hate – These are strongholds of secrecy among the generations, within family homes, and ministries. They have become more prevalent to the point of yielding the mindset that it is okay and is a part of family and ministry culture.

- Incubus, Succubus, Nightmare Spirits – These perverse spirits attack people as they sleep at night. They sexually molest and rape people while they sleep or through their dream realms, or insight terror and fear. They instill demonic impartations and fruit into people to further make them crave for perverse and twisted experiences and have propensities for sin, perversion, blood, ungodliness, etc.

- Spirits of Bondage, Addictive Spirits - particularly cigarettes, marijuana, alcohol, and sex).

- Sex Trafficking, Prostitution, Pedophilia have run rampant in regions as these serve as underground agencies for kidnapping, raping, trading, and selling women and children. Pedophilia has become such an epidemic that pedophiles are seeking to have laws passed where they can marry children.

Gluttony - Gluttony is a principality of unfulfillment in a person, land, or region where it can never get enough. The effects of gluttony can be seen physically, but the empty portal to which it operates, and gorges can only be discerned spiritually. This spirit devours whatever it oppresses. You can see the potential of that person, region, or thing, but they are engorged by the overconsumption of this spirit. The identity has been so filled with excess that it steals the usefulness, healthiness, strength, balance, stability, and purpose of that which it oppresses. This is the reason some people, ministries, and regions, appear to have a lot going on – have a lot of activity and opportunity, but are producing no real fruit. They are full of things that taste good but are not Godly or healthy. The world will have you think more is a success. There is this need to indulge and obtain without even considering the necessity of that matter or thing. Be careful not to allow this principality to seek into your regional revival vision. Stay God-driven, and God-focused, where your appetite is to feast on him. Cancel every way this spirit influences the saints and your ministry, where there is constant teaching and equipping, but minimal desire to walk in the things of God. People will gorge and stay fat – dying on the pews. This kills revival fire.

<u>*Spirit of the Crab*</u> - this spirit grabs hold of people, businesses, regions, refuses to let go. It is a possessive spirit that has no vision and holds others down, so they will not pursue a vision. It often works with gluttony and sexual perversion as the gluttony and perversion are lodged in its claws, which makes deliverance from sexual and gluttonous issues difficult. As you contend with glutton and sexual perversion, break the claws of the crab spirit.

<u>*Spirit Of Infirmity*</u> - Usually generational, territorial, cultural, and operates through a curse. In this day and age, the world systems are designing ways to make us sick, so they can prosper off us being unwell.

- ❖ Allergies, arthritis, asthma, bent body, and spine, bleeding, cancer, chronic diseases, colds, diseases, disorders, epilepsy, feebleness, fungus infections, hallucinations, hay fever, heart attack, impotent, infections, insanity, lameness, lingering physical trauma, lingering spirit, madness, mania, mental illness, oppression, paralysis, paranoia, physical disorder, retardation, schizophrenia, senility, sinusitis, spirits of death, torment, virus, bacterial infections, leaky gut, weakness, wounded spirit, diabetes, blood pressure problems, cholesterol problems, tumors and health problems among the male and female reproductive organs.

- ❖ Due to idolatry and rampant unrepentant sin in America and the world at large, we have an epidemic of malignant diseases and tumors, particularly cancer. Cancer has become an epidemic that is stealing the lives and destinies of people and generations. Cancer has instilled fear in the world such that much of what we eat, clean with, complete daily tasks with, etc., has been marked as an open door to cancer. People have become more health-conscious than ever, yet it has not stopped cancer from wreaking havoc upon the world, as the healthy and the unhealthy have succumbed to cancer. This lets us know that cancer is not just a natural epidemic, but a spiritual matter that must be dealt with accordingly.

Cancer operates as a principality, and it has entered society through rebellion against God and rejection of his will, standards, and laws for our lives. Because we have worshipped the creature, we have created things that are not of God's will and design, and have not adequately governed the land where our environment and earth can be healthy, cancer has come in and wreaked havoc upon the world. Some forms of cancer are manmade to instill sickness for the purposes of feeding mammon (pride, greed, and money) and worldly health care systems (Pharmakia, Nehushtan). Some cancers are a result of things we have created that we deem to be beneficial to us, but really are harmful to our bodies and the earth.

Romans 1:25 Who changed the truth of God into a lie, and worshipped and served the creature more than the Creator, who is blessed for ever. Amen.

Numbers 21:9 And Moses made a serpent of brass, and put it upon a pole, and it came to pass, that if a serpent had bitten any man, when he beheld the serpent of brass, he lived.

Information from Wikipedia: *In the biblical* Book of Numbers, *the Nehushtan or Nohestan)* (Hebrew) *was a bronze serpent on a pole which God told Moses to erect to protect the* Israelites *who saw it from dying from the bites of the "fiery serpents" which God had sent to punish them for speaking against God and Moses.*

King Hezekiah *later instituted a religious iconoclastic reform and destroyed "the brazen serpent that Moses had made; for unto those days the children of Israel did burn incense to it; and it was called Nehushtan"* (2Kings 18:4).

Jesus is who we are to look to for healing.

> *John 3:14-15 Just as those who looked in faith to the serpent in the wilderness were healed, so those who look in faith to the lifted up Son of Man will have eternal life.*

It was not the snake on the pole that healed the people, but their belief that God could heal them that caused them to live. This should be our focus and posture today, "that Jesus is our healer."

Cancer is prideful and haughty. It acts as a Goliath that believes it cannot be annihilated. It also spreads like famine and pestilence that eats up the flesh of the person and their life. It devours until there is no trace of their legacy. It devours:

Finances	Mobility
Progress	Strength
success	relationship
Generational & Spiritual Inheritance	Vision & Promises of God
Identity	Destiny

It is idolatrous and seeks to change people's lives into an image that is far from the image of God in and for their lives. We need to command its haughtiness to fall in the name of Jesus.

> ***Proverbs 16:18*** *Pride goeth before destruction, and an haughty spirit before a fall.*

<u>*Pride* is *gaon* in the Hebrew and means:</u>
1. Arrogance, excellency(-lent), majesty, pomp, pride, proud, swelling
2. Exaltation, majesty, pride
3. Majesty, exaltation, excellence
    A. Of nations
    B. Of God
    C. Of the Jordan
    D. Pride, arrogance (bad sense)

We know that many of our nations have become prideful and haughty. We have taken God out of most everything and have made his laws and standards an option rather than the mandate to which we are to feast on and live by. Many people only want God if it benefits them. Otherwise, many have become their own God or taken up the god of the world in an effort to live by their own prideful will and desires.

> ***2Timothy 3:1-5*** *This know also, that in the last days perilous times shall come. For men shall be lovers of their own selves, covetous, boasters, proud, blasphemers, disobedient to parents, unthankful, unholy, Without natural affection, trucebreakers, false accusers, incontinent, fierce, despisers of those that are good, Traitors, heady, highminded, lovers of pleasures more than lovers of God; Having a form of godliness, but denying the power thereof: from such turn away.*

It is, therefore, wise for those battling cancer and other malignant diseases to search themselves and their generations for root strongholds of pride and haughtiness. Though not always the case, this can be a factor with cancer and other malignant diseases gaining access in a person's life or generational line. Pride and haughtiness may need to be dealt with so that malignant tumors and diseases can be destroyed in the person's life and generational line. Pride and haughtiness may also be the challenge of the people and region the person is ministering to. God may allow disease to bring those persons to true humility and repentance such that transformation occurs in their lives and the person's sphere of influence.

- Allergies are huge in certain regions; could be due to the factories and agriculture environments, or in big cities where a lot of people drive cars and pollute the air with toxins. In some regions, there are more allergies and sinus medications on the shelves than cold medications. The spirit of allergies operates through the stronghold of the spirit of pollution. Moreover, Satan is the prince of the power of the air, so when we do not govern the air, we are subject to his workings. Asthma, respiratory problems, constant colds are caused by pollution that creeps about the earth. Rebuke the prince of the power of the air, especially during allergy season, and claim dominion over him and everything that moves and creeps to bring about demonic infestation as we have dominion over all creeping and moving spirits whether in the air, sea, or land. The more the presence of the spirit of God glows into a region, the more the air will be like heaven as these infirmities are cleansed out of the atmosphere and region. Declare God's glory into the region.

Genesis 1:26-28 And God said, Let us make man in our image, after our likeness: and let them have dominion over the fish of the sea, and over the fowl of the air, and over the cattle, and over all the earth, and over every creeping thing that creepeth upon the earth. So God created man in his own image, in the image of God created he him; male and female created he them. And God blessed them, and God said unto them, Be fruitful, and multiply, and replenish the earth, and subdue it: and have dominion over the fish of the sea, and over the fowl of the air, and over every living thing that moveth upon the earth.

The words *creepeth* and *moveth* are the same word *Ramas*, in the Hebrew and means:
1. To glide swiftly, i.e., to crawl or move with short steps; by analogy to swarm: — creep, move
2. To creep, move lightly, move about, walk on all fours
3. To creep, teem (of all creeping things) to creep of animals)
4. To move lightly, glide about (of water animals) to move about (of all land animals generally)

We must assert dominion over the creepy things that are taking up residence in our region to make the people, land, and atmosphere sick. We must assert authority in this area in order to experience more deliverance, healing, miracles, signs, and wonders, and so our greater works can be maintained and sustained.

Scorpion – Though not always the case, this is a territorial spirit that is usually found in the desert. Though it tends to be an isolated being, it devours other vertebrates and is subject to other forces. Therefore, there are a lot of spirits working in and of its kingdom, such as serpent spirits, python, addler (**Luke 10:19**), the ruler spirit of the Lion (ferocious devouring spirit), and the young lion and dragon (leviathan, behemoth) (**Psalms 91:13**). The scorpion spirits have poisoned lands and atmospheres of many regions with their sting. Its sting can cause a quick death, which is why murder is on the rise, slander is rapid, and is the reason some regions look so dead and desolate in many areas.

The Scorpion Spirit also causes torment among the people and loses spirits of fear and pain. It will be essential to tear down these high places and drive them out of the city along with its imps. Suck out its poison in the land, people, and atmosphere, and decree healing, fruitfulness, and prosperity in its place.

Legalism – This principality works with the antichrist, stronghold of religion, politics, institutionalism, litigation, and corruption. Restricts free choice; restricts the workings of the Holy Spirit; restricts the favor and prosperity of the saints, restricts jobs and moving upward in companies and branching out into one's own business. Causes segregation of communities, churches, and racists of people. Operates as a strong territorial spirit within ministries and people; causes them to feel like they have ownership of people, ministries, organizations, positions, etc. because they are a part of those people's lives or those institutions. Very possessive and will fight to hold claim to their legalities.

REFERENCES

- Dictionary.com
- Olivetree.com
- Matthew Henry Strong's Online Concordance
- Gillen, A.L. (2007, June 10). "Biblical leprosy: Casting light on the disease that shuns." Retrieved from *Answers in Genesis* website at https://answersingenesis.org/biology/disease/biblical-leprosy-shedding-light-on-the-disease-that-shuns/

Kingdom Shifters Product Line & Books Referenced In This Manual

Products available at kingdomshifters.com and amazon.com	
Books (Paperback, Kindle, and e-books available)	
Healing the Wounded Leader	There is an App for That
Apostolic Governing	Dance from Heaven to Earth
Apostolic Mantle	Annihilating Church Hurt
Healing the Wounded Leader	Discerning the Voice of God
Release the Vision	Feasting in His Presence
Birthing Books That Shift Generations	Prayers that Shift Atmospheres
Atmosphere Changes (Weaponry)	Dismantling Homosexuality
Strategies for Eradicating Racism	Let There Be Sight
Kingdom Shifters Decree That Thang	Kingdom Watchman Builder on the Wall
Kingdom Heirs Decree That Thang	Kingdom Keys to Governing Relationships
Fivefold Operations – Manuals I, II, and III	Unmasking the Power of the Scouts – Volumes I and II
Deliverance from the Suicide	Processing Grief & Loss
Books for Liturgical / Interpretive Dance Ministries	
Dance & Fivefold Ministry	Dance from Heaven to Earth
Spirits that Attack Dance Ministers	Dancers! Dancers! Dancers! Decree That Thang
KSM Prayer CD's	
Decree That Thang	Kingdom Heirs Decree That Thang
Teaching and Worship	

www.ingramcontent.com/pod-product-compliance
Lightning Source LLC
Chambersburg PA
CBHW081349230426
43667CB00017B/2773